P9-ARF-957

PLOTS AND CHARACTERS
IN THE FICTION
AND NARRATIVE POETRY
OF HERMAN MELVILLE

PLOTS AND CHARACTERS
IN THE FICTION
AND NARRATIVE POETRY
OF HERMAN MELVILLE

Robert L. Gale

with a Foreword by
Harrison Hayford

ARCHON BOOKS
Hamden, Connecticut
1969

SBN: 208 00906 X
Library of Congress Catalog Card Number: 70-82690
Printed in THE UNITED STATES OF AMERICA

To Christina Dowd Rust,
my affectionate and generous
sister-in-law

TABLE OF CONTENTS

FOREWORD

Next to works of literature themselves, good reference works deserve the gratitude of readers. They are the books that libraries must buy and must put on accessible shelves, because people want to use them. It is hard to imagine having too many good reference works. After a quarter-century dominated by criticism, it is easy to see there can be too much criticism, even about writers whose writings require it. On Herman Melville, besides a half-dozen biographies, there are around a hundred published critical studies (and even more unpublished dissertations, most of them critical). Robert Gale's *Plots and Characters in the Fiction and Narrative Poetry of Herman Melville* is the first published book of pure reference devoted to Melville's writings. For his contemporaries, more valued by Victorian readers, there is a gamut of such works—for Emerson, for Dickens, for Tennyson, for Browning, and later for Hardy. For Melville there is no concordance and, though he is a remarkably allusive and digressive writer, no complete analytical index. No handbook has been published. Mr. Gale's *Plots and Characters* is needed.

This book will help many readers, with needs as obvious as reviewing a book already read, or as necessary as getting an idea of what is in it without reading it; as predictable as locating an elusive character or episode, or as unpredictable as finding a name for a dog (as I did).

Mr. Gale has written full and admirably objective summaries of the plots of Melville's fictional works (stretching the genre to include his sketches and his one extensive review, in a fictional persona). His summaries have little in common with those hackwork trots that litter college bookstores. They are accurate, full, and faithful in emphasis. They are self-effacing. They reflect critical sophistication while imposing no special critical interpretations.

Beyond its reference use, a competent work such as this can bring unexpected dividends of insight. On a first examination, not expecting (as a hardened Melville scholar who has read all the books and enough of the dissertations) to learn much new, I have been surprised to see what is revealed by a simple indexing of his characters. That is, not just the number and variety of his people, but that they are there and that they are real. Melville's earliest readers saw at once that he excelled in striking off character vignettes. As his writing career went on into the 1850's they complained because he had turned away from external South Sea adventure books to satire, allegory, and "philosophy." Twentieth-century critics, however, have revived Melville largely because of his anti-Victorian attitudes. Their articles, books, and dissertations have been devoted to exploring and explicating his thought and his symbolic techniques. Much less has been made of his gift of direct observation and intuition of character and of his ability to establish a character firmly. One use, then, that we may hope from *Plots and Characters in Melville*, is to re-direct attention to Melville's characters. Enough has been made of his thought; too much, perhaps, of the half-truth that his characters are just embodiments of ideas. The disjunction is unnecessary, and without belaboring the point, it can be said that Mr. Gale's index of the characters, by sparely listing them, proves how peopled Melville's world was.

Harrison Hayford

Northwestern University
April, 1969

"Eh!—He's asleep, ain't he?"
"With kings and counselors," murmured I.

—"Bartleby the Scrivener"

PREFACE

This handbook, which is a companion to my *Plots and Characters in the Fiction of Henry James* and my *Plots and Characters in the Fiction and Sketches of Nathaniel Hawthorne*, both recently published by Archon Books, should prove useful in several ways. The reader may wish to have some understanding of the plot or contents of a certain Melvillean novel, short story, or narrative poem before reading it, or he may wish to review the contents of a work after—perhaps long after—he has read it. If he is a specialist, he may wish to review the plots of several works to compare Herman Melville's treatment of certain subjects and themes early in his career and later, or perhaps to compare Melville's treatment of some element with that of another writer. It may be that the reader will wish to refresh his memory of a certain name or the function of a certain person in Melville's crew of characters. If he remembers the work in which the name figures, he can easily find the name in the alphabetized list of characters after the summary of a given work. If he remembers the character but not the work, he can find what he needs in the alphabetized list of all persons in Melville's narratives; the entry there will also enable him to recollect where the character may be found in Melville. Included in the list of characters are all named persons or namable persons (for example, the Starbuck family), and in addition all persons referred to by capitalized nouns (for example, Captain). If the reader wants to review Melville's activity during a certain phase of his career, he may well begin by consulting the chronology of Melville or the chronological list of his novels, short stories, and volumes of verse.

It should be noted here that, in order to keep the chronological list within reasonable limits, the titles of individual narrative poems are not included in it (with the exception of *Clarel*) but may be found in Appendix A. It should also be noted that if a poem tells no story (for example, "The Maldive Shark"), it is not summarized; if its plot is very simple, it is not summarized, although its characters are defined so as to suggest its plot adequately (for example, "The Admiral of the White");

xiv PLOTS AND CHARACTERS IN THE FICTION

and if its plot is very simple but without named characters, it is briefly summarized (for example, "The Berg [A Dream]").

The diligent reader of Melville's plots summarized here will be struck by the truth of Alexander Cowie's conclusion that Melville's "richest experience of the objective world came during the prologue to his literary career"—that is, during his many voyages—that Melville had a mystic strain, as evidenced by his writings about the sea, Eastern matters, children, and weird events; that he was a bold thinker, about violence, love and hate, religious matters, good and evil, and faith; and finally that he was a daring critic, of religion, the affairs of state, literature, and the deeper realities.[1] And the reader who looks through the list of characters identified here will agree with James E. Miller, Jr., who has divided Melville's dramatis personae into seekers, idealists, innocents, primitives, rebels, hypocrites, mystics, and masked and maskless men.[2]

Please note that I have summarized plots and identified all named or namable characters—only from the novels, short stories, and narrative poems. (Names in brackets are supplied from sources other than Melville.) I do not treat any of his non-fictional prose (for example, letters and reviews) or his non-narrative poetry. Also please note that dates in parentheses in the chronological list of Melville's narrative works are dates of first book publication. Titles in italics are of works more than about fifty thousand words in length; titles in double quotation marks are of fictional works under about fifty thousand words in length. Titles in single quotation marks are of poems. Deceased persons are named and identified if, in my opinion, they have a direct bearing on the plot. Statistically oriented readers may be happy to learn that Melville's fiction contains 1,039 named or namable characters and his narrative poetry another 398 characters; in addition, these works have 182 nicknames, pseudonyms, alternate designations, and names of that sort.

[1] Alexander Cowie, *The Rise of the American Novel* (New York: American Book Company, 1951), pp. 395-411.
[2] James E. Miller, Jr., *A Reader's Guide to Herman Melville* (New York: Noonday Press, 1962), pp. 6-15, 231-239.

It is a pleasure to acknowledge most gratefully the financial and clerical assistance provided by Dr. David Halliday, Dean of the Faculty of Arts and Sciences, University of Pittsburgh, and by Dr. Robert F. Whitman, Chairman of the English Department, University of Pittsburgh, and the prompt and professional assistance provided by Mrs. Katherine Y. Armitage, Bibliographer of the English Department, University of Pittsburgh. I am also indebted to Professor Harrison Hayford of Northwestern University, Evanston, Illinois, and to Professor Merton M. Sealts, Jr., of the University of Wisconsin, Madison, Wisconsin, for valuable advice. In addition, I have greatly profited from annotations to Melville's poetry published by Professors Walter E. Bezanson, Hennig Cohen, and Howard P. Vincent. And I should also like to thank, for cooperation which materially speeded my work, personnel of the Melville Project, Newberry Library, Chicago, Illinois; the Berkshire Athenaeum, Pittsfield's Public Library, Pittsfield, Massachusetts; the Troy Public Library, Troy, New York; and the Duquesne University Library, Pittsburgh, Pennsylvania; and my friend and colleague Dr. Ronald T. Curran of the University of Pittsburgh.

Wherever possible, I have used as the definitive authority *The Writings of Herman Melville*, The Northwestern-Newberry Edition, edited by Harrison Hayford, Hershel Parker, and G. Thomas Tanselle (Evanston and Chicago: Northwestern University Press and the Newberry Library, 1968–).

Robert L. Gale

University of Pittsburgh
Pittsburgh, Pennsylvania

CHRONOLOGY

1819   Herman Melville born to Allan and Maria Gansevoort Melvill in New York City, August 1.

1825   Enters New-York Male High School.

1830   Father suffers financial reverses and moves with wife and eight children to Albany, New York; Melville enters Albany Academy.

1832   Father dies in debt and nearly insane; Melville withdraws from Academy and clerks in New York State Bank.

1834   Works on farm at Pittsfield, Massachusetts.

1835   Clerks in store in Albany, enters Albany Classical Academy.

1836   Joins Ciceronian Debating Society.

1837   Teaches school in Pittsfield.

1838   Studies surveying and engineering at Lansingburgh Academy, Lansingburgh, New York.

1839   Ships from New York City on merchantman *St. Lawrence* to Liverpool and return; teaches school in Greenbush, New York.

1840   Visits in Galena, Illinois.

1841   Ships from Fairhaven, Massachusetts, on American whaler *Acushnet*.

1842   Deserts *Acushnet* at Nukahiva, Marquesas Islands; spends a month there; goes to Tahiti aboard Australian whaler *Lucy Ann*; is imprisoned in Tahiti for refusing sea duty; ships aboard American whaler *Charles & Henry*.

1843   Works in Honolulu, joins American navy and ships on frigate *United States*.

1844   Is mustered out in Boston; returns home to Lansingburgh.

1846   *Typee*.

1847   Marries Elizabeth Knapp Shaw in Boston and moves with her to New York City. *Omoo*.

1849   Son Malcolm born. Melville travels to England, briefly visits Paris, Brussels, Cologne, and Rhineland. *Mardi, Redburn.*

1850   Meets Nathaniel Hawthorne, moves to "Arrowhead" farm outside Pittsfield. *White Jacket.*

1851   Son Stanwix born. *Moby Dick.*

1852   *Pierre.*

1853   Daughter Elizabeth born.

1855   Daughter Frances born. *Israel Potter.*

1856   Travels to Scotland, England, Greece, Turkey, and Egypt. *The Piazza Tales.*

1857   Visits Palestine, Greece, Italy, Switzerland, Germany, the Netherlands, and England; returns home; lectures (until 1860). *The Confidence-Man.*

1860   Sails to San Francisco, returns home via Isthmus of Panama.

1861   Father-in-law Judge Lemuel Shaw dies.

1862   Moves with family from "Arrowhead" to Pittsfield, sick with rheumatism, is injured in road accident.

1863   Moves with family to New York City.

1864   Visits Civil War battlefields in Virginia.

1866   Becomes Inspector of Customs at the Port of New York (until 1885). *Battle-Pieces and Aspects of the War.*

1867   Son Malcolm shoots self to death.

1872   Mother dies, fire destroys wife's Boston property.

1876   *Clarel.*

1886   Son Stanwix dies.

1888   Voyages to Bermuda briefly. *John Marr and Other Sailors.*

1891   Dies in New York City, September 28. *Timoleon.*

1922-1924 *The Works of Herman Melville* (London: Constable), 16 vols.

1924   *Billy Budd*

1947   *Collected Poems* (Chicago: Hendricks House; part of new edition of Melville).

1968-   *The Complete Writings of Herman Melville* (Evanston, Illinois: Northwestern-Newberry), 15 vols.

CHRONOLOGICAL LIST
OF MELVILLE'S FICTION
AND HIS VOLUMES OF VERSE

1839

"Fragments from a Writing Desk. No. 1" (1924)

"Fragments from a Writing Desk. No. 2" (1924)

"The Death Craft"

1846

Typee

1847

Omoo

"Authentic Anecdotes of 'Old Zack' "

1849

Mardi

Redburn

1850

White-Jacket

"Hawthorne and His Mosses" (1924)

1851

Moby-Dick

1852

Pierre

1853

"Bartleby" (1856)

"Cock-a-Doodle-Doo!" (1922)

1854

"The Encantadas" (1856)

"Poor Man's Pudding and Rich Man's Crumbs" (1922)

"The Happy Failure" (1922)

Israel Potter (1855)

"The Lightning-Rod Man" (1856)

"The Fiddler" (1922)

1855

"The Paradise of Bachelors and the Tartarus of Maids" (1922)

"The Bell-Tower" (1856)

"Benito Cereno" (1856)

"Jimmy Rose" (1922)

1856

"I and My Chimney" (1922)

"The 'Gees" (1922)

"The Apple-Tree Table" (1922)

"The Piazza" (1856)

The Piazza Tales

1857

The Confidence-Man

1866

Battle-Pieces and Aspects of the War

1876

Clarel

1888
John Marr and Other Sailors

1891
Timoleon

1922
The Apple-Tree Table, and Other Sketches

1922-1924
The Works of Herman Melville, 16 vols. (XIII, *Billy Budd and Other Prose Pieces,* including "The Two Temples" and "Under the Rose," 1924; XVI, *Poems:*

Battle-Pieces, John Marr and Other Poems, Timoleon, &c., 1924)

1947
Collected Poems of Herman Melville

1948
Melville's Billy Budd (and Appendices, including "Story of Daniel Orme")

1968-
The Complete Writings of Herman Melville

PLOTS

'The Admiral of the White,' 1947.
   The Admiral of the White, Captains.

'After the Pleasure Party: Lines Traced under an Image of Amor
   Threatening,' 1891.
   Urania, discontent with her intellectual life once she finds
herself sexually aroused by the sight of a man whom she wants
but who prefers an ordinary peasant girl, is tempted to join a
nunnery but instead prays to the armed Virgin, probably
ineffectually.
   Amor, Urania.

'The Age of the Antonines,' 1891.
   Antonine [Antoninus Pius], Antonine [Marcus Aurelius].

'Amoroso,' 1924.
   Rosamond.

'The Apparition (The Parthenon Uplifted on Its Rock First
   Challenging the View on the Approach to Athens),' 1891.
   Emperor Constantine, Diogenes.

"The Apple-Tree Table," 1856.

For five years after buying his present house, an old mansion in an old quarter of an old American town, the narrator has not visited his locked garret. But then, finding a key in his glen-like old garden, he is impelled by curiosity to fit it into the stair-door keyhole and go up into the hopper-shaped attic, reputed to be haunted. Under the roof is a stepladder leading through swarms of insects to a pulpit-like platform. Through its bull's-eye window the narrator thrusts his head—into the rapturous warmth of the sun! He turns back and examines the contents of the garret and finds among many other odd things an old table of apple-tree wood with three crooked legs terminating in cloven feet. Awkwardly carrying the table downstairs, he bumps his daughter Julia with one leg. She thinks that it is the Evil One's foot and screams. His other daughter, Anna, also dislikes the table; but his energetic wife, to drive their giddiness away, orders the table set up and the girls to sit at it for breakfast and tea. At night, the narrator uses it for a reading table. One Saturday night he is reading Cotton Mather's frightening *Magnalia*, also brought from the attic, and drinking warm punch when he hears an utterly inexplicable ticking. He retires to bed, kicking a chair in his eagerness to escape the sound. In the morning he comes down to a pair of frightened daughters: they too hear the ticking and blame it on spirits in the table, in spite of their mother, who pooh-poohs their silliness and examines the floor, without finding any ticks there. She admits that the sound comes from the table; but insisting that no harm can ensue, she orders Biddy the maid to set breakfast on it as usual. The narrator walks outside and gradually assumes that no evil can come to his innocent family. He returns to his reading at the table, determined to adopt the calm level-headedness of Democritus, who refused while at his studies to be scared by little boys pretending to be ghosts. The ticking starts again. The narrator jocosely invites it to continue, which it does, tauntingly. Finally he sees a sparkling little worm, a shining beetle or bug, emerge from a crack in the warm wood. He puts a tumbler over it and goes to bed. But in the morning, before he can boast much of his bravery to his wife, he discovers that Biddy has tossed the insect into the fire and has scoured the tumbler. The girls cry tremulously at the thought that a bug was ever in a drinking glass of theirs; when they again speak of spirits, their mother sends them to their room to repent. Then she queries her husband, proposes polishing the table, cements the little crack through which the bug appeared, and continues as courageous as Democritus. But that evening the ticking resumes. All four watch—and listen—the narrator oscillating between Democritus and Mather. First they hear the night watchman and then bottled cider exploding in the basement. By two o'clock the narrator's wife is asleep; by four Julia and Anna are also. At six the baker's rap at the door awakens the females, who see the narrator cowering in the corner. Finally a second bug emerges, sparkling like a jewel in a glorious sunset. The girls are thrilled and want to consult Madame Pazzi the conjuress. Instead, the wife calls in the celebrated naturalist Professor Johnson, who windily opines that the bugs came from eggs laid in the living apple-tree wood ninety years before the tree was cut and made into a table, which must now be eighty years of age. Julia lectures to the effect that their bug is proof enough of the glorified resurrection in store for the spirit of man. The bug dies next day and is embalmed in a silver vinaigrette.

Anna, Biddy, Mrs. Brown, Mrs. Democritus, Professor Johnson, Julia, Madame Pazzi.

'The Archipelago,' 1891.
Theseus.
'The Armies of the Wilderness (1863-4),' 1866.
Describes Union and Confederate camps on opposite sides of a valley, tells of a brave Confederate prisoner, then obscurely pictures the tangled fighting and its horrible wake.

[General Ulysses S. Grant], Gray-back, [General Thomas J.] Stonewall [Jackson], [General Robert E.] Lee, [General James] Longstreet, [Colonel John S.] Mosby.

'At the Cannon's Mouth, Destruction of the Ram Albermarle by
   the Torpedo-Launch (October, 1864),' 1866.
      [Lieutenant William B.] Cushing.

"Authentic Anecdotes of 'Old Zack,' " 1847.
   A correspondent is sent to the Mexican front to observe
General Zachary Taylor. Reports sent back to the *Yankee Doodle*
magazine concern Old Zack's calm defusing of a Mexican mortar
shell, his habit of washing and mending his own clothes, a nail put
by a drummer boy under his saddle and later probably sought by
P. T. Barnum for his Museum, an eye-witness description by an
army surgeon of Old Rough and Ready's personal appearance, a
copy of a letter sent by the general to his Mexican counterpart
General Antonio Lopez de Santa Anna after the Battle of Buena
Vista, a pie which an enemy shot caused to fall on General
Taylor's head, Barnum's plan to exhibit General Santa Anna, a
rumor that Old Zack once walked inside the fire of a steamboat,
his implied loyalty, and finally his belligerent eating habits.
      General [Pedro de] Ampudia, P. T. "Peter
      Tamerlane" Barnum, Major [William W. S.] Bliss,
      General [Captain Braxton] Bragg, Brooks, Brooks,
      Secretary [of War William L.] Marcy, Sambo, General
      Antonio Lopez de Santa Anna, a Surgeon of the
      Army in Mexico, General Zachary Taylor, General
      Tom Thumb, Yankee Doodle.

"Bartleby," 1853 (also called "Bartleby the Scrivener: A Story of
   Wall Street")
   The narrator is an elderly lawyer with a snug business on Wall
Street. He deals in bonds, mortgages, and deeds. He is prudent
and methodical. His employees include the scriveners Turkey and
Nippers, and a young office boy named Ginger Nut. Old Turkey
is a careful copyist until noon, then waxes wrathful. Nippers, on
the other hand, is irritable and drunk-acting until noon, then
grows mild. One day, in answer to the lawyer's advertisement for
another scrivener, a pallidly neat, forlorn fellow turns up at the
office. He is Bartleby. The employer gives a portion of his private

office to him, and all is well until one day Bartleby calmly replies to an order to proofread by saying that he would prefer not to. The lawyer is too stunned to dismiss the non-humanly calm man. Days pass. When the refusal is voiced again one morning, Nippers suggest that Bartleby be kicked out. But again the lawyer delays. On an afternoon some days later, Bartleby again prefers not to proofread with his employer, and Turkey offers to blacken the man's eyes. Again the lawyer is reluctant to face the situation. One Sunday morning some time later he happens to go to his office, only to find Bartleby encamped there, partly dressed and refusing to let his employer in. Later the lawyer examines his strange employee's desk and concludes that the odd man has been living at the office day and night, in utter friendlessness and melancholy solitude. A wave of compassion sweeps over the lawyer, who—hopeless though he feels his chances are to be of aid—questions Bartleby the following morning. But Bartleby prefers not to answer any questions, and his manner nettles his employer, who, however, feels superstitious about becoming critical, even though Nippers chafes at the man and Turkey suggests beer for him. The employer notices that Bartleby's eyes are dull and glazed, grows sympathetic, and lets more days pass. Bartleby seems to be a millstone around his neck, however; and so, putting an extra twenty dollars in plain sight, the lawyer tells the fellow that he must be gone in six days. But when the appointed time comes, Bartleby is still in the office. The employer is so dumbstruck that he walks slowly away and into the street again. Returning, he argues, but Bartleby, reluctantly, will say only that he prefers not to quit the lawyer, who in the ensuing days begins to blame it all on predestination and also to feel charitable. Then, however, some of his professional colleagues notice the pale, uncopying scrivener and start whispering about him among themselves. So the employer moves out from under Bartleby to new offices nearer the City Hall, only to have Mr. B—, the new lawyer-tenant of the old place, call on him to report in desperation that the copyist is still there, still refusing to do any copying. When the employer disclaims responsibility, Mr. B— has his landlord turn Bartleby out. Now the fellow haunts the staircase and sleeps in the entry. So his old employer tries once again to talk to him, even offering to find him another job or take him home for a while; but Bartleby prefers not to accept. The employer feels free in his conscience and yet finds himself driving uneasily a good deal in his carriage. Returning at last to his office, he finds a note from his former landlord telling him that Bartleby is now in prison for vagrancy. Rushing to the Tombs, the employer finds his former scrivener, tries ineffectually to talk with him, pays the grub-man to feed him well, and leaves. A few days later the troubled lawyer returns and finds Bartleby lying in the prison yard, dead. Bartleby, it is rumored, was once employed as a clerk in the Dead Letter Office in Washington.

    John Jacob Astor, B—, Bartleby, Monroe Edwards, Ginger Nut, Nippers, Turkey.

'The Battle for the Bay (August, 1864),' 1866.

    Describes Admiral Farragut's brave and successful attack with Union vessels, including his flagship the *Hartford*, on Mobile Bay, during which Farragut loses the *Tecumseh* but captures the Confederate iron-clad, the *Tennessee*.

    Admiral [David G.] Farragut.

'The Battle for the Mississippi (April, 1862),' 1866.

    [Admiral David G.] Farragut.

'Battle of Stone River, Tennessee, A View from Oxford Cloisters (January, 1863),' 1866.

    [General John C.] Breckinridge, [General William S.] Rosecrans.

"The Bell-Tower," 1855.

    In southern Europe near a capital once great but now mouldy, stands the stump of what seems a fallen pine, but it is of stone. Ages ago its story started. The great mechanician Bannadonna, a foundling, is permitted to build a three-hundred-foot bell-and-clock tower of stone, to be the noblest in Italy. He works proudly and secretly. From its completed top he stands erect and views the distant Alps. During the casting of the huge bell destined for the tower, the frightened workmen shrink back. Bannadonna smites the leading culprit with a huge ladle, and a splinter from the dying man flies into the molten metal and weakens the bell-to-be. The complicated mechanism is hoisted with much holiday pomp. Then months of silence follow, during which Bannadonna continues to work in private. Eventually he lifts with a crane a cloaked statue which seems almost to step into the belfry. Two magistrates present at the high platform take notice and are also puzzled by an apparent change in the figure's posture, by a kind of ventilation in its covering, and by a corroded cup nearby. The huge bell-clock has ornate figures personifying the twelve hours. Una, remarks one magistrate, seems to be staring fatally at Bannadonna and looks different from the other hours—in fact looks like Deborah the prophetess in Del Fonca's painting. Bannadonna lightly explains that an artist can make no two objects alike and that Una needs some touching up. He then urges his visitors to descend. When they do so, they seem to hear a footfall, which, however, the mechanician soon explains is merely loose mortar falling from the high stonework. He reascends and works alone through the night installing the clock mechanism. He has promised that at one o'clock the following afternoon the first hour will be marvelously struck, as soon as his mechanical Haman yonder under the cloak is in place. A crowd waits below. At one a dull, mangled sound is heard. Then an awesome silence. The two magistrates rush aloft, accompanied by a spaniel, and find Bannadonna prostrate and bleeding, under the stroke of one, and with his grotesque bell-striking creation impending over him. It has a downcast face, limbs, scaly mail, and manacled, clubbed arms uplifted. Beneath its victim's dead body, which looks like Sisera felled by Jael, is the bell-striker's advanced, spurning foot. The rest is uncertain. Some say that the spaniel was shot at, after which came a sound like a snapped mainspring and a crash of metal. The magistrates ordered the mechanical figure removed and sunk at sea. It was theorized that Bannadonna sought to create a scientific serf, a super-animal, by sheer scientific reasoning and hard work, not by metaphysical philosophizing or incantations or prayer. He wanted to solve nature, steal behind her, and bind her to his hand. He wanted to make a Promethean God of himself. It was further reasoned that Bannadonna, just before his death, became engrossed in touching up Una's face and did not notice that his mechanical monster was gliding up on its oiled tracks to sound the hour. Thus the creature destroyed its creator. The magistrates planned a great funeral for Bannadonna, but when the appointed bell ringer jerked the rope he pulled loose the dead man's bell, which fell with a crash. When examined, it was seen to have a curious defect near its ear. The metal was remelted and a new bell cast. For a year a choir of birds sang in the belfry of the stone tree; then an earthquake shook the entire structure down with a crash.

Bannadonna, Del Fonca, Dua, Excellenza, Haman, Una.

"Benito Cereno," 1855.

The year is 1799. Captain Amasa Delano, commanding a sealer named the *Bachelor's Delight*, is near Santa Maria, an island off the southern coast of Chile. One morning through gray mists and shadows he sees a dilapidated Spanish merchantman in obvious need of help. He causes himself to be rowed over with supplies to the slovenly *San Dominick*, which has "Follow your leader" chalked under its canvas-covered figurehead or beak. Telling his men to return for water and more food, he stays on the Spanish deck, on which are four Negro junk pickers, ten Negro hatchet cleaners, and many other Negroes and a few Spaniards, including Captain Benito Cereno and his Negro attendant Babo. Cereno is sick-looking, weak, and spiritless. Babo seems sad and affectionate, and leaps to his master's every imagined need. The *San Dominick* soon drifts seaward. The Spaniards seem pitiable; the Negroes and Negresses, quite out of control. Captain Delano, singularly undistrustful and good-natured, begins to question his Spanish counterpart. At this, Cereno grows reserved and frequently coughs but manages to explain that his ship, bound from Buenos Aires to Lima with fifty Spaniards and three hundred slaves aboard, encountered gales, plague, scurvy, fever, and accidents which combined to kill all of his officers and many others, both white and black. He speaks ill of his remaining crew-members. Silently critical of Benito's evidently poor seamanship, Delano commends Babo for his friendliness, promises the loan of three of his best men to help the ship get to Concepcion, and walks to the poop with his host and ever-faithful Babo. He sees a Negro boy stab a white lad in the scalp, but Cereno only shrugs impotently. They talk of the Spanish captain's best friend, Alexandro Aranda, who owned and accompanied the slaves but is now dead. When Delano voices sympathy that the corpse could not be kept aboard, his host stares and then faints. Next a gigantic Negro slave named Atufal, a king in his own land, reports to his master as ordered but regally refuses to ask pardon; he must therefore remain in heavy chains. Delano quietly dis-approves. When Cereno and Babo suddenly walk away and begin whispering conspiratorially, the American silently notes this fresh affront. A young Spanish sailor stares intently at him from the rigging. Delano begins to wonder whether his host is an innocent lunatic or a guilty imposter, and concludes that the young captain must be an indecorous, cruel adventurer. But Delano's frosty suspicions soon melt in his sunny good-nature.

Cereno now approaches the American and questions him about his cargo (silks and silver), the size of his crew (about twenty-five in all), and their arms (cannon, muskets, spears, and cutlasses). Delano is annoyed but takes comfort in fearless truth and soon moves off, to avoid being uncivil. In a dark hatchway he suddenly sees a Spanish sailor (later identified as Don Joaquin, Marques de Aramboalaza) with something like a gem sparkling in his shirt. Puzzled, Delano wonders whether the curious Spanish captain has any designs on his *Bachelor's Delight*. Are some of the supposedly dead Spanish sailors really in hiding below? If Cereno is telling lies, what is the truth? Are the Negroes in on the plot? But no. Cereno is a sulking invalid. Delano will have to loan him his second mate to get the *San Dominick* to Concepcion. The American grows tranquil, especially when he sees his whaleboat, the *Rover*, far away but slowly approaching. Suddenly two Negroes, accidentally jostled by a sailor (later identified as

Bartholomew Barlo), dash him to the deck. Instead of looking on, Cereno turns in a fainting cough and is devotedly attended by faithful Babo, whom Delano smilingly offers—in vain—to purchase. Left alone by the two, Delano descends from the poop and walks boldly among the junk pickers. A noble, haggard-looking Spanish sailor sits tarring a strap; another sailor is splicing. Both have Negroes near—white pawns among opposing chess men. Fondly observing a Negress, half asleep, suckling a stark naked, fawn-like infant, Delano notes her typical combination of tender heart and tough constitution. He walks into the starboard quarter-gallery, which resembles a Venetian balcony or a half-wrecked summer-house, and from which he spies the *Rover*, now struggling against a rip tide as dusky noon arrives. Is that Spanish sailor (possibly Luys Galgo, named later) covertly trying to warn him again? Is Cereno in league with his simple Negroes, and does he in talking with Delano malign his intelligent white friends to betray them? An old sailor (possibly Luys Galgo) tosses a knot to him and says in rapid, low English, "Undo it." Delano reminisces, feels uneasy, even fearful, reviews the recent curious events, and then as the *Rover* touches the Spanish ship supervises the dispensing of water, pumpkins, and cider before the enervated but jealous Spanish captain. At one point, some Negroes jostle him, Delano half-humorously threatens them with a gesture, and only the junk pickers can prevent what appears to be developing as an attack on him. Dispatching his men for more water, Delano plans to remain aboard the *San Dominick* and pilot her to an anchorage by sunset or perhaps a little later—under the expected full moon. Now Babo, always near, reminds his master that it is time for him to be shaved in the cuddy and suggests that Delano come along and talk.

The cuddy, a light deck-cabin like an attic over the large cabin beneath, is in complete, bachelor-like disarray—on account of the storms and disasters just ended. Gliding after his master, Babo impresses Delano as being a typical Negro—brisk, noiseless, good-humored, and docile. The servant takes from the flag-locker a piece of bunting—which oddly turns out to be a Spanish flag—and tucks it under Cereno's chin, strops a keen razor on his oily palm, and begins the shaving process. For a second, Delano images the scene before him as that of a white man at a black headsman's block. The two captains discuss the recent gales and adverse currents, and Delano half doubts the Spaniard's story of a two-month delay from Cape Horn. Cereno shakes, and Babo accidentally draws blood from his neck. Combing and clipping finally done, Babo stands back to survey all. Delano walks forward to the mainmast. When the other two emerge, Babo is bleeding from the cheek and complains that his master nicked him in punishment. Delano concludes that slavery breeds ugly passions. A fine-looking mulatto named Francesco announces lunch—pumpkins, biscuit, cider, and Canary wine—during which Babo stations himself behind the American and facing his master, whose every whim he can thus observe and jump to gratify. The two captains discuss the price of sails which the *Bachelor's Delight* will supply the *San Dominick*, and then two o'clock sounds and the wind begins to rise. Determining to get the Spanish ship into the harbor, Delano goes on deck and in his best Spanish shouts orders which Babo repeats. Before the American can return to his Spanish host to confer with him, Babo is there again ahead of him. Seeing his own ship, Delano invites Cereno to have coffee aboard her, but the morose man sullenly refuses. Irked, Delano walks off alone. Soon the two vessels lie anchored together and the *Rover* is hooked along the Spanish gangway. Delano tries to bid a proper goodbye to his curious host, who, however, merely grasps his hand across Babo's constantly interposed body. Again Delano has forebodings until he looks at his domestic ship; then he smiles, all being well—including his conscience.

Delano now steps into his boat, orders it off, and is terribly startled to see Cereno leap after him into it—evidently in an attempt to give the impression that he is being kidnapped. Three Spanish sailors splash into the sea after him as if to rescue him. Babo, dagger in hand, also jumps into the boat in an evident effort to aid his master by attacking Delano. A sooty avalanche of Negroes next pours over the Spanish bulwarks. Wrenching the dagger away, Delano throws Babo down and simultaneously clutches the fainting Spaniard. But then, at last, the innocent American sees all: Babo is trying to stab Cereno with a second weapon. The Negro is quickly pinioned. Delano sees other revolting Negroes on deck, flourishing hatchets among their captured Spanish victims, and sees Spanish boys running for their lives up to the topmost spars. The *San Dominick* wheels, and the end of its cut cable whips the canvas off the beak, revealing a human skeleton for a figurehead. Cereno wails that it is Aranda, his murdered, unburied friend. Delano gets back aboard his own vessel, imprisons Babo, cares for Cereno and the other escaped Spaniards, and then permits his resolute chief mate and some of his men—promised rich shares of booty—to attack with yawl and whaleboat the *San Dominick*, now drifting away by the light of the rising full moon. They give chase, fire murderous volleys into the hatchet-hurling Negroes, board the ill-managed vessel, and soon capture all the remaining slaves.

Two days later, both ships proceed to Concepcion and then Lima, where the vice-regal courts take depositions and pronounce sentences. Mainly from sick Benito Cereno's testimony, the following facts are revealed. On May 20, 1799, his ship left Valparaiso bound for Callao with one hundred sixty Negro slaves of both sexes, mostly belonging to Alexandro Aranda, a crew of thirty-six white men, and in addition some white passengers. Babo, a frail, cunning Senegalese, and Atufal, a powerful former African chief, four Negro calkers (the junk pickers), six Ashantees (the hatchet cleaners), and a few other Negroes planned and executed a sudden revolt against the whites. They immediately killed many, committed atrocities on others, mutilated and murdered Aranda and made his skeleton into a figurehead with "Follow your leader" chalked under it as a terrifying warning, and forced the few remaining Spaniards to sail for Santa Maria in search of badly needed water. They remained there during the evening of August 17. Next morning, seeing Delano's ship, they formulated their plan in the couple of hours before the American came aboard, about 7:30. Cereno had two choices: to do exactly as Babo bid or be instantly killed, along with his American would-be benefactor. Only when Delano was safe aboard his own whaleboat did Cereno—inspired by God and the angels, he believed—leap to safety himself. Cereno then detailed the fates of various casualties, including the old sailor who tried to warn Delano, and a nobleman who had a jewel and was forced to dip his hands in tar. Only six white men and four white boys now remain alive.

Delano, who has accompanied Cereno on a long, mild voyage to Lima, talks with him after the trial. The Spaniard feels that God must have charmed his friend's life. Delano is sorry that he so misunderstood events as to suspect the Spaniard but lightly tells his mournful friend to forget the whole experience. The Spaniard says, however, that since he is human, unlike the blue sea and the blue sky, he can never forget it. Silent Babo is hanged. His body is then burned. And his head is put on a pole in the Plaza, across which is St. Bartholomew's church, where the bones of Aranda are laid to rest and where three months later shadowed Benito Cereno borne on a bier follows his leader.

> José de Abos and Padilla, Akim, Alexandro Aranda, Atufal, Babo, Lorenzo Bargas, Bartholomew Barlo, Captain Benito Cereno, Dago, Captain Amasa Delano, Delano, Diamelo, Francesco, Luys Galgo, Hermengildo Gandix, Juan Bautista Gayete, Ghofan, Martinez Gola, Roderigo Hurta, Infelez, Don Joaquin Marques de Aramboalaza, José, Lecbe, Mapenda, Francisco Masa, Matinqui, Miquel, José Morairi, Mure, Nacta, Nat, Ponce, Raneds, Juan Robles, Doctor Juan Martinez de Rozas, Alonzo Sidonia, Manuel Viscaya, Yambaio, Yau, Yola.

'The Berg (A Dream),' 1888.

The poet dreams that a martial ship is insanely steered into an indifferent iceberg and thus wrecked.

"Billy Budd," 1924 (also called "Billy Budd, Foretopman" and "Billy Budd, Sailor) [An Inside Narrative]"[1]

---

[1] The text used is Herman Melville, *Billy Budd, Sailor (An Inside Narrative)*, ed. by Harrison Hayford and Merton M. Sealts, Jr. (Chicago: The University of Chicago Press, 1962). In earlier editions, Captain Vere's *Bellipotent* is called the *Indomitable*.

Often sailors, walking on docks, will gaily surround their favorite shipmate, who is usually taller and handsomer than the average. Such a one is Billy Budd, aged twenty-one, impressed late in the 1790's off the *Rights-of-Man*. She is an oddly named merchantman whose unruly crew Billy's sweet presence has mollified and calmed wondrously, according to Graveling, her disconsolate captain. But off Billy must go, anyway, and so waving a cheerful goodbye to his mates he accompanies Lieutenant Ratcliffe aboard H.M.S. *Bellipotent*, a seventy-four outward bound. Soon Billy is rated as an able seaman and assigned as foretopman on the starboard watch. He is noble looking but slightly adolescent, a Bristol orphan—as he explains when asked about his parentage—illiterate, naive, exuberant, and fresh. He has one flaw—a liability to stammer.

In April, 1797, mutiny at Spithead breaks out; in May, at the Nore. It is all suppressed after some grievances—not including impressment—are redressed and also because of loyalty in the marine corps and among influential sections of the crews. In the summer, Billy comes aboard the *Bellipotent*, which is on her way to join the Mediterranean fleet. Melville excuses himself at this point for digressing to praise Admiral Horatio Nelson, a naval genius notable for painstaking foresight and for a burning love of glory. The captain of the *Bellipotent* is Edward Fairfax Vere, a bachelor of about forty. He is unselfish, strict, modest but resolute, dreamy (he is called "Starry Vere"), conservatively bookish—even pedantic—unjocose, and very honest and direct. His master-at-arms is a certain John Claggart, aged about thirty-five, thin and tall, with a pallid brow over which dark curls cluster, and possibly of defective blood. His mysteriously unknown past gives rise to rumors that he was a chevalier who got out of trouble with English law by joining the navy, often a refuge for the insolvent and the immoral. At any rate, Claggart is unpopular; he is also, however, swiftly obeyed by his subordinates, who have created for him an underground spy system aboard ship.

Life in the foretop suits Billy, who is most dutiful, especially after he is obliged to witness a flogging. Yet he is troubled because Claggart's police keep finding things amiss with his gear. So one day he appeals for an explanation to a scarred old veteran, a Dansker, who rather likes Billy and who laconically says only that Claggart has it in for the handsome youth. The next day, while the ship is rolling, Billy happens to spill his soup on the newly scrubbed deck just as Claggart walks by slapping his rattan. The master-at-arms has stepped by the mess before he notices that Billy was responsible but then elaborately says, "Handsomely done, my lad!" Billy is so naive that the sarcasm pleases him. What ails Claggart? He is a baffling personality, naturally depraved: he is proud, without petty sin, never mercenary or avaricious or sensual, dangerously lunatic because inconstantly so—in short, mysteriously iniquitous. He hates Billy and yet envies him because of the lad's heroic good looks and his obvious innocence. Matters are made worse when Squeak, a rat-like corporal of the master-at-arms, reports lies about Billy, saying that the foretopman has applied certain critical epithets to Claggart, whose curious conscience exaggerates them and makes him decide to check up on Billy.

A few nights later, Billy is aroused from his hammock by a whisper urging him to come to the lee forechains. Billy is unable to say no. When he arrives, an unknown man, also impressed into the navy, tries to bribe Billy to help in some unspecified way—at which Billy stammeringly tells him to be off. Billy is puzzled when he later sees an afterguardsman who he thinks is the man who spoke mysteriously to him, because the fellow laughs and is open in his manner. The Dansker, to whom Billy guardedly tells part of the strange story, repeats only that Claggart has it in for the handsome sailor. Refusing to be a telltale, Billy quietly remains ignorant, simple, juvenile, and trusting. He has no more trouble with his gear, and Claggart continues to speak pleasantly to him. But what of Claggart? He looks after Billy with his eyes suffused with incipient tears, softly yearning, as though he could love the youth but for fate. While Billy naively refuses to talk about Claggart to other impressed seamen, that monomaniac feels a hidden fire eating deeper into him.

Some time after the *Bellipotent* passes through the Straits [of

Gibraltar], she is detached from the fleet as a scout. She chases an enemy ship, which, however, crowds sail and escapes. Directly after this, Claggart asks permission, cap in hand, to speak with Captain Vere on his quarter-deck. Vere hardly knows his new master-at-arms but finds his first impressions of him distasteful. He is shocked when Claggart, with an air in which grief mingles with determination to be frank, reports that Billy Budd during the chase of the enemy ship behaved suspiciously and then hints that the result might be a repetition of the recent mutiny. Even though he thinks that Claggart is acting like a perjurer he once heard, Vere decides to investigate quietly, calls for Billy, and orders Claggart to stand by. Billy reports to his captain. Claggart hypnotically repeats his accusation. Billy turns as pale as a leper and begins to stammer gurglingly. When Vere, who has been thinking paternally of promoting the lad, tries to calm him by urging him to take his time, Billy's huge fist shoots out like a cannon and Claggart falls dead to the floor, like a dead snake. Aghast at such an Ananias-like judgment, Vere quietly calls the surgeon to verify the death and then—aware that Billy, though an avenging angel, must surely hang—convenes a drumhead court. The surgeon momentarily suspects his captain's sanity and would prefer to turn the case over to the fleet admiral.

Acting promptly and secretly, Vere appoints three officers, convenes a court in the quarter-deck cabin, and briefly describes what happened. Billy then testifies that he bore no malice against Claggart, did not mean to kill him, is sorry he is dead, but felt he had to act with a blow when lied about and when his tongue failed him. Vere says that he believes Billy, who is deeply grateful and who is shortly thereafter taken out under guard. Vere then tells the court, a trifle pedantically but efficiently, that moral scruples vitalized by compassion are irrelevant here in the face of a situation requiring military duty. He warns the officers not to listen to their hearts or consciences, nor to consider Billy's intent. He says that although God may forgive Billy the Articles of War are clear as to the penalty for a sailor who strikes a mortal blow to a superior in rank. Billy's act was mutinous homicide. In addition, Vere explains that the possible proximity of the enemy makes necessary quick action concerning the accused. If the death penalty does not immediately follow, the men will think that their officers are flinching and a deadly relaxation of war-time discipline will result. The uneasy court then sentences Billy to hang in the morning.

Vere personally reports the court's decision to Billy. The precise circumstances of their final meeting are never revealed. Perhaps Vere caught Billy to his heart like Abraham with his son. Probably Billy appreciated Vere's frank spirit. During the second dogwatch Vere tersely reports the events to the assembled crew, and shortly thereafter Claggart's body is honorably buried at sea. The chaplain visits Billy, who in sleep on the upper gun deck has a child's virgin innocence upon his face. Later the chaplain returns, offers what spiritual help he can, but concluding that innocence is better than religion to go to Judgment with kisses Billy's rose-tan cheek and withdraws. At four in the morning all hands are piped on deck. Just before being run up to the mainyard, Billy in clear syllables says, "God bless Captain Vere!" The crew echoes these words. The dawn clouds are fleecy. Billy ascends in rose light, and his body does not twitch. Talking about this phenomenon later to the purser, the physician denies that it should be equated with euthanasia and grumpily hurries off to his sick bay. Billy's body is quickly buried. Awkward seafowl croak a requiem over the spot where it has splashed. To assure prompt resumption of discipline, Vere orders the drum to beat to quarters.

A short time later, while the *Bellipotent* is returning to the main fleet, she engages the French line-of-battle ship the *Athéist*, and Vere is mortally wounded by a musket ball. Dying at Gibraltar, he is heard to murmur, "Billy Budd, Billy Budd," though not remorsefully. Weeks later an authorized naval chronicle reports that Claggart discovered a mutinous plot but before he could report everything to his captain he was stabbed by William Budd, who was undoubtedly a foreign agent and who was properly therefore promptly hanged. But his shipmates in time treasure bits of the spar from which he was hanged, as though they were pieces of the Cross, and in addition one tarry hand writes a ballad called "Billy in the Darbies," which purports to be the doomed sailor's thoughts as he thinks of his death and dreams of falling fathoms down into the oozy weeds.

> Albert, Billy Budd, Bristol Molly, John Claggart, the Dansker, Lord Jack Denton, Donald, [Comte] de Grasse [Francois Joseph Paul, Marquis de Grassetilly], Captain Graveling, the Handsome Sailor, Captain Mordant, Mr. Purser, Lieutenant Ratcliffe, Red Pepper, Red Whiskers, [Admiral, Baron, George Brydges Rodney] Rodney, Squeak, Taff the Welshman, Captain the Honorable Edward Fairfax Vere, Captain Vere, Wilkes, X—.

'Bridegroom Dick (1876),' 1888.

Recounts old Bridegroom Dick's varied reminiscences in the presence of his wife Bonny Blue of a varied life at sea aboard brave old wooden ships off Vera Cruz and later to the coming of the iron-clads during the Civil War.

> Commander All-a-Tanto, Bonny Blue, Bridegroom Dick, Brown, Lieutenant Chock-a-Block, Dainty Dave, [Captain Stephen] Decatur, [Admiral David G.] Farragut, the Finn, Guert Gan[sevoort], Jack Genteel, Glen, Hal, [Captain Isaac] Hull, Jewsharp Jim, [Commodore Thomas] Ap [ap] Catesby [Jones], Laced Cap, Chaplain Le Fan, Lieutenant Long Lumbago, Major, Lieutenant Marrot, Orlop Bob, [Captain Matthew C. or Captain Oliver H.] Perry, Phil, [Admiral David T.] Porter, Rigadoon Joe, Rhyming Ned, [General Antonio Lopez de] Santa Anna, [General Winfield] Scott, Sid, Purser Smart, Starr, Starry Banner, the Surgeon, Lieutenant Tom Tight, Top-Gallant Harry, Captain Turret, Will.

'Buddha . . .' 1891.

> Buddha.

["Burgundy Club Sketches"], 1924. See "The Marquis de Grandvin," "Portrait of a Gentleman," "To Major John

Gentian, Dean of the Burgundy Club," "Jack Gentian (omitted from the final sketch of him)," "Major Gentian and Colonel J. Bunkum," "The Cincinnati," 'Marquis de Grandvin: At the Hostelry,' and 'Marquis de Grandvin: Naples in the Time of Bomba.'[2]

'Camoens,' 1924.
[Luiz de] Camoens.

'Chattanooga (November, 1863),' 1866.
[General Ulysses S.] Grant.

'The Chipmunk,' 1924.
Baby.

"The Cincinnati," 1924.
Members of the Burgundy Club discuss the ribbon of the Society of the Cincinnati and related matter.
Colonel Josiah Bunkum, Dean [Major John Gentian], Fathers, [General George] Washington.

Clarel, 1876.
Part I. Jerusalem.
In his hotel at twilight, Clarel, a serious traveler, kneels and tries to pray, and then looks out over the dreary roofs of Jerusalem. He then talks with Abdon, his host, and then goes to his room, reads, and uneasily sleeps. The [Church of the] Holy Sepulcher and nearby hallowed spots are described. Then the Crusaders, who were both raging and devout. In the morning, Clarel rises to find the garden where Christ after the crucifixion appeared to Mary; seeing exhausted Greek pilgrims here, Clarel has a sympathetic vision of Greek Christians, Levantine Moslems, Indians, and Chinese—pilgrims all. But as he now leaves, he hears rival Christian liturgies. He walks through silent streets, through the Jaffa Gate, and beyond the walls, and meets kindly

[2]For information concerning this abortive work, see Merton M. Sealts, Jr., "Melville's Burgundy Club Sketches," *Harvard Library Bulletin,* XII (Spring, 1958), 253-267.

Nehemiah. This saintly old man (from Rhode Island) has long been a revered wanderer in the Holy Land. Clarel accepts when the simple old man offers to be his guide. For days they ramble over the storied ground and see much. By lower Gihon they encounter three demoniacs, one of whom is bitter Celio, a handsome but hunchbacked doubter. He is a Roman presently living in despondency at the Franciscan convent in Jerusalem. Now at sundown he walks along the Via Crucis, goes past the Ecce Homo Arch, and suddenly thinking that he may be like the Wandering Jew goes out through the Gate [of St. Stephen]. Night catches Celio outside the locked town; so he winds through glens and beside caves, hears some Terra Santa friars, weeps at their words, and then is torn by more doubts till sunrise. At the muezzin's cry, the gate opens, and Clarel, passing through it, sees bitter Celio, who soon, however, disappears. It is Friday, and Clarel and his saintly guide Nehemiah go to the Wailing Wall and see Nathan, an American, there, with his Eve-like daughter Ruth. As evening approaches, his guide tells Clarel about Nathan: he was born in Illinois, worked hard as a farmer in his youth, passed through a period of early religious doubt, observed the viciousness of nature, and finally married a Jewess named Agar and became a convert and then an ardent Zionist, and moved with Agar and Ruth (and a younger child who soon died) to Jerusalem, where he now farms at Sharon even though hostile Arabs surround him. That night Clarel is restless, goes to his roof, sees Abdon at prayer, and learns from him that a sudden shriek which they hear came from persons watching at a deathbed. Clarel learns that Celio has been released from his doubts by death. His body is buried in the Vale of Ashes north of town. Nehemiah, who has accompanied Clarel to the Vale, now takes him through obscure little streets, the retreat of lost, forgotten people. They stop at the old man's sparse room, to which Ruth like a shy bird brings food; after Nehemiah eats a little bread, he sleeps and Clarel steals forth. The next day Clarel goes (with Nehemiah) to the home of Nathan, who stares aloofly at him, and meets gentle, apparently responsive Ruth. On the following day south of town Clarel and his old guide encounter a short, rugged man (later identified as

Margoth), who hammers at the rocky soil and hurls gibes when he sees that he has shocked Clarel. Next are described the stone huts of the wretched lepers inside the wall. Then the two visit famous regions near the Gate of Zion.

Days pass, and Clarel calls often on Agar and lovely Ruth, both of whom are glad to see a fellow-American, and both of whom are depressed so far from home. On a certain mild morning Clarel and his gentle old guide explore the Sepulcher of Kings north of town and while there see a shy, meditative man named Vine; later, after visiting famous sites—Moriah, Jehoshaphat, Siloam, and the Pool of Bethesda—they return with him toward the city. The three visit the Garden of Gethsemane, but Vine is shy, aloof, and imperfectly communicative. At the site of the Passion, Nehemiah reads quietly and then grows dazed. Above the garden the group meets Rolfe, a handsome, genial, wise, and talkative man who as they walk along discourses on comparative religion, ranging from Osiris to Matthew impressively. Now follows a poem about Rama, the Indian who was a god but knew it not; perhaps someone here [Vine or Rolfe?] resembles Rama. Beside a stone where Christ sat when He predicted the fall of Jerusalem, Rolfe sits and speaks of the poverty in the city now. The group tarries, and he inveighs against delimiting scientific researches into legend-rich religions. Then follows the touching story of Arculf the palmer to the Holy Land and Adamnan the abbot of Iona [off Scotland] who befriended him on his return. Clarel, Nehemiah, Vine, and Rolfe now climb a little tower and from its top view the wrinkled city of Jerusalem below and then look [to the east] toward the hellish Dead Sea; when unmoved Nehemiah suggests a stroll to Bethany, Rolfe puts him off gently. When the mild old man walks away, Rolfe tells the other two about a sea captain rendered as meek as Nehemiah by a pair of horrible shipwrecks. Curious now, Clarel tries to get Nehemiah to talk about his past but fails.

The young man, who never knew his mother, finds a substitute in kind Agar and soon falls in love with her daughter Ruth, and she with him. Next Clarel visits the grave of Celio, in the Latin and English Cemetery near Zion Hill; there he encounters Rolfe, visiting the grave of an old friend named Ethelward. Parting from his new friend, Clarel sees various travelers entering Jerusalem and then returns to his room, where he happens to find an enigmatic anti-revolutionary poem by B. L. pasted on a wall and white-washed over. Suddenly tidings come that hostile Arabs long scorned by Nathan have killed him and taken away his body; when Clarel finds that Jewish law forbids his entering a Jewish house of mourning, he sends a note and a ring to Ruth as a pledge of his devotion and decides to join Vine, Rolfe, and several recently arrived pilgrims on a short trip to Siddim, the Dead Sea, Mar Saba, and Bethlehem. Clarel encounters an Armenian funeral, which arouses ominous ponderings. Then on Candlemas morning [February 2] the travelers set out, amid the wrangling of their Arab guide, drivers, and guards, and under the half-cynical, half-pitying eye of Abdon the Black Jew.

Part II. The Wilderness.

The cavalcade goes down Dolorosa Lane and includes the following: Derwent, an Anglican priest, benign and modern; the Elder, a Scotch Presbyterian, sour, self-reliant, and belligerent; a Greek banker, rich and self-pampering; Glaucon, the banker's prospective son-in-law, sweet, rakish, and light-hearted; Mortmain, gloomy and stiff; then Nehemiah on his patient ass; earnest Clarel; dapper Rolfe, riding like an Indian scout; and finally Vine, lagging by himself. As the group prepares to ride out, Glaucon begs that no one will speak the word "Death," Derwent suggests a gay morning canter to Clarel, who, however, is gloomily thinking of immured Ruth, and Mortmain morosely harangues against those who crucified the Savior. Then Rolfe tells optimistic Derwent about skull-capped Mortmain, details of whose life he learned at Abdon's inn: Mortmain, an illegitimate Swede, was ignored (save for money) by his father, participated in revolutionary activities in France, and became prey to hideous doubts. Clarel speaks about Homer to Glaucon, but that gay young Smyrniote has hardly heard of the poet and instead talks about shooting at Nazareth and then sings a love song, to the annoyance of the dour Elder. The party now approaches the ugly little hamlet of Bethany, which, all the same, the Son of God once hallowed with His presence. The guide of the pilgrims is Djalea the Druze, a noble, inscrutable Lebanese; and the leader of the six Arab Bethlehemite guards under Djalea is Belex, a former Turkish cavalryman, now tough and stoical because of misfortunes. The party proceeds through the dangerous region of Adommin [Adummim]; the Druze keeps a sharp lookout, and his men scour the dens about, while Nehemiah tells the story of the Good Samaritan. During a halt in a rocky place, Glaucon sings a ribald song which so offends the Elder that he leaves the party permanently, Djalea speaks to Vine so courteously that Rolfe concludes that the aloof American is noble, and demented Nehemiah startles ease-loving Derwent by trying to clear the area of rocks in preparation for the second coming of Christ. Next comes an essay in verse on the desert—beautiful but horrible, dire and yet holy. The group moves along rather sullenly, except for observant Rolfe, even-tempered Vine, and the placid escort. When a small party of armed Turks approaches on its way to Jerusalem, the wheezing banker and gay Glaucon join it and leave the pilgrims. The diminished group proceeds to the gorge of Achor beneath a cliff near Jericho. By Elisha's fountain the group pauses, and suddenly Mortmain announces that he will spend the night here alone and plan to join the others in a day or two. By the Crusaders' Tower at Jericho the pilgrims make camp for the night and begin to discuss previous visitors here, biblical, military, and legendary; and then Rolfe sympathetically speaks of crazed Mortmain to Vine and the others. In the middle of the night, Rolfe gets up; Clarel silently avoids him and then guiltily wonders why he did so.

Early the next morning, Clarel, Rolfe, and Vine talk with a Syrian monk now in the act of spending forty days on the heights of Quarantania re-enacting the temptation of Christ by the Devil; the ascetic monk tells of his vision of the Savior and His message about God's omnipresence, about goodness, and about the peace that will come before death. Clarel, Rolfe, and offended Vine then see Margoth, the geologist, descending the mountain, in a cave of which he explains he has recently slept and which has provided him with rocky specimens. The Jewish Margoth, though a member of a creditable race, outrages his auditors by suggesting that the region should be scientifically modernized. Gloomy, honest Rolfe and pain-hating Derwent turn to a discussion of science as relativistic. Started by shy Vine, the pilgrims then have a learned talk concerning Hebrews.

On the third morning, in the rain, Djalea leads the pilgrims to the Jordan River; they ride across it with seven bandit-like Arab horsemen, with whom they chat and compare arms briefly. The pilgrims stay near the Jordan for a while—Rolfe, Clarel, and Vine singing a hymn, Nehemiah tasting the water, but Margoth pronouncing Nehemiah a fool and rushing off for some wine instead. The group next encounters a Dominican friar of French background who eloquently defends the Roman Catholic church as the only true protestant institution in modern mad times, as able to adapt, as properly anti-scientific, and as centrally related to all religions. As the Dominican leaves, Margoth shouts derisively after him; then Rolfe and Derwent carefully discuss the future of Rome. As the Arabs cut willows for palm leaves, Clarel approaches Vine, who waxes communicative but then stops, saying to himself that the younger man if plagued by doubts must settle them by himself. As the pilgrims file southward toward the Dead Sea, they see some Apples of Sodom and bitter mist drives at them. They discuss the biblical warning that none should traverse the desolate mountain region of Seir nearby and then see a lovely rainbow over the ugly sea. Derwent points out the location of the lost city of Petra, which Rolfe then describes, since he is the only member of the party who has seen it; then they rouse Nehemiah, who is queerly sleeping under a huge rock, and continue their journey. On a rock face they find a chalked image of the Southern Cross and a mysterious inscription about science and Christ beneath it; they think that it may be by Mortmain and hence proof that the man is alive and well. When in the afternoon their Bethlehemite escort pitches camp a little farther south, between the Judah Mountains and the Dead Sea, Derwent placidly starts reading, to the annoyance of Rolfe, who thinks that the present scene is more challenging than any book. Clarel approaches silent Vine at the salty marge, and soon they are joined by Rolfe, who engages Margoth, the literalist geologist collecting specimens there, in debate as to the origins of the Dead Sea—a debate which, to Vine's mute amusement, Nehemiah's ass brays at noisily. Suddenly Mortmain reappears, descending from Judah, and in spite of a warning "salt-song" from Beltha, one of Djalea's Bethlehemite guards, drinks the alum waters of the Dead Sea. Now follows a prelusive canto on the mystery of iniquity. That night Mortmain launches into a violent recital of the terrible sins of which the Dead Sea seems the concentrated symbol. The others withdraw from him; and while Nehemiah sleeps and Margoth conducts some geological experiments, the others discuss the five sunken cities. In the night Nehemiah dreams that the New Jerusalem has risen from the Dead Sea and is murmurously beckoning him, rises yearningly, walks in his sleep, and vanishes. In the morning Vine finds Nehemiah's lifeless body by the shore, calls the others, and they bury the saintly old man's body with his Book in a bone-scooped trench; instantly comes an avalanche of flinty shards down the mountains and then a frail fog-bow over them.

Part III. Mar Saba.

The pilgrims mount up and, putting the Dead Sea and Siddim behind them, begin to climb the perilous mountains of Judah toward Mar Saba; Mortmain starts to describe the vengefulness of God. Clarel, to change the mood, tells a story told him by Nehemiah of a mild carpenter who once argued with his sole friend and thereafter never left his home until he died. The pilgrims pause now and briefly discuss various conceptions of heaven. Suddenly the party encounters a Cypriote, who has vowed to dip his mother's shroud in the Dead Sea and who proceeds toward it singing with incredible gaiety, to the momentary annoyance of the pilgrims when they think of their dead friend Nehemiah down there. The group rests, with most of the pilgrims talking now about the dangers of the Gnostic preference of knowledge over faith and about historical cycles; Clarel admires the calm of pipe-puffing Djalea while Vine idly crushes and tosses porous stones. Mortmain asks Derwent to lecture them as though they all needed spiritual comfort, and so the cleric urges cheerfulness and rejoicing; but this does not satisfy Mortmain, who therefore demands and gets an unpalatable little exposition of influences shaping the Jewish faith. Clarel follows aloof Vine to a lane among the crags and finds him trembling; the entire group hears the bells of distant Mar Saba; then they see a cairn of stones piled up by silent Vine. They ride on, in single file, until they encounter in a green hollow some tents of Moabites and Ammonites, with whom Djalea serenely parleys before his group is allowed to pass on. Several monasteries, European as well as Middle-eastern, are described, and then Saba, hung in the cliff clefts before the pilgrims now.

Clarel and his party enter Mar Saba, not from below, where the Kedron ravine is, but from the ridge above and through a wall near Saba's towers; they are courteously welcomed by the friars, fed, and assigned beds. But first they are treated to a gay drinking party, at which they meet first a gigantic, colorfully garbed Albanian soldier (the Arnaut) with medals, sword, and thirst for wine, and then a native of Lesbos, an aging, gay epicurean; the visiting pilgrims respond differently to the wine: Derwent, at first reluctant, soon joins in; Djalea absents himself; Rolfe offers quick friendship to the Arnaut; Mortmain remains aloof and soon removes himself; Vine relaxes and drinks; and so does Belex. Rolfe sees a morose Greek timoneer (later named as Agath), whom he persuades to tell his sad story: it seems that the timoneer smuggled an evil Mohammedan, who wanted to escape the plague, aboard his ship *The Peace of God* along with the man's sea-chest, containing blades which turned the ship's compass and caused a wreck from which only the timoneer escaped; later Rolfe hears that the man after his unique escape was beset by robbers near Mar Saba and was robbed and beaten. The revelry continues with songs and recitations by the Lesbian, Derwent, Rolfe, and old Agath. Praising Agath's verses, Derwent begs shy Vine for a contribution, which is brief; then the Arnaut recites a battle song; as Clarel leans from a window and broods on the ebb of faith, a stark litany lifts from Kedron's jail below. Late at night Rolfe stirs, and he and Clarel walk to a railed ledge, see Djalea smoking calmly; to Rolfe's polite query, the Druze explains that in his religion there is no God but God. Rolfe praises Djalea's politeness and then begins to discuss at great length Belex's erstwhile position as Turkish guard of the Church of the Holy Sepulcher and the sudden leaping up there of fire at Easter, which Rolfe, to Clarel's discomfiture, says strains his faith.

Dawn breaks upon a holiday at Mar Saba, and four monks sing of Jeremiah, the Chaldean army, and Zedekiah. Rolfe and Derwent visit the church of the monastery, with its books, manuscripts, and flags. By torchlight that night is performed a masque, in which a muffled monk recites a monologue of the Wandering Jew, who thinks of his centuries of life, of his wife Esther, and of the coronation of Charlemagne which he observed, and who lurches on and on deathless and sleepless; hearing the recital, Mortmain shouts from a peak above "Dies Irae . . ." A lyric in praise of the Golden Age closes the masque.

Dawn comes up, and Clarel in anguish over his religious doubts engages Derwent, who seems strangely serious and touched, in a long conversation finally interrupted by the approach of Anselm, a young monk. Derwent has breakfast and then visits the porch of the minster, where he finds a marble shield depicting a fallen knight miraculously rearmed. Derwent next calls upon Christodolus, the blind old abbot of Mar Saba, who shows his flattering guest jeweled relics and saintly bones, then dozes off. Meanwhile, Clarel, breakfastless, walks out to a rocky grotto presided over by Cyril and containing skulls. As for Derwent, he saunters to the stables, jokes with the Lesbian, and goes with that gay fellow first down to St. Saba's fountain in Kedron's bed and then up past mad Cyril's vault; still higher, they see an eagle drop the snatched skullcap from Mortmain, who is on a top crag, and then see old Agath walking by a chasm. Meanwhile Vine reclines on a stone and sings to a brave palm tree in the crags to bloom green bravely though high over horrors. At this very moment, the Lesbian is telling Derwent about the timoneer, who was attacked once by an eagle which fell into the sea with him and bore off his hat as a prize; Derwent and the Lesbian then visit the gloomy cave, full of hellish inscriptions and long ago occupied by crazed Habbibi. While Derwent and the Lesbian begin to dance below him, Mortmain from the rocks glimpses them, then hears mad Cyril's cry for the password, and finally sees the lovely, cross-like palm, which when he thinks of his black past years seems to wave him on to Lethe. Rolfe hides on a low rock ledge, sees the palm, and remembers when as a shipboy long ago he once deserted in Mendanna's sea [by the Marquesas Islands] and went ashore to be greeted as a god in an Eden, then grew restless and left. In the afternoon, Clarel, thinking again of Ruth, climbs to the tree and there encounters the Celibate, a tall, pure monk who feeds his nimbus of St. Saba doves, listens to his young visitor's statement that he misses women's domestic touch here, and silently responds by letting Clarel read his anti-feminist tract, which also contains hymns and prayers; Clarel looks up, but the Celibate is gone, and then sees Mortmain, Vine, and Rolfe, and the palm again. In philosophical recoil, Clarel muses on love, divine and sexual, in heaven. As the pilgrims prepare to depart in the troubled dawn light, they miss Mortmain and find him in the crags dead, his filmed eyes staring at the Tree; the monks bury his body outside their sacred walls.

Part IV. Bethlehem.

The pilgrim group, reduced by the deaths of Nehemiah and Mortmain but augmented now by the presence of Agath (who rides Nehemiah's ass), the Lesbian, and a scarred, half-Indian Confederate veteran (later named Ungar), moves west, like the three kings of the Orient, through a region of powdery dust, toward Bethlehem. The huge Arnaut, who accompanies them briefly, now gallops colorfully back to Mar Saba and fires his gun twice in farewell; then the others notice that Agath has on his arm a tatoo of the Jerusalem ensign—crosses, palm leaves, crowns, and star. The pilgrims induce the old tar to tell about a volcanic island [Narborough, in the Galapagos] far away, dominated by giant, patient tortoises; Clarel concludes that if men cannot explain such a terrible place, which physically somewhat resembles the area through which they are now passing, they can hardly expect to solve the problem of the next world. Suddenly an evil-looking scorpion appears and terrifies Agath, whom Rolfe calls brave all the same. Keenly watching the sailor is Ungar, who—Djalea tells kindly, inquisitive Rolfe—has drilled both Egyptian and Turkish soldiers; Ungar himself then explains both that he is descended from an English Catholic who helped settle Maryland and who married an Indian and also that after the Civil War (which ruined him financially though he morally disapproved of slavery) he became self-exiled.

And then the pilgrims climb a hill and see Bethlehem before them—olive orchards, vineyard, and old walls. Arriving at the Capuchin abbey of Bethlehem, they pay and tip their Bethlehemite guard (Belex remains nearby), have supper, and retire happily; but first Ungar on the terrace greets the shining stars. As he falls asleep, Rolfe contrasts to himself the present age's agnostic materialism with Bethlehem's faith. After blithe Derwent rouses his friends to see dawn over the valley where the shepherds saw the Star of Bethlehem, Ungar suddenly launches into a bitter denunciation of the materialism and hypocrisy of Anglo-Saxons, far crueller than the traditionally cruel Turks. Before a rude stone monument in the valley, mild Derwent and wild Ungar argue about the worldiness of modern churches. The others at breakfast seem to respect Derwent when, though disquieted, he does not argue further with frowning Ungar. Meanwhile, for distraction Rolfe turns and listens to two strangers at the table arguing about the relative merits of Turkey and Protestant Europe. Next, after saying goodbye to Agath, the sad old sailor who now rides out of town, the party visits the Church of the Star, built lavishly about the site of the manger where Mary gave birth to the Christ child; the guide who points out the details to them is an intense, hollow-cheeked young Franciscan monk from Tuscany (later named Salvaterra) whom Rolfe regards as ardent because he is a novice but whom Derwent inwardly criticizes as effeminate. When Ungar seems to sympathize with the Franciscan, the latter suggests that the soldier's sword is a cross: then Ungar retires to his gnawing thoughts, and Rolfe and Derwent debate on manliness (which Derwent likes but Rolfe calls carnal at times) vs. Christliness. As Vine breathes a few words to Clarel sincerely praising the monk-guide, heavenly organ music ripples and swells about the

church. The whole group emerges from the grotto, finds dead
Nehemiah's ass lapping from a marble basin of holy water, and
says farewell to Salvaterra, who recommends the view of
Bethlehem from the church roof; they ascend to try it, and when
Derwent mentions Naomi's Ruth, poor Clarel, thinking of dead
Nathan's Ruth, his love, is tempted to leave the party and go at
once on to Jerusalem; finally, Derwent and Rolfe discuss the
survival of tradition in the Roman Catholic church. When
Derwent lightly leaves, Rolfe and Clarel discuss Ungar, who they
agree is evidently both a brave soldier and a sound thinker. Then
the pilgrims visit three nearby convents, Greek, Latin, and
Armenian, then the Milk Grotto; then Derwent, Rolfe, and Ungar
debate the effectiveness of religion in the heartless world today.
Now up comes a stranger, Don Hannibal Rohon Del Aquaviva, a
one-armed, one-legged friend of Derwent from Mexico; he lost his
limbs fighting for Mexican freedom but is now jocosely disillu-
sioned and starts a little debate with Ungar but then leaves for a
time. Ungar then launches into a violent statement on the
inefficacy of reform. To Rolfe's courteous question, Ungar goes
on by saying that America will be the scene of a new Adamic fall.
Next, to Vine's question about wickedness, Ungar hints that it is
an ingrained evil which we are all born with; Derwent lightly says
that the sunset is sweet; Clarel is tempted to live for his senses but
then thinks of his star near the horizon. Rolfe tries to defend
Ungar to friendly Derwent. As the group returns to town, Clarel
hears an unknown voice (later identified as that of the Lyonese)
singing of his love Inez. Back in town again, Derwent looks for his
crippled friend Don Hannibal and finds him sitting in a coffin
chatting with a traveling Mexican funeral friar named Brother
Placido. When Clarel goes to his room, he finds that it is to be
shared for the night by the prodigal Lyonese, a gaily sensual,
slightly effeminate singer whom Clarel bothers with serious
questions about sad Judaea; the Lyonese counters with comments
about the witchery of dark-tressed Jewesses, sings him a song
about Shushan [in Persia], retires, and trips out of their room
early, while Clarel dreams of being tugged this way and that by
the lush Lyonese and ascetic Salvaterra. Derwent startles Clarel

on the parapet by praising the soft, warm form of the Lyonese, whom they watch as he leaves town. Unger and Don Hannibal also leave; and Clarel, to while away some time before happily returning to Jerusalem, goes out to David's Well, where he meets a Russian pilgrim who tells him that the Lyonese is Jewish but conceals the fact while traveling among strangers.

On the night of Shrove Tuesday, the day before Lent begins, the group—minus dead Nehemiah and Mortmain—leave Bethelehem; Clarel rather decisively thinks of marrying Ruth and taking her, along with her mother Agar, away from this sad land; the pilgrims pass by the Cistern of Kings, Hinnom, Zion, Rogel (since an Ottoman camp blocks the path past Jeremy's grotto), Ophel, Shaveh, and Siloam, toward sepulchral Jerusalem itself. But they stop at the Jewish cemetery, where Clarel discovers that Ruth and her mother Agar, dead of fever and grief, are that moment being buried under cover of darkness because of their friends' fear of the Turks; dawn then breaks on Ash Wednesday. A dirge now begs death to lead Ruth gently away until her lowly lover can join her.

Five days pass, and Clarel sits senseless, his friends Rolfe and Vine and Derwent reluctantly leaving him to go their necessary ways; Clarel soon sees a group of cheerfully singing Armenians on Palm Sunday, but they remind him only of the earlier Armenian funeral train and of death—of Nehemiah, Celio, Mortmain, Nathan, Agar, and Ruth. And now Easter Sunday, the same this year for Latin pilgrims and for the Armenians, Greeks, Syrians, and Copts; Christ is risen, but where is Ruth?—wonders Clarel, lonely now in the depopulated town. On Whitsun-tide amid the long train of burdened people and beasts walking along the Via Crucis is one who laments that he hears no message from beneath the gravestone. In an epilogue Clarel is adjured to keep his heart, though star and clod battle, and to believe what Faith says, that the spirit rises above the dust.

Abdon, Agar, Agath, Anselm, the Arnaut, the Banker, Beatrice, Belex, Beltha, Benignus Muscatel, the Bey, [George] Calvert, the Celibate, Celio, Christodolus, Clarel, the Cypriote, Cyril, Derwent, Didymus,

Djalea, the Dominican, the Elder, the Emır, the Emir,
the Emir, Ethelward, Glaucon, Don Graveairs,
Habbibi, Hafiz, Don Hannibal Rohon Del Aquaviva,
[Pasha] Ibrahim, Inez, B. L., Lazarus, the Lesbian,
Max Levi, the Limeno, the Lyonese, Mahmoud [II,
Sultan of Turkey], Margoth, Methodius, Mortmain,
Mustapha, Nathan, Nehemiah, the Palmer, the
Patriarch, Brother Placido, the Rabbi, Rolfe, Don
Rovenna, the Russian, Ruth, Salvaterra, the Syrian
Monk, [Count Johann von] Tilly, Toulib, Turbans,
Ungar, Vine, a Wahabee.

"Cock-A-Doodle-Doo!," 1853.

The narrator feels gloomy in early spring, walks on his hillside
pasture, visits the old and new struggling in nature, frowns at the
ugly mists and smog of morning, hears the railroad hooting
by—which reminds him of a recent terrible accident in which a
friend died along with thirty other people—and thinks of a certain
dunning creditor. His calves come out of the barn looking
wretched after six months of cold food. Suddenly a magnificent
crowing from an unseen rooster reverberates through the hills,
seemingly saying, "Never say die!" Immediately the narrator feels
better. He returns home and has a hearty breakfast. When his
lean, mirthless creditor appears, the narrator jokes with him
briefly and then throws him out. The invisible cock crows again,
the smooth, flute-like, golden-throated notes spurting through the
sunny air. The narrator's adversities seem like nothing, easily met
with rapturous defiance. Early the next morning the cheerful man
tries vainly to find the noble rooster, determined to buy it even if
it means clapping another mortgage on his land. He asks an old
man plowing and another who is idiotically mending a wreck of a
stone fence, but no luck. A gentleman obligingly shows him his
ten carrot-colored Shanghai roosters, but none of them is the
noble crower. Days and weeks pass. The narrator mortgages his
estate anew and is served a civil process in—of all places—the
village tavern, where he is trying to enjoy some porter and cheese.
How inelegant! But his sadness is dissipated when the unseen

cock blasts again like thunder with bells attached. One day the narrator's wood-sawyer, a sad-faced, shabby man named Merry-musk with a latent twinkle in his eye, comes by to be paid for work diligently done. The narrator asks him if he knows any gentleman with an extraordinary rooster. Merrymusk says no. The narrator visits poor Merrymusk later, to complete his pay-ments, and sees Trumpet, the man's glittering rooster, which irradiates the man's squalid shanty beside the railroad and even sustains mortally sick Mrs. Merrymusk and their four ailing children. Merrymusk refuses five hundred dollars for Trumpet, which the narrator calls Beneventano after a majestic opera figure he once saw. Merrymusk says that the cock's wild, roof-jarring message is "Glory to God in the highest!" When the narrator visits the shanty again, some weeks later, he finds the place a veritable hospital. In reply to his sympathy, pallid Merrymusk feebly says that he is well, orders Trumpet to crow, and falls back dead. The rooster shakes its golden plumage before the weak children, whose souls follow its imperial music up to the heavens. The narrator walks with the rooster out of the shanty, and watches it deliver a final supernatural note from the roof and then drop dead. The narrator buries them all by the railroad track and on their gravestone sets the image of a lusty cock. He is never in the dumps again.

> Beneventano, Widow Crowfoot, Jake, Merrymusk, Mrs. Merrymusk, Merrymusk, Merrymusk, Merry-musk, Merrymusk, Squire Squaretoes.

'The College Colonel,' 1866.
> The Colonel.

' "The Coming Storm": A Picture by S. R. Gifford, and Owned by E.B.: Included on the N. A. Exhibition, April, 1865,' 1866.
> E[dwin]. B[ooth]., S[anford]. R[obinson]. Gifford.

The Confidence-Man, 1857.
> Aboard the *Fidèle* at St. Louis on April 1, 18—, steps a man in

cream colors. He has come from a long distance and is deaf and dumb, harmless, and simple. The comments concerning charity which he scribbles on a slate contrast oddly with the pasteboard sign of the ship's barber—"No Trust." The mute falls innocently asleep on deck, and a tremendously varied crowd gathers around him curiously, wondering who he is, and then drifts away as the *Fidèle*, looking like an Oriental junk or a floating fort, starts its voyage of twelve hundred miles down the Mississippi River, symbol of the all-fusing West. At one of the first few stops, the mute probably disembarks.

Now a Negro cripple nicknamed Black Guinea hobbles about the deck begging money and sympathy. Some doubt his genuineness, and he carefully describes several honest "ge'mmen" aboard who will vouch for him. They include a gentleman with a weed, one in a gray coat and white tie, one with a big book, an herb-doctor, a gentleman in a yellow vest, one with a brass plate, one in a violet robe, and a soldier. An Episcopal clergyman goes in search of one of the described gentlemen. A few people toss pennies at Black Guinea, who catches them in his mouth like a performing animal. When a wooden-legged man denounces the beggar as a disguised white man, a Methodist army chaplain shakes the doubter, who calls the *Fidele* a ship of fools and hints that his doubts are now planted in all the passengers like thistle seeds destined to sprout later. When the crowd disperses, the Negro stumps out of sight.

Next a man who gives his name as John Ringman, with a widower's weed in his hat, accosts in a side balcony astern a pleasant merchant by name. He is Henry Roberts of Wheeling, Pennsylvania. Ringman tries to remind him that the two are acquainted; when Roberts denies knowing him, Ringman gently suggests that brain fever must have damaged his memory, blandly spins a story of terrible misery and obtains a bank note from the charitable merchant, and then tries to get him to invest in some Black Rapids Coal Company stock certificates. When Roberts, aware of the rare financial opportunity, asks why Ringman does not buy them, that man repeats that he is penniless, seems offended, and leaves. In private Ringman then turns soft, meditative, and unreserved; next he meets at the rail a sophomoric-looking young scholar reading Tacitus, whose cynicism Ringman lectures the youth on before he recommends Akenside. Ringman then reminds the college man that reading Tacitus destroys one's confidence in others and asks whether the youth could trust him. Fascinated though he is, the scholar soon retires.

Suddenly a man in a gray coat and white tie, looking slightly sorrowful but very sanctimonious, appeals without success to a rich, ruby-faced gentleman for money to support Seminole widows and orphans. As the gentleman hurries away, the Episcopal clergyman comes up and is happy to find the white-coated man. Just as they start to talk about Black Guinea, the cynic with the wooden leg reappears. He morosely digresses to tell about a Frenchman of New Orleans who tardily suspects his faithless wife. Then the wooden-legged man derisively repeats his charge against the supposedly crippled Negro, who, says the gray-coated man, is now ashore. The clergyman sadly admits that such talk makes him reluctantly mistrustful, whereupon his auditor urges him to remain confident of others and takes some money from him for the Seminoles. Then he turns to a stranger who in his immaculate, satin-lined coat is the embodiment of spotless goodness and asks him to support his plan for the World's Charity—which he presented in London while he was there to demonstrate his Protean easy-chair—to be organized with Wall Street efficiency. The man of goodness has already given money to aid the Seminoles and now half-humorously and half-pityingly adds more for the larger cause. Then he disembarks to attend his niece's wedding. The man in gray, now alone and turning lethargic, goes to the ladies' saloon and finds a sensitive woman reading there. He appeals to her to have confidence and to prove it by giving twenty dollars for the Seminoles. She does so.

A man (later identified as John Truman) with a ledger-like book appears and asks the college man if he has seen the man with the weed, since he wants to give him ten dollars. When the sophomore sees "Black Rapids Coal Company" in gilt on the book, he stops talking about Ringman and demands the right to buy some of the obviously opulent company's stock. Truman, who has identified himself as president and transfer-agent of the company, is reluctant but finally sells him some shares and tries to sell him others in the New Jerusalem, but the college man considers and then declines, at which, calling him cautious and prudent, the company president bids him adieu. Next, Truman enters a lounging, gaming room and encounters Roberts, the good merchant, whom he allows to persuade him to sell some coal company stock. They sit in silence a while, after which Roberts speaks of a certain pitiful old miser clinging to life and lucre aboard the ship and then speaks of the pitiful Negro cripple. But his friend Truman gently rebukes Roberts for mentioning cases illustrating lack of confidence. So the merchant relates the story told him by weed-hatted Ringman. It seems that he was married to Goneril, a vicious, straight-bodied, cactus-like wife, who dieted on crackers, ham, lemons, and blue clay, chuckled, and terrified people by her evil touch. When she started to exert a baleful influence on their little daughter, Ringman left his wife and took the girl with him. But Goneril tried to have him committed as a lunatic, and he began a life of lonely wandering, relieved—to be sure—by recently received knowledge that Goneril has died. Once again Truman, far from defending Goneril's widower, presents a temperate view of the case and alleges that Ringman's predicament is but another illustration of the need to have an intellectual confidence in Providence. Then the two conversers share a bottle of champagne, but Roberts's resultant statements against confidence upset his companion; and the two, after a kind of reconciliation, part. (The author now digresses briefly on the curious fact that, although nature credibly creates such inconsistencies as flying squirrels and duck-billed beavers, a writer is wrongly expected to produce characters which are unnaturally consistent.) Truman now goes down the corridor to the emigrants' quarters, finds a coughing miser lying there on an old moleskin coat, and—appealing to his greed—talks him into investing a hundred dollars in his friend the herb doctor's Omni-Balsamic Reinvigorator.

In a corner of the ship the herb doctor is talking with a very sick old man, urging him to have confidence in the Omni-

Balsamic Reinvigorator. Reluctant and querulously critical at first, the invalid finally buys six doses, whereupon the herb doctor goes to an ante-cabin and hawks his Samaritan Pain Dissuader. At first he has no success with a surly crowd which gathers about him. But then a sickly young man buys a bottle. Others do the same until a shaggy, backwoods giant limping with a swamp-oak cane shouts in a cavernous voice that no medicine can cure all pains, turns livid, and fetches the herb doctor a heavy side-blow. The herb doctor continues his spiel but soon leaves, whereupon two strangers begin to argue about him. Is he unmasked? Is he a knave? But then he returns and offers half his profits to charity if anyone needing or representing charity will step forward; when none does so, he gives two dollars to a wounded hussar. Then the herb doctor walks forward and interviews a cripple named Thomas Fry, a man on crutches and with paralyzed legs. Asked if he is a Mexican War veteran, the loud, ironic fellow explains that he saw a murder once, was put in jail as a witness, and contracted an incurable disease in his legs, after which the murderer got off anyway through influential friends. When the herb doctor ventures to doubt his story, Fry laughs and says that he will try another; and off he goes, shouting that he is a wounded veteran and gleaning a harvest of coins. The herb doctor lectures him on his lack of patriotism and confidence in the divine general goodness of the world, then without charge gives his auditor some liniment for his limbs, telling him to have confidence. Startled, Fry offers to pay. The herb doctor withdraws and soon encounters the coughing old miser, who is in search of the coal company man who took his hundred dollars. The herb doctor says that he sees that man, whom he names as John Truman of Jones Street, in the very act of disembarking—too late to be brought back. So the herb doctor, saying that the miser should have confidence in Truman and also in the Omni-Balsamic Reinvigorator, sells his new customer a box for two dollars—paid for in clipped coins. Then a wild-looking Missouri bachelor in a bear-skin jacket approaches and stands near the stairs. He and the herb doctor converse, the sick miser clinging to the latter's arm, about confidence in general; the herb doctor praises nature, but the Missourian (later named Pitch) waves his double-barreled gun and talks sarcastically of plagues, floods, and old age—all natural. Pitch so hates boys who have worked for him that he would like to buy a machine to replace them all. When the talk turns to slavery, the Missourian says that all spiritless fools are slaves, whether they come from Maine or Georgia. The herb doctor bids his adversary farewell and gets off at Cape Gira[r]deau.

A stooped little man from the Philosophical Intelligence Office now accosts Pitch and engages him in a long debate on whether all boys are rascals. Pitch says that they are and prefers farm machinery to them; but the P.I.O. man humbly replies that Pitch lacks confidence, that boys are like unfinished sketches, lily-buds not yet in bloom, baby teeth, and sinners not yet saintly. Pitch softens and finally pays three dollars plus passage for a boy worker—his thirteenth—to be sent him from the P.I.O. in two weeks. The agent disembarks at Cairo.

While Pitch stands at the rail, overlooking the twilight miasmas of Cairo and wondering whether the P.I.O. man was a trickster, a seraph-voiced stranger approaches and offers to start a friendly talk. The man, later named Frank Goodman the cosmopolitan, is colorfully dressed in Highland plaid, Emir's robe, French blouse, trousers, maroon slippers, smoking-cap, and Indian belt, and has a fragrant Nuremberg pipe. Pitch jeeringly brands him a puppet and a popinjay; but the other only urges him—*en confiance*—to regard life as a picnic, tells him in a little digression about a sick woman cured by getting her drunk, and invites him to walk with him now and to participate in a hurricane-deck dance later, and even to accompany him to New Orleans and on to London. When Goodman says that Diogenes was wiser to live in the market than Timon was to hide in the pines, Pitch mistakenly regards him as a latter-day Diogenes and shakes his hand. Goodman painfully leaves the misanthrope and soon encounters in the porch of a cabin a medium-sized Westerner (later named Charlie Noble) in well-cut clothes. Remarking that Pitch, whom he saw just now, reminds him of Colonel John Moredock the celebrated Indian-hater, Noble then launches into a long repetition of his father's friend James Hall's remembrance of Moredock and the typical, lonely, self-reliant backwoodsman's belief in Indian perfidy and his Nemesis-like tracking of Indians in the forest primeval. It seems that Moredock's mother and eight of her nine children were massacred by Indians shortly after they moved west from Vincennes to the banks of the Mississippi River in Illinois. Only Moredock was spared, and he became a ruthless avenger. At the end of the long story, Noble concludes that Pitch is a shallow misanthrope whereas Moredock was a profound one. Goodman doubts the whole story and then lectures to the effect that both misanthropy and infidelity spring from lack of confidence, whereupon Noble talks reluctant Goodman into sharing at a nearby table a convivial bottle of wine, which he says men should have confidence in. Of what use is health without cheer, security without society? Goodman then highly praises humor and laughter, at which Noble obligingly laughs at a pauper-boy on the deck below. They praise drink, and Noble repeats in a chanting voice a panegyric he once memorized in praise of the free press—the wine-press, that is! Goodman is delighted. Calling for cigars, they praise tobacco. Noble brands Pitch a misguided misanthrope from east of the Alleghanies and then criticizes Polonius as a detestable, toothless old mischief-maker whose advice to his son is horribly puritanical. But Goodman asserts that Pitch hides philanthropy under surliness and that apparent misanthropes really only lack confidence, which would make them genial. Suddenly announcing that he is going to share a confidence with Noble, who looks pleased, Goodman asks him for fifty dollars, the loaning of which will prove his kindness. Noble is outraged and calls his friend an impostor, at which Goodman dramatically says that he was only joking. (The author digresses to deplore the demand of some readers that fiction, written only to entertain, be faithful to life.) Goodman then tells Noble about Charlemont, who hints that he ruined himself financially to aid a friend. When Goodman asks whether Noble would meanly ignore a friend turned penniless, the man uneasily says no and then pleads a headache and retires.

At once a blue-eyed, red-clover-cheeked, mystical-looking man (later named Mark Winsome) warns Goodman against Noble. But when Goodman wants to know why, Winsome indulges in fuzzy transcendental talk about Egyptians and Arabs, and praises Goodman for his beautiful, loving, truthful soul. Goodman says that he believes beauty and goodness to be compatible and that therefore he has no distrust of that beautiful creature the rattlesnake. He then offers Winsome some wine, but that stoic takes ice water instead and speaks a sentence of Greek. A ragged but unsqualid man comes by, selling transcendental tracts; Goodman buys one, but Winsome sends the man away with a fierce stare. Finally he gets around to explaining that Noble is a Mississippi operator, a term which Goodman prefers not to understand aright. Next appears Egbert, neat, commercial in appearance, and about thirty years old. He is Winsome's practical follower, whose experiences verify the rightness of the mystic's philosophy. When Winsome withdraws, Goodman asks Egbert, in order to illustrate the practical consequences of that philosophy, to pretend that he has money and that Goodman wants a loan. In the dialogue which ensues, Egbert refuses a loan with interest (that would be commercial), a loan without interest (that would be alms), and alms (something is wrong with a man who cries for help). To illustrate all this, Egbert tells about China Aster. It seems that Orchis, a friend who had just won a big sum of money in a lottery, induced China Aster, a candlemaker of Marietta on the Muskingum River, to improve his business by borrowing a thousand dollars from him. Although no interest was asked—in fact, the loan was to be regarded as a gift—China Aster signed a note. Later he had such trouble repaying the debt, which Orchis—after getting married and joining a church—demanded, that he had to sign away his uncomplaining wife's inheritance and mortgage the candlery. He finally fell sick and died. Soon thereafter his wife also died, and their children became the town's wards. On China Aster's tombstone two of his conservative old friends recorded his sad story and closed the epitaph by saying that "the root of all was a friendly loan." Egbert's story of China Aster deeply grieves Frank Goodman, who says that its purpose seems to have been to destroy his confidence. But Egbert says that its theme is simply the folly of friend helping friend and adds that no one should put his fate into the hands of a friend since experiences and books may change that friend. Goodman accuses Egbert of inconsistency, a fault of Winsome's too, and says that he needs money to obtain necessities. Egbert will give him alms if he will act like a London beggar, but not otherwise. In a huff, Goodman hands him a shilling of wood to warm him, and Winsome as well.

Next Goodman walks to the *Fidèle*'s barber shop, arouses the barber (later named William Cream) from a cat-nap, and asks for a shave. Sitting in the chair, he is discomfited by the sign "No Trust" swinging above him. He and Cream debate on the subject of confidence. Cream explains that he has confidence in certain persons—for example, Goodman—but not just anyone. He piles hot suds all over the face of Goodman, to get him to shut up; but after his shave Goodman draws up a written agreement guaranteeing to reimburse Cream for all losses if in turn he will take the sign down. They sign the agreement, and Goodman walks out without paying for his shave, since Cream has his document guaranteeing against such losses. Cream tears up the written document and rehangs his sign.

(The author digresses on the subject of original characters, saying that truly original ones are as rare as Hamlet. They come from life, which combines with an author's imagination to produce them.)

Goodman finally goes to the gentlemen's cabin, lighted by a solar lamp from the ceiling, although it is late and most of the passengers there are in berths trying to sleep. An old man sits at a table reading the Bible. Goodman asks for the book and shows the old man a passage unpleasantly urging people to doubt the goodness of others. But the old man says that the passage, being from the Apocrypha, need not be believed. A leopard-toothed little boy enters and sells the old man a door lock and a money belt, neither of which Goodman is willing to buy. Then he and his old companion agree that distrusting man, God's creation, is like distrusting God the creator. They agree to trust Providence on their voyage. When the old man asks where his life preserver is, the cosmopolitan courteously finds him a stool, hands it to him, and leads him gently to his stateroom in the dark.

> Arrian, China Aster, Mrs. China Aster, Aster, Black Guinea, Daniel Boone, Brade, Brade, Bright Future, Charlemont, William Cream, Deacon, Jeremy Diddler, Egbert, Thomas Fry, Mrs. Fry, Goneril, Francis Goodman, Dr. Green, Judge James Hall, General [William] Hull, the Methodist, Mocmohoc, Colonel John Moredock, Mrs. John Moredock, Moredock, Mrs. Moredock, Moredock, Charles Arnold Noble, Old Conscience, Old Plain Talk, Old Prudence, Orchis, Mrs. Orchis, Philosophical Intelligence Office man, Pitch, John Ringman, Henry Roberts, John Truman, Weaver, Mark Winsome, Wright.

'C—'s Lament,' 1891.
     [Samuel Taylor] C[oleridge].

"The Death Craft," 1839.
     The narrator, Harry the Reefer, is in a torrid calm with heat so intense that tar oozes from the seams of the ship. He approaches the helmsman, only to discover a rotting corpse. The Mate screams that theirs is the Death Craft and leaps into the sea. There are human skeletons on the yards. Suddenly a violent storm lashes the vessel. Sailors rush past him as though they could not see him. The Captain shouts orders in a frenzy. Suddenly all is calm again. When Harry awakens, he is embracing his bride, whom he left a year earlier.
     The Captain, Harry the Reefer, the Mate.

'The Devotion of the Flowers to Their Lady,' 1924.
     Clement Drouon.

'A Dirge for McPherson, Killed in Front of Atlanta (July, 1864),' 1866.
     [General James B.] McPherson.

'Ditty of Aristippus,' 1947.
 Aristippus.

'Donelson (February, 1862),' 1866.
 Describes the successful Union siege of rebel-held Donelson.
 Baldy, Commodore, General [Ulysses S.] Grant,
 Colonel [William R.] Morrison, [General] Lew
 Wallace.

'Dupont's Round Fight, (November, 1861),' 1866.
 [Commodore Samuel Francis] Dupont.

'A Dutch Christmas up the Hudson in the Time of Patroons,'
 1924.
 Tuenis Van der Blumacher, Cousin Chris, Elsie, Hans,
 Katrina, Sharp-Eyes.

"The Encantadas," 1854.
 I. The Isles at Large.
 The Encantadas or Enchanted Isles, also called the Galapagos,
look like a gigantic heap of cinders, the world after a penal
conflagration. They are uninhabitable, solitary, changeless, and
they show for life mainly hissing creatures and wiry thickets.
Their coastline is clinker-bound and lashed by waves, partly
strewn with drifting bits of decay and shipwreck. Whalemen
formerly cruised near but found the tides and winds capricious.
Grotesque tortoises crawl about, looking hopeless and con-
demned. Even when far away, the author sometimes thinks of
those slow-crawling creatures on the evilly enchanted isles.
 II. Two Sides to a Tortoise.
 It is well known that you can turn a tortoise on his back and
see his bright side. But just because of this, do not deny its black
side. Nor if you cannot turn a black tortoise over, should you
deny that it has a bright side. Once, after five months at sea, the
author touches the South Head of Albemarle. A party goes ashore
and returns with three huge tortoises, black as widowers, plated
with dented shells which are shaggy, mossy, and slimy from the

sea. They look as though they had come from beneath the earth's foundations. They resemble Coliseums, walled towns. The author examines them curiously; later, when in his hammock, he hears them stupidly, resolutely crawling above him on deck, hopelessly pushing against immovable objects such as the foremast. Next evening, uneasy though he is at the thought of the tortoises' bleak endurance, he and his shipmates have tortoise steaks and stews, and carve the shells into tureens and the flat calipees into salvers.

III. Rock Rodondo.

The sailors see Rock Rodondo, or Round Rock, which from a distance looks like a sail. It is two hundred and fifty feet high and is visible thirty miles at sea. One morning before dawn they head for its base to fish. The tower-like rock is in uniform layers like entablatures or shelves. Above it fly innumerable sea birds, making a kind of canopy over it. Near the bottom are penguins, then pelicans, gray albatrosses, stormy petrels, and other birds—all making a wild din, through which can be heard the whistle of the beautiful "boatswain's mate." The fish are iridescent and tame, biting the hook like those who trust but do not understand human nature. The sun is up, and it is time to climb the tall rock.

IV. A Pisgah View from the Rock.

From the top of the rock you can look south toward the Antarctic and east toward Quito six hundred miles along the Equator. The Encantadas, the isles of San Felix and San Ambrosio, and the isles of Juan Fernandez and Mas-a-Fuera act as sentinels for South America to their east. Before 1563, Spanish ships going from Peru south to Chile were often lost because of their fear of circling far west. Then Juan Fernandez went west beyond the trades and hence easily south; in the process he found the island now named for him. About 1670 the Encantadas were thus found. This group includes Albemarle (about sixty by fifteen miles in size), Narborough—both of which are visited by whalers—and several smaller isles.

V. The Frigate, the Ship Flyaway.

In 1813 the U. S. frigate *Essex,* whose activities during the war of 1812 were perhaps the most stirring in American naval annals, sighted a mysterious ship off the Enchanted Isles, gave chase, but lost her. She alternately showed American and British colors. The *Essex* is peculiarly associated with the Encantadas. The best authorities on these islands are Cowley, Colnett, and David Porter of the *Essex*.

VI. Barrington Isle and the Buccaneers.

One of the islands is Barrington, which almost two centuries ago was the hideaway of the West Indian buccaneers. They raided the Pacific side of the Spanish colonies, then made for Barrington, with its good water, good anchorage, windlessness (sheltered as it was by nearby Albemarle), tortoises, trees, and grass. A sentimental voyager there once recorded finding seats fashioned out of stone and turf, near the tops of shady slopes. He was pleased to imagine the murderous pirates, some of whom turned buccaneer only because of persecution at home, lounging here philosophically.

VII. Charles's Isle and the Dog-King.

Double the size of Barrington is Charles's Isle to the southwest. A shipmate once told the author about it. A Creole from Cuba who fought for Peru against Old Spain was rewarded by being given his pick of the Enchanted Isles. Choosing Charles's, he proceeded to colonize it, build a capital city, guard it with fierce dogs, and even execute some of his rebellious subjects. When the population declined, he sought recruits from among deserters off whaling vessels. But one day they mutinied against the Creole, killed many of his dogs, and forced him to exile back in Peru. The sailors remained, to create not really a republic, which they forthwith proclaimed, but a riotocracy. After that, wise captains kept well off shore from Charles's Isle.

VIII. Norfolk Isle and the Chola Widow.

Northeast of Charles's Isle is Norfolk Isle, where a woeful event transpired. During the author's first visit to the Encantadas, his ship stopped there for two days to capture tortoises. As they were leaving, a sailor standing on a windlass saw a white object being waved from an inland rock. The captain ran out his spy-glass and saw a human figure. He launched a boat and picked up Hunilla, a Chola—half-breed Indian—from Payta, Peru. She told her wretched story. Three years before, she and her husband

Felipe and her only brother, Truxill, were left on the island by a French sea captain, to boil out tortoise oil. He would return for them in four months. But he never returned. In addition, one day Felipe and Truxill—who did not know their plight—built a little raft and merrily went fishing but capsized and were drowned, while Hunilla helplessly looked on from a cliff. Only Felipe's body was washed ashore, and Hunilla buried it reverently in the sand. On and on she waited for the ship to return, then for any ship. On a hollow cane she recorded the passing days, and also other observations—concerning eggs found, fish caught, tortoises captured, days of sunlight, and cloudy days. She stopped marking after one hundred and eighty days, though more followed. When the captain asked why, she would not explain. Did whalers come? . . . She almost missed seeing his ship because it came to the opposite shore of the humpy island from her hut, her husband's grave, and their dogs—now multiplied from two to ten. But something whispered to her through the enchanted air, and she climbed the rocks, saw the ship, and waved her turban. The captain ordered a boat to go to her hut and get the dried-out tortoise oil. Hunilla went silently to the withered cross which marked her Felipe's sandy mound, then set her tearless, haughty face in a gesture which defied nature's torture. She could take only two dogs—provisions aboard were scarce—and left the others clamorously howling on the beach. The Captain took her to Tumbex, a Peruvian port, sold her oil, and gave her some silver, augmented by little gifts from all hands. The last they saw of her she was riding a gray ass into Payta.

IX. Hood's Isle and the Hermit Oberlus.

Southeast of Crossman's Isle is Hood's Isle, with a vitreous cove called Oberlus's Landing on its south side. Half a century ago Oberlus, a deserter, built a clinker den there, grew potatoes and pumpkins for sale to passing ships, and reverted to a Caliban-like state, sinister and secret and debased. He had a musket and once tried to kidnap a Negro sailor put ashore to obtain food. But Oberlus was pinioned, taken aboard ship, whipped, and put back on Hood's Isle. This humiliation turned him completely misanthropic, and later he craftily kidnapped four sailors, turning them into slaves and then bravoes in a kind of army under his sway. Finally a ship sent four boats ashore for provisions, and Oberlus awaited his chance, smashed three of them, and escaped to Guayaquil in the remaining one. His cohorts in crime were never seen again; they probably died on the way to Peru or were tossed overboard. Oberlus made his way to Payta and was about to persuade a tawny beauty there to return to his princely island domain when the authorities caught him in an act of suspected sabotage and threw him into their grim prison. Melville adds in a footnote that much of his information on Oberlus comes from Porter's *Voyages into the Pacific,* some from on-the-spot authorities, and some from his imagination.

X. Runaways, Castaways, Solitaries, Grave-Stones, Etc.

There is much evidence that these islands have occasionally been populated by deserters who prefer them to vicious captains, by tortoise-hunters who have been reluctantly left behind for lost, by victims of captains' revenge, and the like. The beaches in the group have little post-offices in the form of corked bottles placed on stakes. And there are graves—of those who died at sea but in sight of this desolate land, and of one from the *Essex* killed ashore in a duel in 1813. Sometimes rude doggerel verse graces a grave board.

> The Creole, Felipe, Juan Fernandez, Ferryman, Hunilla, Dame Nature, Oberlus, the Palmer, Captain David Porter, Truxill.

'Epistle to Daniel Shepherd,' 1947.
> Daniel Shepherd.

'An Epitaph,' 1866.
> The Soldier.

'The Fall of Richmond, the Tidings Received in the Northern Metropolis (April, 1865),' 1866.
> [General Ulysses S.] Grant.

'Falstaff's Lament over Prince Hal Become Henry V,' 1924.
> Jack Falstaff, [King] Henry V.

"The Fiddler," 1854.

The narrator, named Helmstone, walks down Broadway cursing his fate: his ambitious poem has been rejected. He encounters his friend Standard, who introduces him to Hautboy, a short, fat, ruddy-faced fellow about forty years of age. Hautboy strikes the narrator as irresponsibly happy. The three attend a circus performance, at which Hautboy laughs gaily. Then they have stew and punch at Taylor's, during which time Hautboy seems sound, sensible, and wonderfully balanced as to feeling and thought. When he excuses himself and leaves, the two friends discuss him, and Standard enigmatically links him to Master Betty, a child prodigy some years ago in London. The narrator scornfully denies any possible resemblance. Suddenly Hautboy returns, and the three go to his room, which is filled with odd, old-fashioned furniture, all of it clean and cozily arranged. He agrees to play his fiddle, which he handles enchantingly. Later, the narrator begs Standard to explain. It seems that Hautboy was a precocious child; he tasted glory but is happier now by far—a genius without fame, who teaches fiddling. The narrator forgets his unwanted poetic masterpiece, tears up his manuscripts, buys a violin, and studies under Hautboy.

   Master Betty, Cleothemes the Argive, Hautboy,
   Helmstone, [John Philip and Charles] Kemble, [Mrs.
   Sarah] Siddons, Standard.

' "Formerly a Slave": An Idealized Portrait, by E. Vedder, in the
   Spring Exhibition of the National Academy, 1865,' 1866.
   [Jane Jackson], E[lihu]. Vedder.

'[Fragment of poem],' 1948.
   Billy [Budd], Tedds.

"Fragments from a Writing Desk. No. 1," 1839.

   In a letter from Lansingburgh [New York], L.A.V. describes three lovely girls to his friend M–.

   M–, the Major, L.A.V., W–.

"Fragments from a Writing Desk. No. 2," 1839.

While L.A.V. rests by a river, a muffled figure hands him a note signed Inamorata and asking him to follow the bearer. He does so, by the river, through a grove, and up to a villa, which he and his guide enter by sitting in a basket and being hoisted aloft to a window. They enter a gorgeous, perfumed room which is like a scene from the *Arabian Nights*. Dominating it is a lovely, white-robed woman on an ottoman. L.A.V. kneels before her, utters words of love, and kisses her passionately. Then he rushes out, because he has just discovered that she is deaf and dumb.

Inamorata, L.A.V.

'The Garden of Metrodorus,' 1891.

Metrodorus.

"The 'Gees," 1856.

The narrator decides to tell his many curious friends what 'Gees are. The word 'Gee (pronounced with a hard *g*) is an abbreviation of Portugee, the corrupt form of the Portuguese. Three hundred years ago Portuguese convicts were sent to colonize the Isle of Fogo, in the Cape de Verdes off the northwest coast of Africa. In time only the 'Gees remained. A typical 'Gee is small, hardy, and thick-skinned; at home he lives on fish, but he prefers ship-biscuit, by means of which American sea-captains can easily entice numbers of 'Gees aboard as green hands. Typical green 'Gees are terribly clumsy; but they regularly show docility, excellent memory, and credulity. Often middlemen supply worthless 'Gees to Yankee skippers who touch at Fogo to add to their diminished crews.

Captain Hosea Kean.

'A Grave near Petersburg,' Virginia, 1866.

Daniel Drouth.

'The Haglets,' 1888.

Tells of the Admiral of the White who after defeating the Plate

Fleet of Spain rushes toward home in his flagship to report the victory, only to sink on New Year's Eve when he runs into treacherous reefs because some sword blades clashing in a case under the ship's compass turn it fatally, while three haglets fly overhead in steady pursuit.

The Admiral of the White.

"The Happy Failure," 1854.

At nine one summer morning, the narrator, a young boy, meets his old uncle at the edge of the Hudson River. With the help of Yorpy, the uncle's old Negro servant, the two load a skiff with a ponderous box and row it upstream ten miles to Quash Island. The box contains a mysterious invention, the Great Hydraulic-Hydrostatic Apparatus, by means of which the uncle means to drain swamps at an acre an hour. When they arrive at the island, the uncle cautions his cohorts to be on the lookout for spies; then he uncrates his invention. The narrator views a convoluted mass of pipes and syringes, coiled like a nest of snakes. The uncle pauses to savor his anticipated fame and praise his Sustainer through years of solitary labor; then they tip the machine into the water. It is a complete failure. The uncle kicks his box and hurls pieces of his invention all over the water. His nephew urges him to try the machine again. But again it fails. The uncle turns pale and pinched, and they row downstream sadly. The old man advises his nephew to try to invent nothing but happiness, then suggests that they return for the old iron, which Yorpy can sell for tobacco money. Yorpy chirps with delight, and the uncle, looking rapt and earnest, praises God for the failure. He becomes a good old man, and his nephew is rendered a wise young fellow by the experience. Much later, when the old man dies, he seems still to be praising God for the failure.

Yorpy.

"Hawthorne and His Mosses," 1850.

A Virginian spending July in Vermont relates that at breakfast his country cousin Cherry gave him a copy of Nathaniel Hawthorne's *Mosses from an Old Manse*. The narrator, who has never met Hawthorne, takes the book to a barn and, lying in the new-mown clover, reads it in ecstasy. The next day he writes this essay, lavishing great praise on the book. He urges fellow Americans to support American writers, especially this Man of Mosses who is not far inferior to Shakespeare himself and augurs well for the future of American letters.

Cherry, Pop Emmons, Nathaniel Hawthorne, Tompkins, a Virginian.

'Hearth-Roses,' 1924.
Love.

'Honor,' 1924.
The King of India.

"I and My Chimney," 1856.
The narrator and his chimney are two gray-headed old smokers. The pyramid-shaped chimney, massively set in the very center of his house in the country, is twelve feet at its base in the cellar and slopes up to a four-foot-by-four-foot top—foolishly reduced by fifteen feet off its original height by a previous owner. Fireplaces are let into it, floor after floor, and its position is such that the house can have no grand entrance hall. The narrator's energetic wife frequently complains because of this fact and also because the upper floors are small, owing to the size of the central, spine-like chimney. But the narrator likes his chimney exactly as it is, likes the way his stairs climb along its sides to a gallery resembling an Elizabethan musicians' balcony, likes his tropical second-landing closet in which he ages his cordials, in fact likes all the old things—Montaigne, cheese, wine, chairs, and neighbors—to remain exactly as they are. His wife, on the other hand, is addicted to the new and to change. She is given moral support by their two daughters, Anna and Julia, first in a short-lived plan to tunnel from the front door through the chimney into the dining-room, which with its nine doors is hard for guests to retreat from and is as confusing as the guests' chambers upstairs. One day the narrator's wife hires a surveyor-

architect named Hiram Scribe to examine the chimney and draw plans for its elimination, at a cost of $500. The narrator hedges. The women pester him. His wife threatens to leave him if the chimney stays. He tentatively gives in but ultimately finds that he simply cannot sacrifice his chimney. Scribe then reports that in his professional opinion the chimney has a secret chamber which undoubtedly contains a hidden treasure. The narrator momentarily recalls a late wealthy kinsman named Captain Julian Dacres, who once lived in the big-chimneyed house but whose will mentioned only $10,000 in stocks. The narrator refuses to succumb. The wife begins to complain that husband and chimney smoke together execrably, then that the heavy chimney is causing the whole house to settle—to which he replies that he and his chimney can settle together at last, as into a vast feather-bed. Scribe returns, measures everything carefully, and tries to conclude scientifically that the chimney must indeed contain a hidden receptacle—until the narrator bribes him with $50 to report in writing that it has no such secret place. The three women keep up the pressure on the pipe-smoking, philosophical narrator, whom notes in the village newspapers and anonymous letters fail to ruffle. Seven years pass since he last stirred from his chimneyed home. He is not sour. He is standing guard. He and his chimney will never surrender.

 Anna, Biddy, Claude, Captain Julian Dacres, Julia, Hiram Scribe, Deacon White.

'In the Desert,' 1891.
 Napoleon [Bonaparte].

'In the Turret (March, 1862),' 1866.
 [Lieutenant John L.] Worden.

'Iris (1865),' 1924.
 Colonel, Colonel, Colonel, [General William T.] Sherman.

Israel Potter, 1854.
 It is appropriate that a rugged, self-reliant man such as Israel

Potter should be born in the eastern part of Berkshire, Massachusetts, a rugged, mountainous area of charcoal-burners, maple-sugar-boilers, and farmers whose temper is shown in the neat, strong stone walls bordering their unproductive lands. In spring and summer the region is musky with upland grass and is alive with wild birds; in autumn, foggy; in winter, blocked with snow. Israel turns eighteen, falls in love with a pretty but faithless neighbor girl (later named Jenny) whom his stern father dislikes, and so runs off and becomes a mild and patient trapper and trader among the Indians. Returning after three years to find his girl friend still coy, because of his father's machinations, he goes off to sea, is shipwrecked once, roves on, becomes a whaler, and returns home again—this time to find the girl married to another man.

So Israel becomes a patient farmer and would probably have remained so but for the American Revolution. After the battle of Lexington in April, 1775, he marches with John Patterson's regiment to Bunker Hill, where he is wounded in the arm, chest, hip, and ankle. By July he is well again, volunteers to join a ship blockading Boston, is captured at sea, and goes by prison ship to Spithead, where he no sooner lands than he escapes by eluding his two drunken guards. He runs through the English countryside, in the lovely spring of 1776, exchanges clothes with a ragged ditcher, and catches rides through several villages toward London eighty miles distant. Caught again within a few miles of London, he begins to despair but again effects his escape and boldly appeals for work to Sir John Millet at an estate near Brentford. This kind man sees that he is an escaped American prisoner but clothes and befriends him, and later finds him employment in nearby Princess Amelia's garden, the superintendent of which, however, is so harsh that Israel once again heads for the road. Soon he obtains work in the Kew Gardens of King George III and once even has a frank little talk with the monarch, who recognizes that he is a runaway American but who does not expose him but instead seems to Israel more warm hearted than his cold-headed lords in council.

Soon gossip impels Israel to move on, and he finds work with a pro-American farmer who introduces him by letter to others of like mind; within ten days or so he is on his way from Charing Cross to Dover on a mission for the Rev. Mr. Horne Tooke, for John Woodcock, and for James Bridges to deliver confidential papers to Dr. [Benjamin] Franklin in Paris. At the Pont Neuf, Israel happens to be stopped by a bootblack who offers to polish his shoes. But suspicious that the man wants to take his secret papers from his hollow heels, the sturdy American kicks him away and rushes to the address given him, where he is soon admitted into the presence of the illustrious Franklin, a neat, hale old sage who is reading a shaggy-bound folio. They begin to talk, and Franklin lectures his guest on high heels, the pronunciation of the word *Seine*, mistrust and restitution, exactness in financial dealings, and business before pleasure. At supper they have plain lamb and peas, for white wine only water, and no dessert, since to the host wine is either a luxury or an indulgence, and pastry is poisoned bread. Franklin gives Israel *Poor Richard's Almanac* and a guidebook to Paris to read, and sends him off to bed. The man of wisdom is a combination of erudition and economy, midway between the Palais des Beaux Arts and the Sorbonne.

Israel's room is large and ponderously furnished, with a marble mantel full of objects which the guest senses he will be billed for touching. A bewitching little chambermaid calls, but feeling slighted she quickly leaves. Franklin looks in briefly, warns Israel about the girl, and then leaves his guest to his dull, didactic reading. The maid later interrupts Franklin and Israel at tea to announce the arrival of a rude man—that is, a flirtatious one—who turns out to be tawny, savage-eyed Captain John Paul Jones. He pleads unsuccessfully with canny Franklin to be given command of the *Indien*, a frigate with which he will rain fire on the British, he says. Seeing Israel and then learning about him, Jones offers the brave, blunt seaman a berth with him out of Brest. Soon talk is interrupted by the arrival of the Duke de Chartres and Count D'Estang, and Franklin whisks Jones off to Israel's room, where the wild captain paces restlessly all night.

On the third day, Franklin suddenly puts some secret dispatches in Israel's hollow heels and sends the patient messenger by diligence to Calais, where that night he catches a packet to Dover. Soon he is back at Brentford, where Squire Woodcock is forced by circumstances to conceal him in a terrifyingly cramped stone closet or cell, built in Templar times, behind his massive chimney. Three horrible days and nights Israel spends thus confined. Thinking at last that the squire, who promised to visit him frequently and release him by the third morning but did not, must have been captured by the police, Israel presses a secret spring and steps into his host's private room. It is draped in funereal black. Israel guesses at once that Woodcock has died. He waits until night, dresses in the deceased's finest suit, and when discovered by members of the household walks calmly past them all like their master's ghost.

Before dawn he changes garments with a scarecrow, escapes some suspicious farmers at daybreak, and at the house of one of several local friends buys some ordinary-looking clothes. But when he gets to Dover he learns to his intense dismay that since relations have suddenly been suspended between England and France he cannot cross over to Franklin in Paris again. A smiling stranger invites him to drown his sorrows at an inn, and in a twinkling Israel is shanghaied into the royal navy and thrust aboard the ship the *Unprincipled*. As this huge seventy-four-gun vessel is going down channel that night, a revenue cutter signals her in distress and asks her for a man to replace some lost off the boom. Israel is chosen. But he is hardly aboard the little British cutter before Jones gives chase with his *Ranger*. Israel fights like a lion against the cutter captain, whom he knocks overboard, and then against two other men, whom he disables. Jones takes the wild, yellow-haired Yankee aboard his ship, recognizes him most joyously, and the two reminisce—taking to each other pre-ternaturally—in the captain's cabin, where Israel sleeps the rest of the night.

On the quarter-deck with Israel as his chosen quartermaster, Captain Jones, a curious combination of hero and renegade, gentleman and wolf, explains that Franklin obtained a commission for him to sail as an uninstructed American naval commander menacing enemy ships wherever he can find them. He quickly captures a large sail off Dublin, bombards a revenue wherry off southern Scotland, sinks a Scottish coaster full of barley, and mysteriously breaks off chasing a large vessel aiming for the Clyde River when both ships are dwarfed by the awesome shadow of the Crag of Ailsa. Next Jones sinks a fishing boat off the Irish coast and flirts with the idea of attacking the twenty-gun ship-of-war the *Drake* off Carrickfergus. But unfavorable winds interpose; so he sails off to the coal-town of Whitehaven, on the Solway Firth. There he and a party of other intrepid sailors, including Israel, land, spike the enemy cannon, and start a spreading fire through many of the hundreds of coal ships in the harbor. Next the *Ranger* crosses the Firth toward the Scottish shore, landing at noon at St. Mary's Isle, one of the seats of the Earl of Selkirk, whom Paul wants to capture as a hostage. When he learns from the nobleman's attractive wife that the Earl is in Edinburgh, Paul politely retires but not until two of his officers demand the right to seize some honorable plunder in the form of silver salvers and the like, all of which Jones later redeems at considerable cost and returns to the fair lady. Next day his ship goes back to Carrickfergus and boldly leads the *Drake* out of the harbor to attack her. The two ships engage in a running fight for an hour; then the *Drake* surrenders, a wilderness of shattered yards and masts, and is taken to Brest. Captain John Paul Jones is highly honored by the King of France. Israel Potter has nothing.

For the next three months, Captain Jones is busy getting a mongrel fleet of nine jealous ships together, with himself at its head in an old Indiaman called the *Duras*. Israel, whose station on her is in her castellated poop with a spyglass, suggests a new name—the *Poor Richard*, which Jones translates into the *Bon Homme Richard*. He tries a foray up the Firth of Forth to lay the town of Leith under tribute, but squalls drive him out again. And then off Flamborough Head, in the waters east of the high cliffs of Yorkshire, his ship engages the *Serapis* from seven to ten o'clock one moonlit evening [September 23, 1779]. Most of Jones's consorts desert him, but the *Alliance* does briefly exchange shots with the *Countess of Scarborough*, partner of the *Serapis*. In addition, however, the *Alliance* unaccountably fires four broadsides into the *Richard*. The *Serapis*, with her fifty heavy guns, and the cocky *Richard*, with her heterogeneous armament equaling that of only a thirty-two-gun frigate, circle each other like cock and hen, like hawk and crow, like chasséing cotillion partners whose repartee is deadly. The moon climbs to see better. The yards of the two ships become entangled, and they fight like murderous Siamese twins. The *Serapis* pours deadly cannonades into the *Richard's* vitals; but at the same time the Americans shoot down from their yard-arms, and Israel, following Jones's orders, drops hand grenades into the main hatchway of the enemy, thus exploding rows of heaped cartridges and killing twenty men in one volcanic blast. When the *Richard* starts to sink, the English captain, [Richard] Pearson, asks whether Jones is striking, to which the swarthy Yankee says that he has not yet begun to fight and shatters the enemy ship's main-mast with a powerful shot. Captain Pearson surrenders, and Jones boards the *Serapis*. Both crews stop killing each other to battle fire and water, their common foe. About ten o'clock, the *Richard*, gorged with slaughter, sinks like Gomorrah. Half of each crew is dead or maimed. Is not civilization but an advanced stage of barbarism?

After several months of inactivity, Jones and Israel sail aboard the *Ariel* for America. But on the way they encounter a British frigate and grapple briefly with her, just long enough for Israel, hearing a boarding order, to swing himself onto the enemy craft by her spanker-boom. Then the two craft separate, and he is alone among enemy seamen. All night he tries to mingle anonymously among one gang after another, but all reject him as a crazy, meddling interloper. He is finally brought before an officer but, calling himself Peter Perkins, talks his way out of trouble, is released as a crazy—but highly able—British seaman, and serves at the maintop until the ship puts in at Falmouth. There, joining a crowd ashore, he sees at Pendennis Castle gigantic Ethan Allen, who seized Ticonderoga but was later captured during a valiant attempt to take Montreal and was thereafter brought to England in ignominious chains. Threats that he will be hanged do nothing to silence this magnificent mountain man, who answers scorn with scorn. Israel wants to aid him but is recognized by Sergeant Singles, the man who married his mountain Jenny and who now innocently calls out Potter's name. Nimble Israel talks his way out of being arrested by a suspicious sentry, goes back to his ship and helps paint her hull, drops overboard the same night, exchanges his sailor garb for some clothes abandoned beside a pond, and rushes toward the safety of crowded London, a safe desert for persecuted men.

For thirteen weeks Israel works a few miles from the city as a brick-maker, half buried in a slimy pit like a gravedigger. Then with a few coppers in his pockets, he walks on to London. Then forty-five wretched years pass in that grimy Dis where the sun is eclipsed by belching smoke and neither marble nor flesh nor the sad spirit of man can remain white. He works in a variety of capacities—as warehouse porter, chair-bottomer, park attendant. He saves money for passage home but squanders it to marry a bakery-shop girl who nursed him to health after he was run over at one time. In all they have eleven children, ten of whom die, as does their mother finally. In 1793 the French war makes employment in London easier. But in 1817 peace discharges work-hungry hordes back from Waterloo. Israel has been half demented ever since a rotten beam in a crazy hovel fell on him. He brokenly recalls waving fields of his youth and tells his lone son about his New World home. The boy circulates the story. It is finally believed. And in 1826 father and son leave Moorfields and embark for Boston, through the aid of the American consul.

Home again, Israel Potter wanders with his son to the Housatonic region, finds almost everything changed, finally locates his parental hearthstone—disturbed by a stranger's plow— and sits out his days, without medals and forgotten.

> Colonel Ethan Allen, Princess Amelia, Bill, James
> Bridges, Molly Bridges, Duke de Chartres, the Laird
> of Crokarky, Duchess D'Abrantes, Count D'Estang,
> [Louis XVI] King of France, Dr. [Benjamin] Frank-
> lin, George III King of England, Lord General [Sir
> William] Howe, Sir Edward Hughs, Jack Jewboy,
> Jim, Colonel Guy Johnson, Captain John Paul Jones,

the Hessian, Kniphausen, Captain Martindale, Mungo Maxwell, Colonel McCloud, Sir John Millet, Captain Parker, General John Patterson, Captain [Richard] Pearson, Phil, Israel Potter, Mrs. Israel Potter, Potter, Mrs. Potter, Potter, [General Israel] Putnam, Rev. Mr. Shirrer, Jenny Singles, Sergeant Singles, the Countess of Selkirk, the Earl of Selkirk, Rev. Mr. Shirrer, Jenny Singles, Sergeant Singles, Admiral [Pierre André de] Suffrien [Suffrien Saint-Tropaz], Tidds, Rev. Mr. Horne Tooke, General [George] Washington, Lieutenant Williamson, Squire John Woodcock, Mrs. Woodcock.

"Jack Gentian (omitted from the final sketch of him)," 1924.

Describes the gossip that Gentian is becoming infirm in mind and body, but adds that he is ever loving and kind.

A Croesus, Tom Dutcher, Major Jack Gentian, Mrs. Jones.

'Jack Roy,' 1888.

Larry o' the Cannakin, Jack Roy.

"Jimmy Rose," 1855.

The events happened long ago. The old narrator, a conservative man named William Ford, who has a youngish wife, two daughters, and a maid named Biddy, inherits a great old house in New York on a narrow street which was once fashionable but now is haunted by the aged. The house is changed: it has lost its pulpit-like porch, the heavy shutters have been replaced with Venetian blinds, and its cellar bricks are blackened with age. But its rooms are the same as ever. The largest parlor has old-fashioned French wallpaper, with peacocks and roses. A leak from the eaves has spread through the paper, giving the peacocks a bedraggled air. One of the original proprietors of the place was a man named Jimmy Rose. He was born to a moderate fortune; rich, happy, handsomely rosy-cheeked, hospitable, and eloquent, he sustained at the age of forty a loss of two vessels from China and suffered complete financial ruin. He then disappeared. The kindly narrator, wanting to aid him, learned that Jimmy Rose was hiding in an old house on C— Street. But Jimmy, desperate and armed, refused to admit the narrator, though he was now his only friend. Twenty-five years passed. When the narrator saw him again, it was because the proud fellow through a sense of duty had crawled out into the open to face his bitter doom. From an unknown source he had been receiving an income of seventy dollars a year, off the mere interest of which he lived, on a single daily repast of milk and meal. In addition, he used to visit the homes of more fortunate friends at tea-time, partaking of much bread and butter while regaling his tolerant hosts and hostesses with cavalier talk of European affairs and modern literature. He hid the frayed cuffs of his frock coat and pantaloons by edging them with worn velvet. He was pitied, but those who sustained him with their alms of tea and toast should have banded together to make an independent little income for him. All the same, the roses constantly bloomed in his cheeks, his compliments struck the ear of vanity charmingly, and his smile—fabulous in his days of prosperity—was still rich. The narrator finally recalls that when Jimmy lay dying, he was attended devotedly by the gentle daughter of a rich alderman. The narrator visited Jimmy and found him a trifle peevish, surrounded by books brought by well-meaning friends. The narrator is now often reminded of Jimmy—and his rosy cheeks and proudly courteous manners—by sight of the wallpaper of peacocks and roses in his faded old house.

> Arabella, Biddy, William Ford, Mrs. William Ford, Miss Ford, Miss Ford, Frances, General G—, James "Jimmy" Rose.

'John Marr,' 1888.

Tells in prose and verse about John Marr, who is wounded by pirates and retires from the sea to the frontier in the prairies, only to lose his wife and child to a fever, at which time, unappreciated by his farmer neighbors, he apostrophizes his former shipmates.

> John Marr, Mrs. John Marr, Marr.

'The Lake,' 1924. See 'Pontoosuce,' 1924.

'Lamia's Song,' 1891.
> Lamia.

'Lee in the Capitol (April, 1866),' 1866.

General Lee is summoned to the United States Senate; when at the close of his testimony he is asked if he has anything else to say, he is imagined as urging the Senators to believe that the South wants peace under the law, desires that Northern triumph be not pushed too far, that the Civil War was fated to be, and that Southerners naturally fought for their region.

> [General Ulysses S.] Grant, [General Thomas J.] Stonewall [Jackson], [General Robert E.] Lee, [General John] Pope, [General William T.] Sherman, [General James E. B. "Jeb"] Stuart.

'L'Envoi,' 1924.
> Amigo.

'L'Envoi: The Return of the Sire de Nesle. A.D. 16—,' 1891.
> The Sire de Nesle.

"The Lightning-Rod Man," 1854.

Just as a wild storm of thunder and lightning breaks over the narrator's house in the mountains, a stranger clatters at his door. He is lean and gloomy, with blue-shadowed eyes. He walks, dripping wet, into the middle of the room. He has a wooden staff along which is a copper rod mounted in two glass balls. The narrator calls him Jupiter Tonans and thanks him for brewing the wild storm. But the stranger starts a lecture on the danger from lightning in this region, tells the narrator to avoid standing at the cozy hearth or near the walls, and while the storm crashes overhead offers to write up an order for a lightning-rod at a dollar a foot. But the confident narrator rebukes him violently as a peddler of indulgences from divine ordinations, says that he will stand at his ease in the hand of his God, and notes that the house is unharmed and a rainbow is now appearing. Black with rage, the salesman attacks his host with his rod but quickly gets tossed out. All the same, the peddler still profits on the fears of men hereabouts.

Jupiter Tonans.

'The Loiterer,' 1924.

Tells of an absent, vernal girl eagerly expected to return.

'The Lover and the Syringa Bush,' 1924.

Eve.

'Lyon, Battle of Springfield, Missouri (August, 1861),' 1866.

[General Nathaniel] Lyon, Corporal Tryon.

'Magian Wine,' 1891.

Miriam, Solomon.

'Magnanimity Baffled,' 1866.

The Victor.

"Major Gentian and Colonel J. Bunkum," 1924.

Discusses the pride of Major Gentian in his Society of the Cincinnati ribbon, the bravery of its wearers, and Colonel Josiah Bunkum's valorous but senseless scheme of distributing spelling books throughout the South because the Bible says "My people perish through ignorance."

Colonel Josiah Bunkum, Major [John] Gentian, John Hancock, [General George B.] McClellan.

'Malvern Hill (July, 1862),' 1866.

[General George B.] McClellan.

'The Marchioness of Brinvilliers,' 1891.

[Marie Madeleine Marguerite d'Aubray,] Marquise de Brinvilliers.

'The March to the Sea (December, 1864),' 1866.
> [General Ulysses S.] Grant, [General Judson] Kil-
> patrick, [General Robert E.] Lee, [General William
> T.] Sherman.

Mardi, 1849.
> Part One.

The narrator tires of whaling after three years aboard the *Arcturion* without any success; so he tells the captain when west of the Galapagos that he wants off. When the captain says only that he may leave the ship if he can, the narrator takes the hint, talks a Skyeman named Jarl into joining him, and they stock the bow-boat with water, biscuits, salt beef, and much equipment, and slip away, planning to sail west a thousand miles to the Kingsmill islands of coral. One moonless midnight they lower the boat, shout "A man overboard!", and row away, seemingly in search of the man overboard. They are soon alone in a watery world. Jarl rarely speaks but is dull, mechanical, and witless. On the third morning the narrator has an inexplicable sense of fear. A week passes. What if they have missed Kingsmill and the Ratak chain? They observe a great variety of fish, especially sharks. They handle their water carefully, and Jarl tediously stitches all his old clothes. On the eighth day comes a calm, which lasts four days, and then comes a blessed breeze. On the fourteenth day Jarl gives up chewing his tobacco. He and the narrator observe a shovel-nosed shark and his entourage of pilot fish—a symbiotic marvel which is upset when they kill the hated shark.

At twilight on the sixteenth day, they sight a deserted-looking brigantine, board her, explore the littered decks and cabin and forecastle, and hear disturbing groans overhead. In the morning, stalwart, tatooed, ear-pierced Samoa and his ugly old termagant of a wife Annatoo, natives of the Pacific islands, descend from the maintop and foretop, and in broken English explain that the ship, named the *Parki*, from Lahina, on the coast of Mowee, Hawaii, was in quest of pearls and shells four months before but lost all of her crew in a massacre when murderous Cholos attacked her in a Pearl Shell Island harbor. Samoa repulsed the attackers by musket fire but suffered a grievous wound in his arm and had to amputate and cauterize it afterwards himself, and Annatoo saved herself by hiding in the yards. The two afterwards pillaged the cabin, only to argue unmatrimonially over the spoils, which Annatoo artfully concealed all over the *Parki*. Eventually, however, they made their peace. When the narrator and Jarl boarded the flapping brigantine, her two sailors thought at first that they were ghosts. But the narrator quickly lectures them, takes official command, tells them that the ship belongs to her Hawaiian owners, and determines to sail ever westward with the trades until they hit Kingsmill. In the absence of any navigational instruments, they cannot return to the Pearl Shell Islands for revenge or to Hawaii to give over the ship. The narrator relishes his first command: he takes his turn at the helm, mounts aloft to lounge, hooks an Indian swordfish aboard—a deadly chevalier among frightened shoals of lesser fish—and hangs its bayonet over his hammock as a souvenir, and even finds—and conceals—a cask of aromatic brandy. They steer along the Equator by dead reckoning as well as possible. Annatoo has taken a fancy to Jarl and also stands regular night watches until the narrator can no longer tolerate her filching of items—log reel, boxes of sundry things, even compass—and therefore as commander incarcerates her nightly. After a long calm, the *Parki* is suddenly smashed by a Pacific storm, during which a block at the end of a madly whipping shroud strikes Annatoo in the head and she is instantly washed overboard and lost. The decks are awash, the pumps delay the inevitable, but finally the ship sinks. The three survivors provision and launch the chamois-like lifeboat.

Afloat again in the little shell. One night later they observe the entire sea on fire, glowing with phosphorescent and putrescent animal matter. On the ninth day after that, they detect evidence that they are near land but then see a thirty-foot double canoe full of odd-looking natives. When they overtake the strange craft and exchange bits of cloth for presents, a fight ensues, during which the narrator kills with a cutlass Aleema, a priest and the leader of the other party. Inside a tent in a dais in the strange canoe the narrator finds a beautiful, white-skinned, golden-haired, blue-eyed girl—Yillah—whom he persuades to come with him and with Jarl and Samoa. The crew of the double canoe, Aleema's fourteen sons by fourteen wives, pursues but only ineffectually. The narrator and his four friends voyage on for several days, accompanied by shoals of merry silverheads, bonitos, wriggle-tails, and trigger-fish.. He gradually learns Yillah's story: born at Amma, the beautiful girl was taken at an early age to Oroolia, the Island of Delights, where she became a flower (so she was told and dreamily believed); then she returned to Amma and was enshrined as a goddess in the temple of Apo in the glen of Ardair. With only Aleema for a guardian, she grew lonely in her valley, with its shady pool surrounded by cliffs. One day the priest told her that she was to be sacrificed in a vortex off the shore of Tedaidee. But the narrator rescued her, at the expense of his clean conscience, since he committed murder for her and now tells her insincerely that he comes from Oroolia and knew her as a child. They drift and love; then one day they see innumerable islands and follow several native praus to one of them—never more, they think, to roam.

The happy natives pick up the narrator's little boat and carry it ashore and into the trees. It seems that the narrator resembles Taji, a god at last returned to the islands of Mardi here. He puts on a bold front, admits that he is the god, and explains that Yillah has come from the sun, Jarl from the sky, and Samoa from a reef. King Media immediately invites him to be his guest at the isle of Odo, where the party quickly goes for a gigantic feast in a well-shaded temple. It all seems a dream. Taji is only one deity among many and hence is well advised not to rear his crest too high. He wanders over Odo at night and loves to contemplate Yillah's beauties by day. Their lush viands come in engraved and fired gourds; they relish fruits and light wines. Media is a pleasant host but sees his guest as a peer, not a superior. Media appears only genial but in reality, when his practices are fully studied, is ruthless. He rejects a proposed jury system, orders a rebel beheaded, and forces certain enslaved drudges to live in rotten caves and to toil without hope. All the dead are buried at sea, beyond the outer reef. A certain fixed-eyed incognito stares at Yillah.

Taji keeps thinking guiltily of Aleema, the priest he killed, and is distressed when Yillah murmurs of whirlpools and mosses vaguely remembered. One morning she is gone. A search of several days, ordered by Media, produces no clue; and Taji raves, goes into a trance, and then decides to rove throughout Mardi in search. King Media says that he will accompany his divine guest; and he arranges for the Mardian historian Mohi, the learned mystic Babbalanja, and the minstrel Yoomy, along with Vee Vee the dwarf and six paddlers, to go as well. The flotilla is composed of three ornately carved canoes. First they visit Valapee, or the Isle of Yams, the monarch of which is the ten-year-old Peepi, who has inherited the diverse spiritual qualities of sundry intestate dead. Valapee places a special value on human teeth. Soon leaving, Taji's party passes under a craggy rock called Pella, and while under it they discuss the evanescence of fame. Next they are overtaken by a canoe of Queen Hautia, who sent enigmatic flower messages to Taji while he was still with Yillah at Odo, and whose paddlers now tell him with more flowers of the bitterness of absent love and to beware of Hautia.

They rush on to the island of Juam, whose history includes the fratricidal monarch Marjora. The present ruler is the effeminate Donjalolo, whose fate like that of other Juam kings is to be incarcerated in the glen of Willamilla, which has a palace of the morning, a palace of the afternoon in a natural grotto (where Babbalanja soliloquizes on death, eternity, possible immortality, and mutability), and two deeply sequestered houses for Donjalolo's lush harem's thirty wives (one for each night of the moon). Not finding Yillah, Taji and his group after three days with Donjalolo leave to visit his tributary islands but are quickly recalled to participate in a gigantic feast for twenty-five gluttonous kings. One delicacy is a gourd of marzilla wine in which is dissolved King Marjora's heart. Then dancing women, sedative incense, and dreams.

On their way to the next island, Mohi tells the other voyagers about the Plujii, invisible spirits which are blamed for all adverse circumstances and events, and then about the soporific island of Nora Bamma. Again Queen Hautia's flower-bearers overtake Taji, and again he ignores her message—this one concerning love, death, and joy. Next Mohi tells about Ohonoo, the island of Rogues, a place settled by exiles—good or bad?—from a region of exiles and a place now featuring the rare sport of surfing. The party lands at Ohonoo, whose king is Uhia, a highly ambitious monarch. From there the party goes past Tupia, on the way to which Mohi wrangles with Yoomy, who tells about Tupian pygmy flower mannikins. And then they all land at Mondoldo, whose fat, jolly king is Borabolla. He eats constantly, is intermittently gouty, and likes Jarl uncommonly well. While at Mondoldo, Samoa performs a successful operation on the skull of an injured sea diver named Karhownoo, who, however, dies. Samoa regales his auditors with a story—believe it or not—of a wounded man part of whose brain was replaced by that of a pig; the man recovered but soon grew swinish and died in a year. Taji and his friends attend not only the diver's burial at sea but an almost simultaneous wedding ceremony, in which the bride is tied by flowery gyves and the groom is anchored to a heavy stone. Just as Taji is about to leave Borabolla of Mondoldo, three of dead Aleema's sons—the rest have perished of thirst at sea—appear in their double-keeled prau, see their father's killer, and rave for revenge. Taji himself, haunted by visions of the floating green corpse, swears that the story of the murder is a lie and then becomes delirious because of guilt and also because he is thus reminded of his lost Yillah. Once again Hautia's flower-bearing messengers float by with a gloomy message—the lily is crushed.

The next morning Taji prepares to depart. He leaves unhappy Jarl behind, to remind Borabolla of him. Samoa, tiring of the trip, also stays back, planning to return to Odo but reportedly killed by three arrows later instead. Media, Babbalanja, and Yoomy sail forward with Taji, who continues to feel a nameless dread of Hautia. They all talk of nocturnal paradises, types of devils possessing mortals, and blunt and ambiguous authorities (for example, Bardianna and Yamjamma).

Part Two.

Now the questers are heading for the isle of Maramma, which has a challenging central peak named Ofo. When they land, they find a blind, white-bearded old guide named Pani, who publicly rebukes all pilgrims seeking to climb Ofo without his aid but who privately admits his susceptibility to mortal doubts. Taji's group encounters a variety of pilgrims (for example, wealthy Divino, healthy Fanna, and a brash youth full of hope to ascend Ofo), passes through noxious woods, traverses the sandy burial place of former pontiffs, and visits a sacred lake whose islets feature idols to dozens of gods—each a rival of the others. Finally they all arrive at the temple of Oro, see the other pilgrims approaching it, and—powerless to help him—watch a sincere young man led away by the authorities for alleged impiety. At this, Babbalanja morosely lectures on human strife and spiritual uncertainties. Then they visit the studio of a mercenary icon-chiseler and canoe-maker named Hevaneva. Babbalanja then tells a nursery story about nine blind men who try to find the main trunk of a widely rooted banyan tree; when each thinks that one trunk is the main trunk, King Tammaro dismisses them, saying that finding the trunk is too much even for a person with eyes. Taji's party glides on to an island where the pontiff Hivohitee is reported to be; they proceed through a foul grove, and then an ugly man with a jawbone necklace gestures that the minstrel Yoomy is to visit in his tall, dank pagoda. Only after Yoomy emerges from the gloom and leaves with his friends does he realize that the old man was the pontiff sought; Babbalanja drily explains that many describe the religious Hivohitee but few have seen him.

Suddenly Hautia's flower-bearers overtake Taji and tell him that Jarl is dead. The morose narrator then apostrophizes dreams, which he is full of, from past, present, and future; he is fated, he says, to have them and describe them. The group leaves fruitless Maramma. Media cheers the others by calling for pipes and tobacco, and they puff long and wildly. Soon they arrive at the isle of Padulla and meet a long-nosed, crooked, hump-backed antiquarian named Oh Oh, whose museum of relics contains a tremendous variety of objects, the old manuscripts of which especially intrigue Babbalanja. He begs for a sheet from an old work by Bardianna himself but is refused by Oh Oh, who then gives him a rubbishy-looking old work called "A Happy Life." Babbalanja finds its non-religious exhortation to goodness ecstatically moving. The group then visits a hungry miser named Jiji, who collects teeth in pelican pouches but has to beg a yam from Vee Vee. As they sail away, Yoomy sings some love songs and Babbalanja, quoting numerous sources, discourses to the effect that fame is an accident but merit is an absolute. It seems that many Mardians hoard dental money—that is, collections of teeth—and inordinately pride themselves on their tapa clothing. Proof of the latter habit comes when the party lands at the isle of Pimminee, which is the location of an aloof society stressing dress. Taji and his friends cannot hope to find Yillah there; but they are amused by Nimni, the foremost of the Taparians, who with his wife, Ohiro Moldona Fivona, and their three daughters, named A, I, and O, hold open house to show Taji their Pimminee aristocracy. The swarm of guests parade their tapas and flirt their furbelows vivaciously. But when the visitors leave, Babbalanja can say only that the Taparians are full of their snobbish selves and hence are quite empty.

On their way to the isle of Fossils, Babbalanja regales his companions by theorizing on the origin of the world. As they move along, the hiss of three almost murderous arrows inspires Taji to confess that he killed Aleema and that the priest's surviving sons are therefore pursuing him. Media wishes that he did not know this secret. Hautia's couriers then glide up with a message concerning the sting of remorse and the joys of love. Seeing Vee Vee accidentally fall and hurt his arm, Babbalanja discourses at great length on the distinction between fatalism and necessitarianism, on the omnipresence of the god Oro, on man's consequent presumed irresponsibility, and on the joys of the righteous life. Media then drinks to the stars, his fellow immortals. Yoomy sings about the sun and siestas at noon. And the party proceeds to the island of Diranda, presided over by Kings Hello and Piko, who thin their exploding populations by war games held while they share their throne convivially. They hide Taji's canoes so that their visitors must stay and watch one gory set of games on the Field of Glory. More whizzing arrows signify that Aleema's avengers are still on Taji's trail as the group leaves Diranda. Babbalanja delivers a lecture on the apparent fixity of the sun and on his own apparent identity. Then, over tea, tobacco, and wine, Mohi discourses on the mercenary sorcerers of Minda, who foment quarrels to augment their employment.

Approaching the big island of Dominora, Media explains that its king, Bello of the Hump, interferes in the politics of various kingdoms in the neighboring island of Porpheero (which is full of exploding volcanoes), likes to call every last little island he sees around Mardi his own, used to impress canoers from the blustering island of Vivenza into his own navy, but was defeated militarily by Vivenza. Media goes on to explain that Vivenza is a green, tropical, promising island to the west and that Vivenzans are youthful, brave, and boisterous, but might not have defeated Dominora if that island kingdom had not been also occupied fighting other enemies. The group wanders through Dominora looking vainly for Yillah. The region is beautiful; but its people are poor and hungry, there are many riots, and rioters and strikers are betrayed. King Bello has a fancy state canoe, annually weds himself doge-like to the big lagoon, but notices with alarm that the lagoon seems anxious to marry Vivenza to the west. As Media and his group sail away, Babbalanja discourses on pride, they all drink a good deal of intoxicating wine, they discuss disembodied spirits and nature as a phenomenon rather than a substance, and Media—though a divinity—seems drunk. They approach Kaleedoni, a country touching on Dominora and full of brave, friendly, devout, philosophical, and frugal people. This land, also called Verdanna, is a kind of rebellious step-child of King Bello. Babbalanja next lectures to his friends encyclopedically on physiology and evolution; Yoomy sings a rather erotic song; and the party approaches Kolumbo, which contains Kanneeda to the north and arrogant Vivenza to the south. Babbalanja predicts the coming independence of Kanneeda from Dominora far to the east and uses the topic as an excuse to dilate on the cycles of history.

Vivenza boasts that it is a republic where all are born free and equal, a proposition which Media calls false. The group visits the Temple of Freedom, sees a man with stripes on his back hoist a similarly striped tapa standard, observes big-browed Saturnina with eyes like panther hollows, finds a huge company of persons filling themselves with red wine from a gigantic gourd, and then sees a gaunt Hio Hio lunatic named Alanno (who talks of trouble in Dominora, to the annoyance of Babbalanja) and a fiery youth (who harangues a crowd from the shoulder of his own father by reading an anonymous manuscript on cyclical republicanism, poverty, wisdom, suffering, isolationism, and the inevitability of wars). Media and Babbalanja accuse each other of having written the document just read. Then the group proceeds to southern Vivenza, a hot region of serfs and overloads which threatens secession if northern Vivenzans interfere. Nulli, the fiery-eyed spokesman of the area, calls the visitors incendiaries and claims that his taro-plant toilers are happier than northern workers. Media says that it is easy for outsiders to rail at the south, that wrongs are often products of a certain kind of soil, that customs support evil, and that a prudent remedy seems impossible to devise. Taji laments that Yillah is to be found neither in the north of Vivenza nor in its south, both of which sections are as curiously interrelated—says Babbalanja—as semi-independent members of a cuttlefish.

Media and his friends now sail south of southern Vivenza, past green isles under a tropical sun, and along the coast of Kolumbo of the south with its leafy woodlands like a green ocean. Media and Babbalanja argue as to whether tyranny would be a blessing here. Yoomy adds that Vivenza will have its real test later in history. They sail on, their beards turning frosty and the cape looming icily ahead and then the Andes as they swing north again. From the shores they hear a chorus singing of gold in the Promised Land; Babbalanja calls gold the only poverty and adds that Yillah would never be seen where gold is. Yoomy counters the song from the Promised Land with a song on the curse of the glittering metal. Now sailing far eastward, they come close to Orienda, where song and science first dawned. King Bello is the curse of the exploited place now, and Yoomy laments that Yillah is not to be found there. So they proceed southwest to the vast island of Hamora, where they again hear Bello's bugles. West of Hamora they are hit by a sudden storm. No Yillah there. Taji now pauses to explain that he has been sailing without chart through the world of the mind and would rather have his quest end in failure and wreck than give it up. Yoomy then sings of the immortality of remembered joys. They come upon a frothy island inhabited by Doxodox, reputedly wise; but when Babbalanja interviews him, Azzageddi meets his match: Doxodox is a mass of verbosity.

Weeks pass as they sail on and on. Then, during a sudden mist, an assassin makes a trial at stabbing Taji but fails and falls overboard. Hautia sends another flower message. The party lands at Hooloomooloo, an island full of cripples, with whose king, named Yoky, they have a meal of twisted foods. Babbalanja lectures on the dissimilarity of standards of judgment, on the unlikelihood that Mardians are supremely important in the cosmos, on the infinitude of unknowns beyond the ken of man, and on the lack of new elements to be discovered by questers throughout Mardi. Then he recites his revered sage Bardianna's will and testament, which is full of bequests and denials. The next day, in Sooloo's sea on the way to King Abrazza, the party is buffeted by an appalling death cloud, which causes Babbalanja to ponder on mortality. In a little while they come to the island of Bonovona, ruled by the demigod bachelor Abrazza, who pities the fallen but aids no one and banishes all things uncongenial to him. In his pleasant date grove, Media and the others converse with Abrazza, to whom Babbalanja at great length explains the career of Lombardo, author of the immortal *Koztanza*. Lombardo often seemed inert but only the way a potent lion does which crouches and waits. He bought vellum and quills, wrote carefully—never dashing off his lines—and often burned early drafts, did not outline in advance, liked wine but drank none while working, wrote only by daylight, grew very tired, and ignored so-called advice from critical friends and professional critics alike. He never bargained with his wares, carefully rewrote, and then when he had agonized enough published the admittedly imperfect final version, aware that he needed bread and yams. Now his work lives after him. That night Abrazza entertains the group at a glorious supper—supper always being better, because longer, than mid-day dinner. Even Babbalanja partakes of the wine, soon grows drunk, complains that wine is fine at table but bad in bed, laments the plight of the laborer, and even insults Abrazza. But when the king calls the guards, Media defends his philosopher, and the party breaks up.

The next morning Abrazza pleads an indisposition and fails to see his guests on their way. They sail on, past an island of mangrove trees. Saying that Yillah will not be there, Media orders the boats to go on. At full moon, Babbalanja says to hell with Hautia and calls for long lives all around, and also wine. But when he laughs, the others prefer tears. In the morning Babbalanja turns black-browed and faints. No trace of Yillah. Yoomy becomes gloomy, lamenting that he was happy when the group started on its voyage last spring but that now autumnal nights take away his gaiety. Suddenly a bowsman, in the act of singing merrily, falls and is drowned in the nocturnal waters. The party discusses death, to Media's consternation. A lovely morning follows, and a mild old man greets them and invites them to the blooming island of Serenia, which visitors should be sad ever to leave. The old man lectures them on the serene religion of the place, a creed taught by Alma and based on love, charity, and little formal government. Babbalanja, Yoomy, Mohi, and Media are tremendously moved by the old man. Babbalanja has a midnight dream of soaring with a pair of luminous angels through spirit-haunted space imbued with sadness and tranquillity. He describes the vision to his friends and then announces that he will remain forever in Serenia.

Taji and the others continue the search for Yillah, on and on, through many isles, but in vain. Then they meet Hautia's phantoms once more, and this time the message is that through their queen Taji may perhaps find Yillah. So they rush on to Flozella a Nina, Hautia's flowery, incense-laden, nymph-filled isle; passing submerged wrecks, they beach there. When he sees Hautia, Taji recognizes the incognito from Odo, resists her blandishments, flowers, and wine for a while, but then succumbs to her, feeling that perhaps in this way he will learn something about Yillah. Then Mohi tells of a youth named Ozonna who sought his lost love Ady on the isle of Flozella, only to find that she evidently was hidden effectively among Hautia's maidens, all of whom resemble each other. All the same, Hautia urges Taji to sin with her, be merry, dive for pearls in flambeau-lit caves, and dissolve his woes. Media, Mohi, Yoomy, and Vee Vee return to Odo. Later, when Taji sees in the queen's hand Yillah's rose pearl, he rushes off to a cavern in a hill, sees a whitish vision in its eddying waters, and plunges after it—to no avail, because fierce currents drive him back. Suddenly standing before him are Mohi and Yoomy, ordered there by Media, who is staying at Odo to quell sedition but who wants them to rescue Taji from the queen and take him to Serenia permanently.

However, when Taji gets into the boat, he points it away from Serenia and toward the deeps beyond. Unable to dissuade him, Mohi and Yoomy leap into the water and swim ashore. Taji races on, pursued by a shallop with three armed specters. Arcturus the red star looks down.

A, King Abrazza, Adondo, Ady, Alanno, Aldina, Aleema, Alla Mal(l)olla, Alma, Almanni, Amoree, Annatoo, Queen Aquella, Aquovi, Arhinoo, Atahalpa, Prince Atama, Queen Azzolino, Babbalanja, Ned Ballad, Bardianna, Batho, King Bello, Berzilli, Bidi Bidie, Bidiri, Blandoo, Boddo, Boldo, Bomblum, Bondo, Bonja, King Borabolla, Borhavo, Botargo, Queen Calends, Darfi, Dedidum, Demorkriti, Chief Dermoddi, the Despairer, Diddledee, Dididi, Diloro, Divino, King Donjalolo, Donno, Doldrum, Doxodox, Prince Dragoni, Dumdi, Fanfum, Fanna, Fee, Fiddlefie, Fidi, Finfi, Flavoni, Fofi, Foni, Foofoo, Fulvi, Gaddi, King Grandissimo, Grando, Hanto, Queen Hautia, King Hello, Hevaneva, [. . .] Hivohitee MDCCCXLVIII, Hohori, Hummee Hum, I, Queen Ides, Jarl, Jarmi, Jiji, Jiromo, King of Kandidee, Karhownoo, Karkeke, Karkie, King Karolus [I], King Karolus [II], Karrolono, King Klanko, Konno,

Krako, Kravi, King Kroko, Kubla, Lakreemo, Lanbranka Hohinna, Larfee, Livella, Logodora, Lol Lol, Lombardo, Lucree, King Ludwig, King Ludwig the Debonair, King Ludwig the Do Nothing, King Ludwig the Fat, King Ludwig the Great, King Ludwig the Juvenile, King Ludwig the Pious, King Ludwig the Quarreler, King Ludwig the Stammerer, Manta, Prince Mardonna, King Marjora, Mark, Marko, Marmonora, Bill Marvel, King Media, King Media, Midni, Minta the Cynic, Mohi, Mondi, Nimni, Nina, Queen Nones, Nonno, Noojoomo, King Normo, Nulli, O, Ohiro Moldona Fivona, Oh Oh, Ononna, Oram, Prince Ottimo, Ozonna, Paivai, Pani, Parki, Peenee, King Peepi, Pendiddi, Pesti, Philo, Phipora, King Piko, Pollo, Pondo, Lord Primo, Quiddi, Rabeelee, Prince Rani, Ravoo, Raymonda, Rea, Ridendiabola, Roddi, Roe, Roi Mori, King Rondo the Round, Roo, Roonoonoo, Rotato, Samoa, Saturnina, Sober Sides, Solo, Taji, Talara, King Tammaro, King Taquinoo, King Teei, Titonti, Tongatona, Tooboi, Toooorooloo, Topo, Prince Tribonnora, King Uhia, Vangi, Varnopi, Vavona, Vee Vee, Queen Velluvi, Verbi, Vivo, Voluto, Vondendo, Voyo, Willi, Wyndodo, Xiki, Yamjamma, Yamoyamee, Yillah, King Yoky, Yoomy, Zenzi, Zenzori, Queen Zmiglandi, Znobbi, Zonoree, Zooperbi, Zozo, Zuma.

'The Margrave's Birthnight,' 1891.
  The Margrave.

"The Marquis de Grandvin," 1924.
  A fictive essay in praise of the Marquis de Grandvin, who is visiting America from France.
  B. Hobbema Brown, [Major] Jack Gentian, the Marquis de Grandvin.

'Marquis de Grandvin: At the Hostelry,' 1924.
  The Marquis de Grandvin, a genial Frenchman, speaks about

Italian politics, then summons shades of famous artists to debate on the nature of the picturesque, and finally recommends a story to be told by his friend Jack Gentian.

> Fra Angelico, [King] Bomba [Ferdinand II, King of the Two Sicilies], Adrian Brouwer, [Count Camillo] Cavour, [John] Constable, Leonardo [Da Vinci], [Admiral] De Reyter, Carlo Dolce [Dolci], Gerard [Gerrit] Douw, Agnes Durer, Albert [Albrecht] Durer, King Fanny [Francis II, King of the Two Sicilies], [Giuseppe] Garibaldi, [Major] Jack Gentian, the Grand Duke of Florence, the Marquis de Grandvin, Franz Hals, [Jan Van] Huysum, Frater Michael Angelo [Buonarroti], Phillis, Pope [Pius IX], [Nicolas] Poussin, Raphael [Sanzio], Rembrandt (also Rembrant) [Harmens Van Rijn], Salvator Rosa, Sir Peter Paul [Rubens], [Lo] Spagnoletto [Giuseppe Ribera], Jan [Havicksz] Steen, Swanevelt, [David the younger?] Teniers, [Jacopo Robusti] Tintoretto, [Admiral Cornelius Van] Tromp (also Trump), [Willem I?] Van der [de] Velde, [Sir Anthony] Vandyke [Van Dyke], [Diego Rodriguez de Silva y] Velasques [Velasquez], Paola [Paolo] of Verona [Veronese], [Antoine] Watteau.

'Marquis de Grandvin: Naples in the Time of Bomba . . . , ' 1924.

Major Jack Gentian describes the festive street crowds in Naples, the intimidating fortresses and intimidating troops there, a charming singer, a dancing flower girl—she gives him a rose which slowly fades—smoking Vesuvius, beach jugglers and tumblers and singers, an urchin named Carlo who criticizes Bomba's troops in a song, a canopied priest with hidden host, and finally the deliverer of Naples—Garibaldi—yet to come.

> Agrippina [the younger], Andrea, Apollo, [King] Bomba, Bourbon-Draco, Captain, Carlo, Donna, His Excellency, [Agniello] Falcone, [Francis II, King of the Two Sicilies], [Giuseppe] Garibaldi, Major Jack Gentian, Queen Joanna [I of Naples], Masaniello,

Merry Andrews, Nestors, a Peri, Punchinello, Salvator Rosa.

'The Martyr, Indicative of the Passion of the People on the 15th Day of April, 1865,' 1866.
    [President Abraham Lincoln].

Moby-Dick, 1851.

"Call me Ishmael," says the narrator, as he opens his long account, which begins when he leaves Manhattan one December a few years ago and cures a fit of depression by proceeding to New Bedford to find a whaler to sign aboard. He seeks lodging at Peter Coffin's wild and chilly Spouter-Inn, where the humorous landlord assigns him as a roommate to Queequeg, a tatooed Polynesian prince with whom Ishmael soon gets along most cosily. The next morning, a sleety Sunday, he goes to Father Mapple's Whaleman's Chapel and hears a salty, moving account of Jonah which the venerable preacher delivers from his sea-laddered pulpit. Back again at the Spouter-Inn, Ishmael and Queequeg look at a book together, divide and share their worldly goods, smoke the Polynesian's tomahawk pipe, and retire almost like man and wife to Coffin's huge matrimonial bed. On Monday they wheelbarrow their chests to the wharf and board a schooner to Nantucket, where they stay at Coffin's cousin Hosea Hussey's inn, called the Try Pots. They relish the chowder there, and next morning while Queequeg consults his heathen idol Yojo for information on the best whaling vessels, Ishmael talks with Peleg and Bildad, two owners of the *Pequod*, and signs aboard her. Peleg explains that her temporarily absent commander, Captain Ahab, lost a leg to a monstrous whale, is now half sick and half well, is godly and ungodly both, and has been in colleges and among the cannibals. When Ishmael points out that the name Ahab was that of a wicked king in the Bible, Peleg says that Ahab's crazy, widowed mother provided her infant's name and that the captain is stricken but humane, and has a wife and child. Back at the Try Pots, Queequeg is discovered conducting a Ramadan, during which he fasts, sits bolt upright all night, and seemingly communes with his little black idol. Next morning he goes to the wharf with his devoted friend Ishmael and is hired as harpooneer on the *Pequod*. On the way back, the two men are encountered by Elijah, a mad and tattered, pock-marked prophet who hints at a dire fate if they sign with fated Ahab. A misty dawn or two later, after the ship is fully provisioned for a cruise of at least three years, Ishmael and his Polynesian mate fancy that they see four or five shadowy seamen dart aboard but are not certain. Then, piloted out of the harbor on a chilly Christmas Day by Peleg and Bildad but carrying a still-invisible Ahab, the gaunt *Pequod* plunges like fate into the Atlantic.

Once his ship is launched, the narrator can pause to discuss cetological details, as he often does again later. Then he identifies the officers and their harpooneers. Starbuck is first mate. He is a tall and earnest Quaker from Nantucket, thirty years of age, married and with one small son. He is conscientious and reverent, and has chosen Queequeg for his harpooneer. Stubb, the second mate, is a happy-go-lucky, pipe-puffing Cape-Codman. Always jolly and cool headed, he chooses for his squire Tashtego, a Gay Head Indian of noble blood and great pride. Flask is third mate. From Tisbury, in Martha's Vineyard, this short, stout, ruddy-faced fellow is pugnacious and always looking for excitement. His harpooneer is Daggoo, an enormous, coal-black Negro whose experience is limited to Africa, Nantucket, and the whaling industry. Finally moody, stricken Ahab appears on the quarter-deck. He resembles a man cut from the stake before the fire has ruined him utterly. A thin scar threads its way from his gray hair down his neck. A few days later, and the whaler rolls through a bright Quito spring. After arguing with Stubb briefly, Ahab hurls his pleasureless pipe overboard. Next morning Stubb tells Flask that he dreamed Ahab kicked him with his ivory leg; Stubb compares the blow to the slap of a knight-creating queen. Next fat-cutting is described, and then dining protocol at the cabin table, which is the scene of wild, lip-smacking feeding. During the now pleasant weather Ishmael takes his turn at the masthead, where, a hundred feet above the silent deck, he presumably watches for whales but is tempted into dangerous pantheistic musings. Shortly after breakfast one day, Ahab assembles the entire crew, nails a gold coin to the mast, and offers it to the first man to sight Moby Dick—which he describes as a white-headed whale with a wrinkled brow and a crooked jaw and three punctures in his left fluke. The hypnotized men shout their loyalty when Ahab vows revenge on the creature which dismasted him. When Starbuck objects that he has shipped for profit not vengeance upon a dumb brute, Ahab counters by explaining that the outrageously strong whale represents inscrutable malice and that he must strike through the mask to the principal, even if it means striking through the sun. Starbuck, quelled, lowers his honest eye but inwardly hopes that the blessed influences will stand by him, since his very soul has been overmanned by a madman. By midnight the sailors, livened by the grog with which Ahab has plied them, sing and dance and fight.

Ishmael now hears more about Moby Dick, the deadly, terrible, tremendous whale, which seems ubiquitous, immortal, and consciously malicious, and is the object of Ahab's mono-maniacal hate. Its whiteness, like that of the albatross, the white steed of the prairies, and the albino man of the Hartz forests, is weird and demonic. But Ahab determines to pursue this terrifying creature and so, deciding against rounding Cape Horn, makes for the southern tip of Africa in order to be in the equatorial Pacific in time to hunt there. One sultry afternoon while Ishmael is weaving a mat—its warp seems necessity, his hand free will, and Queequeg's woof-hitting sword chance—Tashtego sights a sperm whale. Suddenly five dusky phantoms dart from the after-hold onto the deck. Their leader, old Fedallah the Parsee and an intimate friend of Ahab, joins the captain's whaleboat in unsuccessful pursuit of the whale, alongside the crews of Starbuck, Stubb, and Flask. The five strange seamen are tiger-yellow like aborigines from the Manillas, and Fedallah is turbaned, steel-lipped, and funereally jacketed. That night Star-buck, Ishmael, Queequeg, and other drenched sailors bob through the black hours miles from their *Pequod* before it rescues them at dawn. Soon, southeast of the Cape of Good Hope, the whalemen encounter another ship. It is the *Goney*. Ahab asks for news of

Moby Dick; but when the *Goney's* captain is about to shout something through his trumpet it falls into the sea. Later the *Pequod* gams with the *Town-Ho*, aboard which a curious set of happenings once occurred. When her ugly mate Radney insulted Steelkilt, the fierce Lakeman broke his officer's jaw, led an abortive mutiny, and was flogged by Radney when their captain mysteriously resisted administering punishment himself. Steelkilt then planned to murder Radney, but suddenly Moby Dick appeared; Radney gave chase and was chewed to bits by the fatal whale. Soon thereafter Steelkilt escaped to Tahiti and beyond.

The narrator now returns to the subject of whales in general and discusses monstrous pictures of whales, less erroneous depictions, then true ones in various media; next he describes brit, the minute yellow substance on which the right whale feeds, and then the frightful giant squid—a vast, pulpy mass with innumerable hideous arms radiating from a central core. Daggoo mistakes a squid for the white whale, and four boats lower in pursuit, but to no avail. The search provides an occasion for the narrator to discuss whale-lines, once made of dusky hemp but now more often of golden Manilla rope. Next day, in the Indian Ocean now, Stubb lowers once again, for a huge sperm whale. Tashtego wildly rows, the line blisters the mate's tough hands, dart after dart flies into the quarry, and it is soon wallowing in its heart's blood. That night Stubb enjoys a rare whale steak, cooked to order by Fleece, the superstitious old Negro cook. Meanwhile countless sharks are rending and gobbling hunks of the dead whale outside at water level. The Sabbath which follows is broken by a scene of incredible butchery on deck, as the busy crew beheads the victim, cuts its blubber into strips, and prepares to try out barrel after barrel of oil. Ahab stands before the severed head and begs it to speak of the sights it has seen in the fathomless depths. Soon thereafter the *Pequod* gams with the *Jeroboam*, which has just lost its chief mate Harry Macey to fierce Moby Dick, and which is now plagued both by a malignant epidemic and also by a lunatic Shaker prophet called Gabriel, who shouts dire warnings to Ahab when he tries to deliver a letter addressed to dead Macey. Cutting into the whale is a dangerous business, because sharks are all about the bobbing body. Queequeg gets onto the back of the carcass and is tied securely by a monkey-rope, the other end of which is securely fastened to Ishmael's belt. The two men are thus Siamese twins. Are we not all interdependent in this curious life? Next, Stubb and Flask kill a right whale and talk for a long while over it about mysterious Ahab and his devilish aide Fedallah. When the right whale's head is hoisted onto a yardarm opposite which is another containing the sperm whale's head, the narrator is inspired to contrast the two heads—the right whale is Lockean, stoic; the sperm whale, Kantean, platonic. In either case, a whale head, with its prairie-like brow (if nut-like brain), is a veritable battering-ram, a container of oil resembling the great Heidelberg tun. Tashtego cuts into the sperm-whale head and repeatedly shoves a bucket into the ever-deepening hole for the oil therein; then suddenly he falls into it, the hooks holding the head to the yardarm tear out, and the enormous mass drops into the sea. Queequeg dives to the rescue and with his keen sword delivers his mate with all the skill of an obstetrician.

In due time the *Pequod* meets with the *Jungfrau*, out of Bremen. Her captain is Derick De Deer. As their gam ends, both ships sight some whales and soon give rival chase to a humped old bull. The German whaleboat is slowed, and the *Pequod*'s three harpooneers hurl their darts simultaneously at their agonized victim. Flask mortally goads it with a lance through an ulcer on its flank, even though Starbuck protests. Soon, however, the old carcass mysteriously sinks, and Queequeg cuts loose just in time. The narrator now turns to a discussion of the honor and glory of whaling in general, the technique of pitching lances of steel and wood into a whale once it is harpooned, the whale's fountain-like spout, and finally its tail. By this time the *Pequod* is approaching the straits of Sunda, which divide Sumatra from Java and through which Ahab plans to pass on his way toward the Philippines and the coast of Japan. Through Sunda also passes a veritable armada of whales, including some at the edges pursued by fierce Queequeg but others safe within that dally in amorous delight *more hominum.*

A few weeks later the *Pequod* encounters the *Bouton de Rose*, a French whaler full of sailors so ignorant that Stubb is able to talk them out of their precious but unsuspected treasure of ambergris within a diseased whale's corpse. But soon Ahab, little interested in profits, orders him away. A few days later Pip the little Negro boy from Alabama replaces an injured after-oarsman when Stubb lowers his boat after another whale. As luck would have it, Pip is rapped out of the boat by a harpooned whale and becomes so entangled in the line that the rich prize must be cut loose. Stubb is so furious that he orders Pip to stick to the whaleboat hereafter, but the poor lad jumps again later, in fear, is left alone a while in the awful immensity of the sea, and when picked up has become insane.

When sperm oil cools and congeals, it must be squeezed back into a liquid state. Oh, what joy! The blubber is minced and boiled in the huge try-pots placed inside some colossal masonry on deck. Then the warm oil is decanted into casks, which are then stowed in the bowels of the ship. Finally the decks are scrupulously scrubbed white again.

One day Ahab stops in front of the doubloon riveted to the mainmast. The coin shows three Andes summits, one with a flame, another a tower, and the third a crowing cock. The captain reads in the coins signs of his firmness, volcanic energy, and victory. Starbuck finds in the high peaks evidence of the Trinity. Stubb concentrates on the zodiacal arch over the mountains, while Flask sees nothing of symbolic value anywhere on the coin. The Manxman mutters in front of the mast a while, and Pip solemnly declines the verb "look." Suddenly the *Pequod* encounters the *Samuel Enderby* of London. Her captain, a down-to-earth, bluff fellow named Boomer, lost his right arm while chasing Moby Dick but according to his testimony and that of his surgeon Dr. Jack Bunger bears no ill-will toward the whale, which they both regard as awkward rather than malicious. Ahab concludes the gam by pushing Dr. Bunger aside and rushing headlong back to his vessel.

The narrator next disgresses on the following subjects: supplying whalers, a glen in Tranque in the Arsacides islands which is hung all over with carved whale bones, whale skeleton measurements, fossil whales, and the possibilities that the whale's magnitude will diminish and that the leviathan will perish. Then we learn that Ahab shortly before the *Pequod* sailed fell and his displaced ivory leg nearly pierced his groin. Leaving the *Samuel Enderby* just now, he wrenches the ivory again and therefore orders the ship's all-purpose carpenter to fashion him another one. The fellow files away, sneezing lustily as he breathes the bone dust. Ahab advances to watch near the vice bench, and close by is Perth the blacksmith at his forge. The captain soon returns to his cabin, where Starbuck reports that the oil in the hold is leaking. Saying that he is all aleak himself, Ahab nevertheless reluctantly orders the casks inspected by the harpooneers. Sweating all day below decks, Queequeg catches a terrible chill, turns almost mortally feverish, and orders the carpenter to build him a coffin, which he placidly gets into in order to try it for size. Pip stands by, sobbing and beating his tambourine, calling himself a coward and praising Queequeg for his gameness. Suddenly the savage rallies, convalesces briefly, and then leaps up—well again. He now uses his coffin for a spare sea-chest.

The *Pequod* meanwhile glides northeast toward Formosa and then enters the huge Pacific, which rolls eastward for a thousand leagues. With one nostril Ahab smells the musk from the Bashee isles and with the other the salt of the waters in which hated Moby Dick lurks. He rushes off to Perth the blacksmith with a leather bag full of race-horse shoe-nail stubbs, to be forged into rods for the shank of a special harpoon. Next Ahab gives Perth his razors to melt and fashion into a harpoon barb, which the delirious captain tempers in some blood from heathen Tashtego, Queequeg, and Daggoo. Now the sea turns pleasant, but beneath its sun-gilt surface lurk monsters. The *Bachelor*, a glad Nantucket ship, comes into view, absolutely full of sperm oil and heading home. The *Pequod* lowers regularly for whales and slays several. Ahab mortally wounds one and notes wonderingly that as it dies it swings its head toward the setting sun. That night, still in the whaleboat, passionless Fedallah tells his fated commander the following: that neither hearse nor coffin can be his, that before he dies he must see two hearses—one not made by mortal hands and the other made of American wood—that Fedallah will precede his captain to death, and finally that only hemp can kill Ahab. These predictions make the man laugh deliriously.

One day, while the *Pequod* is approaching the Equator, Ahab sights the sun through his quadrant, suddenly becomes discontent with the instrument for telling where one is but not where one will be, and dashes it to the deck. On the evening of that summery day the ship is lashed by a furious typhoon, after which the corposants play lividly over the yardarms while the crew is wrapped in sacred awe. Ahab advances to address the spirit of the fire. Later, when Starbuck asks whether to send down the main-topsail yard now that the wind is loosening it, Ahab orders everything lashed against the rising tempest, while Stubb and Flask take the storm more simply and Tashtego aloft mumbles about rum. Starbuck is momentarily tempted to take a musket and shoot his insane, tormented, sleeping commander. In the morning it is learned that the ship's compass was turned by the lightning; therefore, calling for a lance, a maul, and a sailmaker's needle, proud Ahab makes a new one. A few hours later he orders the log heaved, but the line, spoiled by alternate heat and wet, soon snaps under the weight.

The *Pequod* now steers southeast toward Moby Dick's peculiar grounds. Suddenly the cry is heard of a man falling overboard from the mast. The life buoy is hurled after him. But both objects sink from sight. Queequeg offers his unneeded coffin as a new life buoy; so it is lidded and caulked, on Starbuck's orders, by the astonished, muttering carpenter. On the morrow the *Rachel*, commanded by Captain Gardiner of Nantucket, is descried. She is seeking survivors; it seems that during the previous afternoon one of her whaleboats engaged Moby Dick, who tugged it out of sight or sank it. Merciless Ahab refuses to join the *Rachel* in a two-day search for the missing persons, who include Gardiner's young son.

Day and night now, with Fedallah ever nearby, Ahab stands on deck or paces its planks, his slouched hat shading his moody eyes, until a sea hawk swoops down and flies off with it. Next a ninth whaler rolls by. She is the *Delight*, miserably misnamed because she is in tatters and with five of her crew dead because of an attack by Moby Dick only a day before. When her captain shouts that the harpoon is not forged which can kill the white whale, Ahab madly flourishes his special lance and orders his ship forward. And yet soon he drops a precious tear into the wild Pacific and reminisces before an entranced Starbuck about the girl he married when he was more than fifty years of age, calls himself a forty years' fool for being a whaler, and says that he can see his own child in Starbuck's eye. But when Starbuck replies that they can surely now return to Nantucket and have reunions with both their families, blighted Ahab heartlessly crosses the deck and stands ominously near Fedallah.

The next morning Ahab, evidently smelling the sperm whale, suddenly sights the snow-hill hump of Moby Dick, loudly claims the doubloon for himself, and orders all boats but Starbuck's after the enticing quarry. The white whale reveals himself disportingly and then bites Ahab's boat in two, tossing the frenzied captain out and scattering his crew, including the unabashed, unblinking Parsee.

On the second day Moby Dick is again sighted, and Ahab is off again, leaving Starbuck in charge of the *Pequod*. This time the whale furiously charges the three boats seeking him and soon hopelessly tangles their lines, dives, surfaces, and smashes the tiny vessels into chips. Ahab is plucked from the sea, but his ivory leg and also Fedallah are gone. Starbuck begs his captain to desist, but the soul-proud man vows to dive through the globe itself to slay his enemy.

The dawn of the third day is fair and fresh, and not until noon is Moby Dick sighted once again. Sharks now appear, but shaking his mate's hand Ahab lowers a final time. He sees the Parsee lashed to the whale's back by the fouled lines. The whale is thus the hearse prophetically promised by Fedallah, who thus goes before his master. But Ahab, possessed by all the fallen angels, rushes on and plants his special dart in his enemy's flank to the socket. Moby Dick writhes and smites the whaleboat, knocking two oarsmen to its side, where they cling, but tossing a third man free and clear. The crew propels the weakened boat forward, but then it splits and ships water. The vengeful, malicious whale now turns on the *Pequod* and butts a fatal breach in her starboard bow. Ahab now recognizes his ship as the hearse of American wood spoken of by Fedallah. Moby Dick returns to Ahab. He stabs again at his enemy, but as the stricken whale moves away the harpoon line loops around the man's neck and he is instantly bowstrung out of sight. A moment later the triple-masted *Pequod* goes down, and the shroud of the sea rolls on.

The third man, tossed away from Ahab's whaleboat, was Ishmael. The *Pequod's* suction pulls him close, but the black bubble spits out Queequeg's coffin, on which Ishmael floats for a day, and then the *Rachel* finds him, another orphan.

Captain Ahab, Archy, Azore Sailor, Belfast Sailor, Betty, Captain Bildad, Captain Boomer, Bulkington, Dr. Jack Bunger, Cabaco, Walter Canny, Captain, Captain, Captain, Captain, Aunt Charity, China Sailor, Johnny Coffin, Peter Coffin, Mrs. Sal Coffin, Sam Coffin, Deacon Deuteronomy Coleman, Nathan Coleman, Daggoo, Danish Sailor, Derick De Deer, Dough-Boy, Dutch Sailor, Elijah, Willis Ellery, Enderby, English Sailor, Fedallah, Fifth Nantucket Sailor, First Nantucket Sailor, Flask, Fleece, Fourth Nantucket Sailor, French Sailor, Gabriel, Captain Gardiner, Gardiner, Gardiner, Samuel Gleig, the Guernseyman, Captain Ezekiel Hardy, Mrs. Ezekiel Hardy, Harry, Hay-Seed, a High Priest, Hosea Hussey, Mrs. Hosea Hussey, Iceland Sailor, Ishmael, Jack, Jenny, Joe, Jonah, Jonah, King of Kokovoko, Lascar Sailor, Lazarus, Robert Long, Long Island Sailor, Harry Macey, Mrs. Harry Macey, Seth Macey, Maltese Sailor, the Manxman, Father Mapple, Captain Mayhew, Mounttop, Old Gay-Head Indian, Don Pedro, Captain Peleg, Perth, Mrs. Perth, Perth, Perth, Perth, Pip, Portuguese Sailor, Queequeg, Radney, Mrs. Radney, St. Jago's Sailor, Don Sebastian, Second Nantucket Sailor, Sicilian Sailor, Snarles, Dr. Snodhead, Spanish Sailor, Starbuck, Starbuck, Starbuck, Mrs. Mary Starbuck, Starbuck, Steelkilt, Stiggs, Stubb, Sub-Sub, Nathan Swain(e), Tahitian Sailor, John Talbot, Miss Talbot, Tashtego, Third Nantucket Sailor, Tistig, Tranquo, Usher

'Monody,' 1891.
   [Nathaniel Hawthorne?].

'Montaigne and His Kitten,' 1924.
   [Michel de] Montaigne.

'The New Ancient of Days: The Man of the Cave of Engihoul,' 1924.
   Eld, the Man of the Cave of Engihoul, Jones III, Jos, Mahone, the Pope, Joe Smith, the King of Thule.

'Off Cape Colonna,' 1891.
   [William] Falconer.

'Old Counsel of the Young Master of a Wrecked California Clipper,' 1888.
   Master.

Omoo, 1847.
   In mid-afternoon the limping narrator signs aboard the *Julia*, a Yankee-built Australian whaler, and thus escapes the natives of Typee. His wild native costume prompts many questions from the crew, some of whom he knows from earlier voyages. Sickly young Captain Guy, dubbed "The Cabin Boy" and "Paper Jack" by his disrespectful men, leaves nautical matters to his mate, rough-and-ready, sharkish little John Jermin, who is half drunk all the time but knows his work well. Long Ghost, a tall, bony, wandering ship's surgeon—retired from duty after an argument with Guy—a vicious New Zealand harpooneer named Bembo, and an unbelievably ugly carpenter, called Beauty and also Chips, are also aboard the leaky but bouncy little barque, whose crew are few and supplies worse. A couple of days after leaving Nukuheva, the *Julia* anchors at the island of St. Christina (Hytyhoo), where the

native rulers declare the ship taboo—to keep girls from boarding and causing disorder—but where several crew members temporarily desert the first night. Then they sail north to the island of Dominica (Hivarhoo), where Guy looks for more deserters and just for fun fires his pistol at the natives. At a bay called Hannamanoo they encounter a white renegade named Lem Hardy, with a blue shark tatoo and a colossal local reputation. The narrator digresses on the subject of tatooing at Hivarhoo.

Soon the *Julia* sails west into strange waters, with her sick crew, but finds no whales. Jermin studiously conceals their position, and Guy remains out of sight. The narrator, still an invalid, plays chess with Long Ghost—an irrepressible prankster—reads the man's books, and become familiar with the forecastle—and its cockroaches and tame rats. Forecastle levity is momentarily stopped by the death of two sick shipmates, one after the other. Both are buried at sea, and the crew turns somewhat superstitious, especially Van the Finn, who predicts that soon not a quarter of the crew will still be aboard. Suddenly the weak captain grows sicker, and Jermin abruptly veers off for Tahiti. Meanwhile, the crew continues to plague poor Ropey, a former baker's apprentice from London and later Australia. Chips the carpenter, with his cohort Bungs the cooper, steals liquor from a cask in the hatchways. The *Julia* rides triumphantly through a spicy gale east of Tahiti, which washes the cookhouse of Baltimore, the Negro cook, completely loose from its moorings. Jermin shoots the sun with a rusty quadrant while he is drunk and while he checks the time with a broken chronometer. All the same, they soon sail past the beautiful coral island of Pomotu. The narrator discusses coral, pearls, coconut oil, and the aroma of the sweet islands. Next morning: shimmering, lush Tahiti. But the men must remain aboard ship, because Guy, now on a stretcher and with Jermin in attendance, orders himself taken ashore and the ship under Bembo to put to sea.

The men are so irate when the captain leaves that Long Ghost and the narrator are hard put to restrain them from mutiny. The narrator suggests a round robin, that is, a petition, which sixteen men sign and send to Wilson, the British consul ashore. But when that functionary appears aboard, he proves to be unsympathetic, queries the men about their mate Jermin and the food in a prejudiced way, and orders the ship to prepare for a three-months' voyage for whales. The narrator now hopes to persuade the crew to refuse duty but not to mutiny. Instead, they all get drunk and listen indecisively to Jermin's suggestion that they go whaling and drinking, perhaps never to return for sick Guy. Soon Bembo and an ex-convict from Australia named Sydney Ben get into a violent fight. Early the following morning the sleepy men discover sullen Bembo sailing the *Julia* straight toward a coral reef and turn her in the nick of time. They jump on him and would kill him but for the intervention of drunken Jermin, who locks him in a scuttle. In the morning, Jermin grows impatient and takes the *Julia* into the risky harbor of Papeetee, finally aided by Jim the native pilot. Wilson boards, blusters, and finally transfers under arrest all rebellious seamen—including the narrator and Long Ghost—to the nearby *Reine Blanche*, a magnificently built French man-of-war full of dainty, unprofessional sailors. The prisoners remain aboard for five days and nights, and are fed badly.

Then the mutineers are taken ashore, are quizzed by Wilson, and upon refusing to return to duty are marched along a beautiful road under the careless eye of a fat native guard named Captain Bob to the Calabooza Beretanee—that is, the British jail. They are put into stocks made of two huge logs. Soon they are given more and more freedom by Bob, who trades sea biscuit brought by Rope Yarn from the *Julia* for breadfruit and even lets them go into nearby groves of oranges for baskets of the fruit. The narrator digresses on the villainous French at Tahiti, British connivance with the French there, Polynesian elephantiasis, and the beauty of young Tahitian girls. One day Dr. Johnson, Wilson's crony, visits the calabooza, listens to the complaints of the prisoners, and sends them some medicines—including a little laudanum.

After a couple of weeks in jail, the men are haled before Wilson again. He reads some trumped-up depositions designed—without success—to frighten them into agreeing to sail on the

Julia. Back to the calabooza, where they are visited by three
French-trained priests, one of whom, Father Murphy, sends some
clothes and white bread to the prisoners. Long Ghost and the
narrator share some French brandy with the priest and hence will
always think well of him. Finally, after three weeks, Guy and
Jermin collect a new crew and set sail in the *Julia* without the
unrepentent rebels, who soon conclude that the consul wants
them to disperse without further ado. So they pick up their
chests, which Jermin was kind enough to leave behind with a
native friend, and—reluctantly, it must be said—begin to enlarge
the circle of their activities.

To each white sailor a native friend attaches himself loyally.
The idle crew members jovially steal from ships in the harbor and
have moonlight picnics with the proceeds. They debate the
virtues of missionaries. The narrator bows to a bevy of white
ladies on the road and almost causes faintings. The men attend
worship in a spacious, native Christian Church, which features
noise and an anti-French, pro-British sermon. The narrator
comments on the hypocrisy of the natives in matters of religion,
their mode of dressing, missionaries in Tahiti, segregation of
white children and Hawaiian children, indolence and white men's
diseases in Tahiti, and finally the evil and hopelessness rampant
there. Melville quotes many authorities and also presents
anecdotes of his own.

When Dr. Johnson next calls at the calabooza, Long Ghost
throws a fit, in order to be assigned to more comfortable
quarters; but when they prove barren of extra food he returns to
the jail. One day, about three weeks after the *Julia*'s departure,
the men crowd after Wilson to force him to feed them. His
behavior convinces the narrator and Long Ghost that they should
accept employment as field hands for some white farmers in the
valley of Martair on nearby Imeeo island. So after bidding their
cronies farewell, off they go one night. Soon they are helping a
Yankee named Zeke and a Cockney called Shorty cultivate sweet
potatoes, turnips, yams, and sugar cane. But most of the time
they are off in the hills with their friendly hosts looking at
curious trees and flowers and a weed-grown cemetery, hunting

wild bullocks and boars, and indulging in rousing nocturnal feasts. All the same, the occasional hoeing and weeding they do proves too arduous; therefore, after Zeke sells a great heap of potatoes to a passing ship, the narrator and Long Ghost bid their saddened employers goodbye and head for the inland village of Tamai, where they witness a vivid native dance in the moonlight. After a few days, they hear of the approach of authorities seeking white vagrants; so they return to Martair for a hearty supper and soon proceed toward Taloo—by easy stages along the beach. They stop for food at the hut of a loving old pair, dubbed Darby and Joan, and soon are greeted by three pretty maidens, who escort them to the village of Loohooloo, whose chief Marharvai welcomes them to his dwelling and offers them a most pleasant dinner of rolls, fish, poee, fruit, and relishes. Afterwards the narrator strolls through a nearby grove of coco palms, which are blessed trees of many uses. He and Long Ghost are enjoying themselves; so they stay a few days, then bid a rather touching adieu to the bright-eyed girls—notably lovely Marhar-Rarrar—and continue by canoe toward Taloo, examining the curious coral reefs as they go. After about ten days from the time they first left Zeke and Shorty, they are close to Taloo, near which they spend the night in the bamboo coop of Varvy, a local dealer in contraband liquor—made by boiling and fermenting a yam-like root. Long Ghost becomes especially tipsy, has quite a hangover in the morning, and is missing his boots for good measure. Varvy cannot locate them anywhere.

The two companions hike barefooted over a hot, sandy tract to Partoowye, a hospitable village near the harbor of Taloo. They are made welcome by a very kind, hospitable, Christianized native named Ereemear ("Jeremiah") Po-Po, who provides for his friendly wife Arfretee, a beautiful but cold young daughter—Loo—a dandified son, twins, and other persons in his spacious home of cane and palmetto leaves. The white men eat well, remain several days, and enjoy rambling through the eighty-house settlement, at the end of which is the residence of Queen Pomaree Vahinee I. Long Ghost gets too amorous at one point with reserved Loo, who quietly stabs him with a thorn. The visitors inspect a local sugar plantation run by a white man named Bell, whose wife is surpassingly beautiful. The visitors also attend the Taloo chapel, where Po-Po is a deacon, and later witness a native criminal court proceeding against one Captain Crash. Finally they push their way into the presence of slovenly Queen Pomaree herself but are promptly dismissed.

Unable to persuade the queen to commission them in her navy, Long Ghost and Typee decide to leave. They have spent about five weeks in Partoowye. The narrator wants to ship aboard a whaler called the *Leviathan*, everything about which—its appearance, crew, and food—he likes. So he asks the captain, a tall, robust man from Martha's Vineyard, who over a bottle agrees to take him on but not Long Ghost. That individual when told everything commends the Vineyarder's penetration. Just before he ships out, the narrator bids an alcoholic farewell to Po-Po, Arfretee, little Loo, and finally his lanky companion. The Pacific Ocean looms ahead.

Adeea, Antone, Arfretee, Atee Poee, Baltimore, Beauty, Bell, Mrs. Bell, Bembo, Betty, Black Dan, Bill Blount, [Admiral Armand J.] Bruat, Bungs, Captain Bob, Carpagna, Nathan Coleman, Captain Crash, Darby, Dick, Dunk, Farnoopoo, Farnow, Farnowar, Major Fergus, Flash Jack, Captain Guy, Lem Hardy, Ideea, Jack, Jack, John Jermin, Jim, Jingling Joe, Joan, Joe, Dr. Johnson, Josy, Kitoti, Kooloo, Lefevre, Dr. Long Ghost, Long Jim, Loo, Billy Loon, [King] Louis Philippe, Lullee, M'Gee, Mack, Mahinee, Mai-Mai, Marbonna, Marhar-Rarrar, Marharvai, [J. Antoine] Merenhout [Moerenhaut], Monee, Mordecai, Mother Moll, Father Murphy, Navy Bob, Noomai, Old Gamboge, Old Mother Tot, Paraita, Pat, Poky, Pomaree [I], Pomaree II, Pomaree III, Queen Pomaree Vahinee I, Pomaree, Pomaree, Poofai, Deacon Ereemear Po-Po, Pot Belly, Pritchard, Rartoo, Reine, Robins, Rope Yarn, Salem, Shorty, Stubbs, Sydney Ben, the King of Tahar, King Tamatoy, Tammahamaha III, Tanee, Tati, Admiral

Du Petit Thouars, Tonoi, Tooboi, Typee, Utamai, Van, Varvy, Victor, Viner, the Vineyarder, William, William, Wilson, Wilson, Wymontoo-Hee, Zeke.

'On the Photograph of a Corps Commander,' 1866.
[General Winfield Scott Hancock].

'On Sherman's Men Who Fell in the Assault of Kenesaw Mountain, Georgia,' 1866.
[General William T.] Sherman.

'On the Slain Collegians,' 1866.
Boy.

"The Paradise of Bachelors and the Tartarus of Maids," 1855.

I. The narrator rounds a London corner one day and comes upon the veritable oasis of the latter-day Templars' cloisters. Formerly the Templars were rough, mailed knights. Now they are affable lawyers, and their Temple is a bachelors' refuge, a pleasant place to be invited for dinner. The narrator's host is R. F. C. In all, nine attend the gay banquet, which flows with oxtail soup, claret, turbot, sherry, roast beef and other meats, ale, tarts, and puddings—all soberly supervised by a headwaiter with a head like that of Socrates. The guests relate pleasant stories and seem to know no pain or trouble. After snuff the time comes to break up, and the entranced narrator tells his host that the place is a Paradise of Bachelors.

II. Next the narrator reports visiting one winter day a paper mill in New England, near Woedolor Mountain, beyond a dusky pass called the Mad Maid's Bellows-pipe and a gorge named the Black Notch. In the seedsman's business, he wants to buy envelopes to put seeds in and send them far and wide. In a hollow called the Devil's Dungeon, beside Blood River—which provides the power—the narrator finds the mill and beside it dormitory-like buildings which house the pale girls who work there. He recalls the pleasant Paradise of Bachelors back in London—so very different from this scene. Blanketing his faithful horse Black against the numbing cold, he enters the mill and sees blank-looking girls tending monstrous, animal-like machines. Suddenly a dark man (later referred to as old Bach) drags the narrator outside and vigorously rubs his frozen, white-spotted cheeks with snow. When the healthy pain returns, the narrator feels that his cheeks are being bitten by Actaeon's hounds. Going back inside, he is next led on a tour by an officious young lad named Cupid, who shows him the water wheel, turned by the blood-red water, then the cutters which chop rags in the lint-filled rag room, and finally the $12,000 paper-making machine. The narrator times the process: nine minutes from eggy pulp through successive cylinders to perfect sheets of foolscap. There is a fascinating, repulsive inevitability in the evolution of finished paper. All about gleam the pale faces of the girls. The dark man explains that they are all maidens, because married women are unsteady workers. The narrator retrieves his horse and buggy, departs, and back at the Black Notch pauses to contrast once again the Paradise of Bachelors and this veritable Tartarus of Maids.

   Old Bach, Cupid, R. F. C., Socrates.

'The Parthenon,' 1891.

   The poet sees the Parthenon from a distance and then closer; he relates its beauty to that of the Greek courtesan Lais and then thinks of its architect Ictinus and then of Pericles.

   Aspasia, Ictinus, Lais, Pericles, [Baruch or Benedict]
   Spinoza.

'Pausilippo (in the Time of Bomba),' 1891.

   [King] Bomba [King Ferdinand II of the Two
   Sicilies], Silvio [Pellico?].

"The Piazza," 1856.

   The narrator has moved to the country, into an old-fashioned farmhouse, solidly built seventy years ago and with a magnificent view of Greylock. But the house lacks a piazza. Shall he build one to the east where the hills start, to the south where the apple trees are, to the west looking toward pastures and maples? No. It

shall face north, because to the north is Greylock, a Charlemagne
of mountains. In March it is cold facing north, but not repellent.
Looking out that way then is like facing Cape Horn again, with
frost in one's beard. And in the summer the slanting grain all
about is like the sea. Under certain light a spot on the
northwestern hills is like a mole on a pale cheek. The further end
of a rainbow rests there. Is it a glen? a grotto? It seems glazed, as
though a window were there. Once, a light gleams off it as though
from a newly shingled roof. The narrator reads *A Midsummer-
Night's Dream* and thinks of Titania. But then he grows sick and
must keep to his room, which does not face toward the curious
spot. One September morn, recuperating, he happens to notice
millions of cankerous little worms feeding on a beautiful Chinese
creeper in bloom by a post of his piazza. Then he sees a
golden-glowing window on the mountain and determines to look
at it close up. He mounts his horse, canters along thinking of
Spenser and Don Quixote, follows an old goat, and goes on foot
past a sawmill and flowers and a pool and finally an orchard.
Beyond a craggy pass is a low-storied, gray cottage with a peaked
roof. Is this fairyland? Is Una inside? But through the doorway he
sees a lonely, pale girl, seated and sewing by a window. She is
Marianna, an orphan who lives with her brother, a hard-working
man always absent by day and exhausted at night. She points out
to the narrator a marble house off yonder—his own abode—and
wonders what happy, charming man lives in it. It is lovely by
sunset, she explains dreamily. When the narrator counters by
remarking that the rising sun gilds her house, she denies the
romantic assertion and realistically criticizes its roof and
chimney. A cloud casts a shaggy shadow across her work. A
second cloud blots out the impression of her dog nearby. The
narrator comments on the absence of singing birds here near the
top of the mountain. She mentions her lonesomeness and
sleeplessness, and says again that she would like to see the happy
being who lives in the house yonder. When she wonders why she
so much wants this sight, the narrator replies that he too knows
nothing and therefore cannot answer her. So now he walks to her
fairyland no more: by day he observes the scene before him as

though his piazza were an opera box; but at night the curtain falls, there is no light from the mountain, and dark truth comes to him.

Dives, Marianna.

Pierre, 1852.

Pierre Glendinning, the only son of Mrs. Mary Glendinning, a rich, haughty, beautiful widow, is just emerging from his teens. The two live in a manorial mansion called Saddle Meadows, in a town of the same name. Both of Pierre's parents are descended from French and Indian War and also Revolutionary War officers, even generals, and battles were fought around Saddle Meadows. Pierre and his doting mother have a jolly, sunny breakfast, during which he playfully calls her Sister Mary, jokes with one of their servants, and eats voraciously. Then, kissing her devotedly and ordering a big, old-fashioned phaeton drawn by gorgeously groomed colts, he drives off to visit Lucy Tartan, his docile little fiancée, of whom Mrs. Glendinning approves.

Lucy's father is dead, and the girl lives with her mother in the city but visits her Aunt Llanyllyn, a Saddle Meadows widow who has a cottage near the Glendinning estate. Being a matchmaker and liking Pierre, rich Mrs. Tartan approves of her daughter's summer vacations in the country. Lucy has a couple of brothers, naval officers whom one happy day Pierre told with embraces all round that he would soon be their brother-in-law. This particular morning, Pierre and Lucy take the phaeton into the pleasant countryside, lie on the grass, and kiss and talk. When Lucy suddenly asks him to tell her more about a certain dream of his—about a mysterious, dark face which kept intruding between them—he grows angry and expresses both his devotion to her and also his regret that he ever shared such a secret with her. Frightened, she weeps, vows eternal love, and begs him to hold her hand hard and forget the dark face. They return to her aunt's home, and Pierre goes at the girl's request to her room for a portfolio of her sketches and sees her snow-white bed. Later that day he visits a grove near his mansion, communes with a gentle pine tree and a dark hemlock nearby, and ponders on the subject of grief.

And how did Pierre encounter the mysterious countenance in the first place? Once, when he escorted his mother to a sewing circle conducted by the benevolent Miss Pennies, he suddenly heard a shriek when his name was announced and later saw a marvelously radiant face in candlelight gazing at him from amid a snowy group of sewing maidens. He queried his mother, who abruptly told him to think only of Lucy; then he changed the subject. But for two days, Pierre kept on wrestling with his problem: why should such a face, dark and entrancing though it was and the source of such a piercing scream, haunt him? Soon, however, he resolved to drive the phantom from his mind and partly succeeded, though his secret was such that when he chanced to encounter poor Lucy he told her about the strange face and his reaction to it. Now back to the present. Pierre enters the dining room and finds his mother with a wine bottle; she tells him that she now wishes him to wed Lucy as soon as he decently can. He is delighted at the news and is not less so when the girl comes calling, with a basket of strawberries. Rather haughtily, Mrs. Glendinning thinks of her as a childish creature after all when compared to herself, whose husband when he wed her was a mature and manly thirty-five. That evening, when Pierre is about to knock on Lucy's door, a muffled stranger hands him a letter and hurries away. At first the young man thinks that he will go talk with his fiancée and read the letter later, but instead he returns to his room, pauses a moment in hesitation, then breaks the seal of a tear-stained missive—from a girl who says that she is the unacknowledged daughter of his own sainted father. Pierre is aghast! Recovering from his shock, he vows to defend the strange girl against the world. Her name is Isabel Banford, and she is now living three miles from town near the lake.

Pierre now finds that his revered father's reputation is smashed. The young man suddenly remembers that when his father lay dying, he clasped and unclasped an ashen hand and spoke in seeming delirium of his daughter. Pierre also recalls in detail how his aunt, Miss Dorothea Glendinning, once told him about a youthful portrait of her brother, the lad's father. It seems that Ralph Winwood, a cousin of the older Glendinning, secretly dashed off the painting when Glendinning dropped in at his studio between rumored visits to a certain mysterious French emigrant who then strangely disappeared. Winwood then quietly gave the picture to Dorothea Glendinning, who later explained to her nephew that his mother much preferred an older, more sedate portrait of her husband. Eventually the aunt gave the painting which she long cherished to Pierre, when he was fifteen. Tactfully, he never asked his mother why she disliked the more romantic picture of her husband. Nor did they ever discuss that gentleman's early life. Now, suddenly, Isabel's letter casts a lurid light through all the ambiguities and explains his father's dying comments about a daughter, his Aunt Dorothea's story about the painting, and his mother's dislike of it.

Pierre rushes out into the black night, returns long after midnight—feeling all charred within—and hides his father's portrait in a chest. His world is topsy turvy. His father's image is blasted. And now even his thoughts concerning his mother are different: she seems wrapped in glittering pride, and he doubts that she would welcome Isabel, whom, however, vowing to follow his heart rather than his head, he resolves to see. He also decides never to reveal his secret to his mother, because doing so would be a blow to her pride, would destroy her fond memories, would thus cause her terrible grief, and would not aid Isabel. After waiting leadenly for the slow dawn, Pierre falls asleep for a while, awakens to an awareness of his duty, and writes Lucy that he is obliged to absent himself a while. When he goes for breakfast with his mother, she instantly notices a change in him, guesses that something is amiss, and begs him to share with her any secret trouble he has. Then the Rev. Mr. Falsgrave, the dainty, pleasant local clergyman—who incidentally admires Mrs. Glendinning inordinately—comes in for breakfast too. He and his hostess discuss what to do about a married servant who has got another servant—named Delly—with child, at which time Pierre wonders whether the man's two children, one legitimate and the other proscribed, should shun or love one another. Mrs. Glendinning takes a very hard, Old Testament line, while her clergyman hedgingly says that circumstances differ in such a way as to make a universal ruling difficult to render. Pierre leaves the two to discuss their problem and vows to help his sister, even though he is in anguish at the thought of thereby hurting his Lucy.

Finally evening comes and Pierre can see Isabel. When he goes to the lake, he recognizes the red farmhouse as one rented by Walter Ulver, ruined Delly's father. He knocks at the door. Dark Isabel, apparently alone, receives him, and they briefly kiss. She is the girl who screamed at the Miss Pennies' sewing circle. She weeps; he vows eternal loyalty to her; and then she begins to tell her story, while the sound of walking is intermittent upstairs above them. She remembers a dull, dumb house of which pictures of French chateaux remind her later. An old couple cared for her, and there was a cat and there were many empty rooms, perhaps haunted. She was afraid and sad. Then there was another house, this one amid farm buildings. There were many people about, but Isabel still knew no joy. Some of the occupants seemed savage and demented, and the place was filled with the sounds of chains. Then she drove for a couple of days with a pleasant-looking woman and soon began to live in a small place with a close-knit family. Years passed. Did she cross an ocean? Then a man identified as her father came once in a while, kissed her tenderly, but then was reported as dead. Money for Isabel's keep stopped coming, and the girl was put into another house and did chores, spinning, and weaving there. One day a peddler came by and sold her a guitar, which she quickly learned to play. She plays it now for Pierre, and he is enthralled by its mysterious music. He kisses her and leaves, promising to return next evening.

Pierre goes to his room, rests fitfully, and then has breakfast with his mother, who talks coldly with him for a while—he denies that he and Lucy have had a lovers' quarrel—and then warns him to beware of being offensive. Next Pierre plunges into the woods for miles and finally comes to a curious rock he knows which is balanced on another rock. He daringly crawls under the upper one, which could of course teeter down and crush him; while there he prays to be killed instantly if he ever behaves in a way unbecoming a man. He soon emerges haughtily and walks on and on, turning over the story of Isabel in his mind. He cannot exonerate his father, ever. It is sad that his sister—he does not doubt her identity—should now be a servant for the Ulvers. Isabel's ineffable expression haunts him. She is shrouded in mystery, but he must not pry. Strange—the two indulged in no real embrace. Nor can they, ever. Yet to him Isabel is transfigured in the heaven of Love.

Evening arrives, and Pierre goes to Isabel again. He wants to be affectionate but finds himself strangely shy. She tells him how their father left a handkerchief behind after his final visit. She treasured it, learned to read, and deciphered the name *Glendinning* in it. She also explains that she once peeped into the guitar which the peddler brought—from the Glendinning house, she later ascertained from the man—and saw the name *Isabel* gilded on one side of the interior. She speaks frankly to Pierre, as she explains matters, because though he is a man and she a woman there is no sex in their immaculateness. She believes that the guitar belonged to her mother. She whispers the word *mother* to it, and its strings seem to sparkle a responding melody. Pierre is quiet, intrigued by his dark-haired sister, who now explains that successive jobs as a chore girl brought her closer and closer to Saddle Meadows, and that she intended never to disclose her identity to him but saw him once while she was sewing at the Miss Pennies. Then, though she knew that haughty Mrs. Glendinning would never welcome her—Pierre agrees—she decided to write her brother. Pierre vows his delight, his love, and his devotion to the truth. When Isabel tells him that the pacer upstairs is poor, shamed Delly, whose baby died and whose parents have disowned her, Pierre promises to help the girl, whom he writes a brief note of sympathy. Then after he and Isabel share a simple meal, he leaves to go to the home of the Rev. Mr. Falsgrave, who is surprised to have a visitor at such an hour but admits him and tells him that he and Mrs. Glendinning plan to expel Delly Ulver from the community. Politely rebuking the unchristian man, Pierre departs solemnly.

On his way home, the confused young man repents the folly of disturbing good Mr. Falsgrave. In his room again, Pierre reads Dante's lines about abandoning hope, then Hamlet's lines about the curse of having to set disjointed times right again. Pierre must acknowledge his sister, must keep his mother from knowing who that girl is, and must shield his dead father's reputation. The young man wallows in gloom.

Finally Pierre decides that he will pretend he has married Isabel and this in spite of the fact that Isabel never so much as mentioned her need for money even. God seems to urge him to this resolve. He feels certain that Isabel knows nothing of Lucy, whom the unwarned lad is fated to lose along with his good name. Has his curious habit of calling his mother Sister Mary habituated him to fictitiousness, which he will now continue by calling his sister his wife? Pierre must save the reputation of his father, who when dying surely repented his vile act. And Pierre must keep his proud mother from being ridiculed in the eyes of the world. Suddenly a thought: his father died so quickly that his old will, leaving all to his wife Mary Glendinning, is still in force. That proud woman will surely disinherit Pierre. Suddenly he thinks of tender Lucy's lovely form and is immensely saddened.

Fated Pierre resolutely goes to Lucy, raps on her snowy bedroom door, and bursts in to tell her that he is married. She faints, revives, and orders the monster away. He goes to his mother, tells her the same story, and listens to her arrogant tirade, which ends with his permanent dismissal from home. Next he goes to the Black Swan Inn, writes his mother's servant Dates and asks for certain possessions to be sent him, and then orders the astonished old innkeeper to prepare rooms for himself and his wife that night.

In broad daylight Pierre now goes to Isabel, who judges from his terrible appearance that he has injured himself for her. He explains that deception is necessary, that the two of them will go with ruined Delly to the distant city next day, and lets slip accidentally that he has lost something. Isabel presses him for an answer, but he only embraces her, kisses her burningly, and then whispers in her ear what he has done. Meanwhile, Mrs. Glendinning is visited by uncomforting Falsgrave, whom she imperiously ejects. She suspects that Pierre has married the slut who screamed in the Miss Pennies' sewing circle. Mrs. Glendinning tells Dates to send Pierre whatever he wants and later visits Lucy, who lies inert on her snowy bed like one drowned. At sundown in the Black Swan, Pierre breaks into his chest in search of needed gold but finds his hated father's smirking portrait, which he burns along with other mementoes of his dead past.

At dusk Pierre goes to the Ulver farmhouse and takes Isabel, along with Delly, to the inn for the night. At four in the morning the trio flees Saddle Meadows forever, by coach and four, leaving the innkeeper to mutter in deep melancholy at the sadness of this wedding party.

Sour with doubts and sad at the ruins left behind, Pierre finds in the jolting coach part of a pamphlet called "Chronometricals and Horologicals," by Plotinus Plinlimmon, and reads it while Isabel and Delly sleep. The essay explains that a Greenwich clock does not indicate the correct time in China; neither is ideal Christian (chronometrical) conduct acceptable in contemporary (horological) society, though it would be admirable for one even if he is only temporal to behave in an eternally praiseworthy way.

Pierre plans to live for the time being in a house once offered him by his cousin Glendinning Stanly. Glen is a rich young man of twenty-one recently returned from Europe. He and Pierre used to be immensely devoted to each other but had something of a falling out, reflected in decreasingly affectionate letters and then a long silence. Glen, however, in a recent burst of generosity wrote to say that Pierre would be welcome to use a town house he inherited as a "Cooery" for himself and his bride Lucy, whom Glen evidently once liked a great deal. Just before leaving the Black Swan, Pierre dashed off a peremptory letter to his cousin asking that the proffered house be aired and a minimum of domestic utensils provided, and reported that he and his wife—a sincere, appreciative lady though not Lucy—together with a girl needing protection, would soon be taking up temporary lodging there until he found employment. He also mentioned rumors concerning his broken engagement and his being disowned but gave no explanation.

The stage enters the big, flaring city at twilight, and the wheels clash on the pavement, the stones of which are as hard as hard

hearts. Their driver turns surly when Pierre shouts that they must
have passed the lights of the house which cousin Glen has surely
prepared for them. But after an argument, supervised by an
increasingly suspicious policeman, they fail to find the place, and
Pierre, his two female charges, and their luggage are uncere-
moniously dumped in a side street. The policeman goes to the
precinct house with the three, and while the girls remain there
Pierre finds the house which Glen promised; but all is dark and
locked up. Pierre seeks a carriage in the main avenue and happens
upon the handsome house in which Glen has his own apartment.
The sound of music and merriment floats down. Pierre forces his
way past a servant, confronts his dandified but rather masculine
and very firm cousin—whom he has not seen for some years—but
is rudely denied any help and is ordered from the premises. The
bewildered young man finds a hack and returns to the police
station, which is now a madhouse of drunks, prostitutes, flailing
policemen, and others. Pierre manages to rescue Isabel and then
Delly, and goes with them by hack to a fairly respectable hotel
for the night.

It is now time to summarize Pierre's literary career to date.
Having a poetic nature, the young man published some sonnets,
meditative verse, and moral essays in magazines. He was praised
by editors and approached by the publishers Wonder & Wen, who
wanted to publish his works—at his expense. Girls asked him to
write little songs in their albums. He was once invited to speak at
the Urquhartian Club for the Extension of Knowledge, which
convened at Zadockprattsville. His portrait was sought, and one
editor asked him to have a daguerreotype taken. Biographers
looked him up. But humble Pierre refused all and before leaving
Saddle Meadows took satisfaction in burning all such appeals to
his vanity.

Pierre's literary productions, though very commonplace because the lad has not had enough time to dig down through the
rubbish and get to the gold, have nevertheless earned him respect,
deference, and some little money. He used to glory in his dollars
from the *Gazelle Magazine*, because they came from his work and

were not inherited. He also bought cigars with his payments. But he was careless with his manuscripts, which he scattered about at Saddle Meadows.

In the lower, old-fashioned part of the city is a tall, ancient building called the Church of the Apostles, near which is another tall structure. They have been converted into rattletrap offices and now house rather unsuccessful lawyers, artists, and other musty professionals called the Apostles. Three nights after his arrival in the city, Pierre is discovered sitting at twilight in the rear building behind the Apostles. His grandfather's old camp bed is there, along with some other battered furniture. Outside his window is a wilderness of tiles, slate, shingles, and tin. Isabel and Delly are also living there. The group has three meager rooms. Isabel and Pierre sit in the descending darkness, their arms about one another comfortingly. When Isabel tries to encourage him to write, saying that he told her that he had done fine things at Saddle Meadows, he gloomily calls his former writing useless but says that he will try anew.

Pierre found these quarters through a childhood acquaintance of his, one Charlie Millthorpe, the refined and sweet-tempered son of a poverty-stricken tenant farmer at Saddle Meadows. Pierre and Charlie often played together when they were little. A couple of years after his father's death, Charlie sold out and moved with his frail mother and three sisters to the city, where he has been supporting them all by law work and by writing. He is now a transcendental member of the Apostles and is idealistic and optimistic in his conversations with his old friend from the country.

Pierre now attempts to write a comprehensive treatise, to reveal neglected truth and make money for himself, Isabel—who is studying to become his copyist—and their maid Delly. His book will be based upon his varied reading and a great deal of original thought. But he is quickly interrupted by three dreadful pieces of news from home. His mother went insane and has now died. The day after he left, she made a new will leaving all of her Saddle Meadows property to hypocritical Glendinning Stanly. And in addition Glendinning is now said to be the suitor of Lucy, who, recovering from her awful sickness, is now living in town with her mother. Pierre sinks into the depths of despair, blames himself for his mother's death, and worries because one of his parents died weighed down by grief and now the other has died weighed down by hate. Pierre recalls that Glen always liked Lucy, who now must regard the ruffian as the best person available to her. Storming out of his little apartment for a walk to hide his feelings from Isabel, Pierre encounters Plotinus Plinlimmon, the author of the pamphlet on chronometricals and horologicals. The fellow is a combination of Apollo and Saturn, cheerful and yet non-benevolent, and inscrutable. Millthorpe pointed him out to Pierre once and offered to introduce him, but the young man declined; yet he does want to see more of the philosopher, whose expression seems to say to him, "You vain fool, you silly ass, quit!" Pierre has looked high and low for the misplaced pamphlet by Plinlimmon but cannot find it. (Much later, a rummaging clothesman found it in Pierre's surtout.)

Summer has flown. Autumn touches the land and leaves. Now frosty winter is here. Pierre huddles before his desk wrapped in countless ragged garments and tries to write. He is learning to stand alone. He has found his own orbit and must fight out his battle here. He rises early, washes in icy water and polishes his limbs with a towel, eats very little, leaves stove and fuel for Isabel and Delly, and scratches his quill across his paper. Behold Pierre, a civilized man compared to the healthy Indian down in Texas! Is Pierre building a book or unbuilding his own body thus?

Try though he does to banish thoughts of Lucy, Pierre cannot. Then one day comes a letter from Miss Tartan, in which she professes her continued love for him, saying that she will always respect his desire to keep some mysterious secret from her, insists that she believes he still loves her, and vows that she is coming to live with him—and the person he is with—though he might murder her when she arrives. She will be his cousin. When Isabel comes in and Pierre tells her that a nun-like girl is coming to stay with them, the dark girl swoons, then expresses jealousy of the other—whose fair hair and blue eyes she has dreamed about—but agrees to continue to be Pierre's evil angel and to welcome—and serve—his good angel. Pierre believes that somehow Lucy has guessed he is not married. He wonders if somehow a mysterious God is present with him. Hearty Millthorpe bustles in, supervises the delivery by a tip-happy porter of Lucy's easel and trunks, tells Pierre that he has settled certain bills for the writer of the unpublished *Inferno*, and rushes out. Pierre firmly tells puzzled Delly that his *cousin* Lucy Tartan, whom she will remember from Saddle Meadows, is coming and that Isabel is his *wife*. When alone, Delly fears that she is trapped in a nest of sin and begs God for pity.

Shortly after the trio prepare her room, pale, firm Lucy arrives but is prevented from entering by Glen and Frederic Tartan, the girl's older brother, a naval officer, until Pierre bursts onto the stairs and outfaces the two furious men. He tells them that Lucy wishes to live there and that he will make no explanations. Several Apostles drag Glen and Fred away. Soon Mrs. Tartan arrives, alternately pleads with her daughter and threatens her, and when neither course avails casts her off utterly, with a terrible malediction. Lucy is sustained by the invisible wings of love. Isabel mechanically serves her but occasionally kneels before her, when the pale girl says the word *mother* and the dark one's guitar vibrates in sympathy.

A couple of days after her arrival, Lucy is recovered sufficiently to announce that she will earn money by drawing likenesses. Pierre is encouraging but suggests that she charge only a little for each sketch. When Isabel enters and touches him, he starts, and the two come close to arguing, until she forgets her jealousy and then suggests that she can give quitar-playing lessons—at which Pierre laughs but then embraces her. Lucy happens to see them. All this time Pierre has been worried because both Glen and Fred are the sort to seek personal revenge against him. They will not go to the law for satisfaction. What force or wile will they use instead? After all, Pierre has insulted a brother and also a lover. But he welcomes their attack and would commit murder in his own defense. Meanwhile, he and Lucy are never alone together; yet when he and Isabel are, they are now somewhat embarrassed. He slaves away at his book, utterly alone deep down and without any real sympathy from anyone. He writes on, like a proud ship heading consciously for a great wreck. He is indifferent to all praise or censure. Then his eyes begin to distress him; and one stormy night, while he is walking for relief, he experiences vertigo and faints. There comes to him a vision of the Delectable Mountain back home. It was renamed the Mount of the Titans. Near its inaccessible summit is a fierce outcropping shaped like armless, broken-browed Enceladus, the potent Titan, struggling from its earthy confines to defy the heavens above. Like Moses smiting his rock, Pierre forces a personal meaning to yield from his image of the Mount of Titans: Enceladus, son and grandson of incest, is a mixture of heaven and earth, and it is fitting that he should seek to regain his birthright by force.

Pierre talks the two girls into taking a walk and a sail in the bay. On the way to the wharf, they enter an art gallery, which is showing many imported paintings. One is a fair copy of Guido's "Cenci." Another, called "The Stranger," seems to both Isabel and Pierre to be a portrait of their father. As they walk on, wild thoughts assail Pierre. How does he know that Isabel is really his sister? Her whole story seems enigmatic. The three take a boat past the crotch of the twin rivers and into the Atlantic. Suddenly feeling unwanted, Isabel tries to plunge overboard toward France but is restrained. They all return home, where Pierre finds two letters. One is from Steel, Flint & Asbestos, his publishers, who now call his book a blasphemous rhapsody and intend to sue him for costs and all advances paid him. The other letter is from Glen and Fred, who challengingly call him a liar. Pierre strides blackly past both Isabel and Lucy, goes to the room of one of the Apostles and takes two pistols, and storms up a glaring avenue until he sees both Fred and Glen. When Glen smites him with his cowhide, Pierre—who calls himself the fool of truth, virtue, and fate—shoots and kills him and soon is in prison awaiting death by hanging. Isabel, with a vial of poison, and Lucy come to see him. When Isabel identifies herself as Pierre's sister, Lucy shrivels and falls dead. When Fred and Millthorpe enter the cell, Pierre lies dead of poison, and Isabel says that all is over but that they know him not. She drops the empty vial and falls lifeless upon Pierre, her black hair running over him like vines.

Miss Angelica Amabilia, an Apostle, Asbestos, Isabel Banford, Bettie, the Bishop, Brandt, Casks, Christopher, Clara, Clarissa, Count, Cranz, Dates, Doc, Douw, Donald Dundonald, Mrs. Dunker, Edgar, Falsgrave, Falsgrave, Rev. Mr. Falsgrave, Fletz, Flint, Flitz, Dorothea Glendinning, Mrs. Mary Glendinning, General Pierre Glendinning, Pierre Glendinning, Pierre Glendinning, Glendinning, Mark Graceman, Crantz Jacobi, Kit, Mrs. Llanyllyn, Marie, Marten, Martha, Martha, Charles Millthorpe, Millthorpe, Mrs. Millthorpe, Miss Millthorpe, Miss Millthorpe, Miss Millthorpe, Moyar, Ned, Nellie, Peter Pence, Miss Pennie, Miss Pennie, Plotinus Plinlimmon, Rowland, Glendinning Stanly, Steel, Susan, Frederic Tartan, Lucy Tartan, Tartan, Mrs. Tartan, Tartan, Delly Ulver, Walter Ulver, Mrs. Walter Ulver, Mrs. Van Lorn, Vivia, Professor Monsieur Volvoon, Wen, Ralph Winwood, Wonder.

'Pontoosuce,' 1924. (Formerly called 'The Lake.')

Thinking of death in nature, the poet by the lake is kissed by a rosy, vernal spirit which tells him that after death comes life cyclically again.

"Poor Man's Pudding and Rich Man's Crumbs," 1854.

The narrator listens without enthusiasm to his poetic friend Blandmour's comments about Poor Man's Manure (snow, which is the only fertilizer for poor farmers' fields), Poor Man's Eye-water (melted snow for afflicted eyes), Poor Man's Egg (a cup of cold rain water), Poor Man's Plaster (medicine made of simple, natural elements), and finally Poor Man's Pudding. To taste this last item, the narrator goes to the old, damp house of William Coulter, who chops rich Squire Teamster's wood for seventy-five cents a day. Coulter's pregnant wife Martha, although she is sick and feeble, proudly offers the narrator what hospitality she can; and when her husband returns at her insistence for a hot mid-day meal, they share rank pork, rye bread, and a weak pudding made of rice, milk, and salt all boiled together. Later, knowing that she would resent any offer of money, the narrator shakes her cold hand, looks into her resigned eyes, and leaves. That evening over a cup of tea in front of a blazing fire, he tells his friend Blandmour that if ever a rich man speaks encouragingly to him of a poor one—well . . .

During the following summer, in 1814, the narrator goes to London and in the company of a civic official visits the scene of the Guildhall Banquet given by George the Prime Regent of England to honor various princes shortly after the Battle of Waterloo. It is now the day after the sumptuous feast. Famished people who have blue tickets are being permitted to rush at a certain hour into the hall and lap up the remains of the feast—pheasants, pasties, porkpies, jellies, and the like. While watching, the narrator and his guide are nearly crushed and must escape by a side door as the murderously hungry mob howls through the halls, which have aristocratic banners looking down like Dives on Lazarus. The narrator's guide continually remarks on the good fortune of starving Londoners who are able to gnaw the leavings of princes and duchesses. In the fresh air again, the narrator revives, surveys his torn clothing, is put into a hack, and goes back to his rooms. He heartily prays that heaven will save him from both the Poor Man's Pudding and the Rich Man's Crumbs.

> Alexander of Russia, Blandmour, Blandmour, Blandmour, Mrs. Martha Coulter, Martha Coulter, William Coulter, William Coulter, the Duchess of Devonshire, Frederic William King of Prussia, George the Prince Regent of England, Jehu, the Lord Mayor of London, Platoff the Hetman, Squire Teamster, the Duke of Wellington.

'The Portent, (1859),' 1866.
   John Brown.

"Portrait of a Gentleman," 1924.
> A brief sketch of Major John Gentian.
> Major John Gentian.

'Presentation to the Authorities by Privates, of Colors Captured in Battles Ending in the Surrender of Lee,' 1866.
> [General Robert E.] Lee.

'Rammon,' 1947.[3]

When Solomon's disdainful son Rehoboam is crowned, penitent Jeroboam offers his allegiance but is spurned. This action further saddens Rammon, a precocious son of Solomon and Rehoboam's half-brother, who has been thinking of the novel doctrine of immortality promulgated by Buddha, whose teachings the Princess of Sheba has brought to Jerusalem. Rammon turns to Zardi, a pleasant Tyrian improvisator, for an explanation of this doctrine. But it is not long before Rammon notes the shallowness of Zardi, who sings him a song of "The Enviable Isles," a place where both sorrow and glee are lulled.

> Buddha, King Hiram [I], Jeroboam, Jethro, Prince—,
> Prince Rammon, Rehoboam, the Princess of Sheba,
> Solomon, Zardi.

'Rebel Color-Bearers at Shiloh: A Plea against the Vindictive Cry Raised by Civilians Shortly after the Surrender at Appomattox,' 1866.
> [General Ulysses S.] Grant, [General Thomas J.] Stonewall [Jackson], [General Robert E.] Lee, [General George B.] McClellan.

Redburn, 1849.

Wellingborough Redburn, the young narrator, has long dreamed of going to sea. Advertisements of imminent sailings, reminiscences by his now dead father—once an importer in Broad

---

[3] The text used is the one contained in Eleanor M. Tilton, "Melville's 'Rammon': A Text and Commentary," *Harvard Library Bulletin*, XIII (Winter, 1959), 50-91.

Street, New York—sights of real-life travelers, pictures, books, and especially an intriguing glass ship—complete with rigging and a little glass sailors—all feed his imagination. His older brother gives him a gun to sell, his old shooting jacket, advice to look out for himself (who else will?), and the address of a friend in New York. So, saying goodbye to his mother and three sisters, the young lad takes a steamboat 180 miles down the Hudson River and eventually docks in the rain, a cold, wet, hungry fellow embarrassed at his inability to pay more than a dollar for the two-dollar boat ticket. But his brother's friend, young Mr. Jones, feeds Redburn well and the next day takes him to oddly jolly Captain Riga of the *Highlander*, bound for Liverpool. He signs Redburn aboard as a green hand for three dollars a month. The boy pawns his fowling piece for two dollars and fifty cents, buys some stationery and writes his mother, gets some items for a sea wardrobe, and the next morning reports to his ship. Through the whole day and night following, he has only water for food.

The next morning—in early June—they are off. Redburn, faint with hunger, is ordered to clean out the pigpen and then slush down the main-topmast. A steam tug takes them down the river past the Narrows, with its decayed old fort high to the right. Poor Redburn though busy feels wretched, thinks of his father, once opulent and then bankrupt, and wishes he too were dead. The chief mate and the second mate choose watches, and Redburn is chosen last. He is so seasick that when a muscular, handsome lady's man of a Greenlander offers him a cannikin of rum, he accepts it in spite of his juvenile temperance pledge. The men stand their watches, hoist sails to cheery wordless songs, and begin to talk of former voyages. Redburn feels a little better, although he does not join his mates in a sociable smoke. He talks about church and good books with one of the sailors, but when he queries the man about the puzzling bells aboard ship, the only answer he gets is a guffaw. Suddenly a drunk sailor rushes up the scuttle and pitches himself overboard to a quick death. The men begin to talk about the future in such a way as to frighten Redburn, and he lashes back by accusing them of fear because of their dead mate. A venomous, bullying little sailor named Jackson warns the lad to steer clear of him or he will kill him. Forlorn and miserable, Redburn finally falls asleep with his face between his knees, in the drowned man's bunk.

Redburn helps scrub the decks and then reports for a breakfast of mush, molasses, and coffee but gets none, since he has neither spoon nor cup. He is fascinated by diseased little Jackson, who is compact of malignity, physical weakness, and horrifying stories of sin and evil, and who seems to hypnotize almost the entire crew by his starved-tiger eye. The man envies Redburn his youthful health. The second day out is beautiful. The sky and sea are deep blue. Redburn begins to make some progress, even though the sailors' lingo puzzles him and he has to clean out the chicken coop and bed down the pigs aboard. Then he dresses up and starts to pay a social call upon Captain Riga, but the chief mate spins him around and sends him quickly back off the quarter-deck to the men's great delight. Later observation confirms Redburn's opinion that Riga is really no gentleman: he swears, dresses badly, and seems to have dyed his hair while he was in port earlier. The sailors ridicule Redburn because of his wardrobe—fashionable pantaloons, high boots, leaky hat, and shooting jacket. In addition, he has no cutlery and has to trade a silk handkerchief for a rusty pot from a passenger. But he is thrilled when the *Highlander* speaks to a Hamburg vessel sailing west, and he is pleased when Max the Dutchman compliments him for the manner in which he loosened the skysail. Gruff Max loans him two books, one on sea disasters and the other on delirium tremens. Other crew members include Thompson the Negro cook, who is proud of his messy cook house and reads a Bible there, and Lavender the mulatto steward, formerly a barber and now a handsome dandy with a string of broken hearts behind him. Another is Jack Blunt, whom Jackson reproachfully calls an Irish Cockney and who superstitiously consults a dream book every morning before taking pills and applying hair oil. Then there is Larry, a whaleman who talks fondly of the Indian Ocean and reviles "snivelization"; also Gun-Deck, an affected little man-of-war man who boasts of his military and amatory exploits.

One night the *Highlander* rams another vessel, owing to the drowsiness of the lookout men. Another noon, during a dark fog, Redburn is ordered to toll a dismal warning bell. Suddenly he sees some whales and is disappointed: they seem too small to be able to swallow men as one did Jonah. Redburn is thrilled when off the Grand Banks he watches the men take soundings and from three hundred fathoms down bring up sand from the bottom. And he is terrified when after a storm off the Banks their ship encounters a wreck, with green, grassy, swaying corpses lashed to the rails. Jackson flings curses in its wake, but Max and Blunt hope that the souls of its dead are safe. The crew have fun spread-eagling an unwary, gloomy cabin passenger until he promises money for drinks. Another cabin passenger is a young girl, thought to be the daughter of a Liverpool dock master on her way back home; she flirts with paternal Riga all the way over. None of the twenty or more steerage passengers is of any interest. One little stowaway, a six-year-old lad returning to England after the untimely death of his father in America, the crew welcomes with open arms. Gradually Redburn becomes somewhat more nimble at jumping into the rigging; however, some processes and nautical terms remain mysterious to him. He examines the binnacle, harness cask, capstan, booby hatch, and fife rail, but is never allowed to stand at the helm.

After thirty days at sea, the *Highlander* comes in sight of Ireland, then Wales, and finally the Mersey River, the famous bell buoy, and Liverpool, which Larry pronounces a big city but which disappoints Redburn, who is also surprised when Max's wife Sally greets him there—surprised because Max left his wife Meg in New York. Led by Jackson, the men go off to Handsome Mary Danby's Baltimore Clipper, where they board sumptuously at company expense. Redburn likes England thus far but wonders where the famed manor houses are. Meanwhile, Riga stays at the Arms Hotel, frequents the theater, entertains fellow captains aboard his ship, and often is found drunk under his table at four in the morning. The sailors' duties are light: minor chores from dawn until mid-afternoon, with time off for meals ashore, and the remainder of their time free. The narrator next dilates on the subject of maritime reforms, which seem impossible when nothing runs but Congressional mouths.

During the six weeks that the *Highlander* remains in Prince's Dock, Redburn walks all about Liverpool, part of the time trying to find places located in a prosy old guidebook which his father purchased there in 1808 and which the boy has brought along. But after several fruitless attempts—he fails to find Riddough's Hotel, where his father stayed—Redburn concludes that every age makes its own guidebooks and that what guided the father cannot help the son almost half a century later. He returns to Handsome Mary's for some tea. In his spare time he admires the big stone docks, visits tidy little droghers and observes Germans awaiting passage to America, talks with a cultured Lascar sailor named Dallabdoolmans from the Indian vessel the *Irrawaddy*, boards an unpainted Dutch galliot, and worships in a chapel ship. He also visits an old church on land. The bells please him, but a nearby morgue is appalling. In the cellar of a warehouse on a dingy street called Lancelott's-Hey he finds a starving woman and her three shriveled children, one of whom is dead in her skinny arms. Redburn cannot interest any authorities in their plight, gives them some bread, cheese, and water, and then is almost sorry for doing so, since he is only prolonging misery which he cannot cure. A few days later the stench from the cellar informs him of death on the premises; he looks in and sees only glistening quicklime. The observant young man also sees dock beggars of various sorts, maimed war veterans, clothes dealers, recruiters, pawnbrokers, tobacco smugglers, immigrant Irish laborers, proud Negroes freely stepping along the streets of the unprejudiced city, a Chartist, and a gentlemen's club from which he is ejected when he looks in. One afternoon he takes a delightful walk in the country, enters a church, and then passes a cottage; the occupants, including lovely Matilda, invite him in for tea and buttered muffins. His dreams that night are entrancing!

The next day, Redburn makes the acquaintance of young Harry Bolton, a small, neat, rather effeminate young man with a mysterious, aristocratic past, who says that he is an orphan from

Bury St. Edmunds, has inherited a great deal of money, has been a midshipman in the East India service, and wants to sail before the mast aboard the *Highlander*. They become close friends, and Harry finances a brief trip for the two of them to London, during which they go to an opulently appointed place which Redburn rightly dubs Aladdin's Palace and where Harry evidently loses a huge sum of money gambling. They quickly whirl by train north again to Liverpool.

The *Highlander* prepares to leave for America. The mate is sarcastic to Redburn when the lad returns tardily to duty. Harry is hired. Five hundred emigrant passengers ship in foul conditions. One drunk sailor is slung aboard by a crimp, for pay, but is soon discovered to be dead in his bunk and burning phosphorescently. He is quickly buried at sea by the crew, all of whom but raucous Jackson are aghast at the event. The most unusual passenger aboard is a handsome, fifteen-year-old Sicilian lad named Carlo, who draws the most enchanting airs from his hand organ. Reburn is sad to learn that dainty Harry Bolton, in spite of his boasts, proves to be incapable of climbing aloft in the rigging; when the other sailors discover his incurable fear, they treat him with terrible contempt. Harry wonders what he will do for a livelihood in America. Should he sing? Should he become a scrivener? Meanwhile, Jackson has grown too sick to continue performing his duties; so he sits idle, smoking in the faces of fellow sailors who are now without any tobacco, and cursing the universe.

The emigrants are jammed into a foul-smelling hold. They must cook at only one stove, which, to be sure, is a big one and which is planted over the main hatches; but it must be kept extinguished much of the time. The Irish aboard mistake Ireland, as they pass it, for America. Among the emigrants are two widowed Irish sisters, Mrs. O'Regan and Mrs. O'Brien, each of whom has triplet sons. Soon a famine develops aboard the ship. The emigrants are close to starving, and inhumane Riga provides only a minimum of aid and threatens to flog anyone who steals food. Next, a dreadful fever breaks out, and many deaths occur. Meanwhile, two babies are born. Thus, we come and go. The mate courageously nurses the sick, and some of the crew obey the order to descend into the steerage to cleanse it of unspeakable defilements. Scenes of grief are past all telling. Then, when the ship is off Cape Cod, sick Jackson emerges from his pallet, joins his mates in reefing the sails, and suddenly—spouting blood from sin-lacerated lungs—falls from the topsail-yard to a yeasty death in the sea.

Four months after leaving America, the *Highlander* is off the New Jersey coast. A pilot, with the smell of the land in his beard, boards her, and the emigrants are ordered to jettison all bedding, douse the lower decks, and scrub and fumigate all, or face the prospect of a weeks-long quarantine. The cabin passengers can afford to be privately disembarked, and Carlo sings his way off. The others get away more slowly. Once the ship is knotted to the pier, her men are free to hit the city, where Redburn and Harry buy pies, doughnuts, and ginger pop to share in their dingy, deserted forecastle. Learning from Mr. Jones that he is urgently wanted at home again, Redburn tries without success to obtain a job as clerk for Harry through a New York friend named Goodwell. The two shipmates report to Riga for their pay, but the vicious captain tries to charge Redburn for lost time and hammers dropped overboard, and is willing to pay Harry only a dollar or so, which the high-spirited youth flings in Riga's face. Soon the two friends must part, forever. Years later, while on the Pacific Ocean, Redburn learns that his immaculate friend Harry Bolton was crushed to death between a whale and a whaling vessel off Brazil.

> Betty, Bill, Billy, Jack Blunt, Harry Bolton, Brandy-Nan, Bridenstoke, the Marquis of Bristol, Carlo, Dallabdoolmans, Mrs. Handsome Mary Danby, Danby, De Squak, Colonel Digby, Daniel Dods, Tobias Drinker, the Duke [of Wellington], the Duke, Lord George Flagstaff, Patrick Flinnigan, Lady Georgiana Theresa, Goodwell, the Greenlander, Gun-Deck, Jackson, Betsy Jennings, Jonathan Jones, Jones, Mrs. Jones, Judy, Miss L—, Captain [Georg H. von] Langsdorff, Larry, Lavender, Tom Legare, Lord Lovely, Mary, Matilda, Max the Dutchman, Meg, Molly, Morille, Ned, Mrs. O'Brien, O'Brien, O'Brien,

O'Brien, Mike O'Regan, Pat O'Regan, Teddy
O'Regan, Mrs. O'Regan, Parkins, Pat, Pat, Peggy, Jane
Redburn, Martha Redburn, Mary Redburn, Walter
Redburn, Mrs. Walter Redburn, Wellingborough Red-
burn, Redburn, Redburn, Captain Riga, Rigs,
[William] Roscoe, Sally, Sampson, Miguel Saveda,
Bob Still, Sweeny, Thompson, Madame Vestris, the
Marquis of Waterford, Senator Wellingborough, Wilt,
Wood.

'The Released Rebel Prisoner (June, 1865),' 1866.
  [General Turner] Ashby, [General Ambrose P.] Hill,
  [General James E. B. "Jeb"] Stuart.

'Rip Van Winkle's Lilac,' 1924.
  Rip Van Winkle comes down from the Kaatskills to find a lilac
tree in front of his door where a willow used to be. Earlier, an
artist found the lilac and the dilapidated house more picturesque
than the nearby new church, of which a passing parishioner is
proud. In time, the lovely lilac immortalizes Rip.
  Washington Irving, [Joseph] Jefferson, Rip Van
  Winkle, Mrs. Rip Van Winkle.

'The Rose Farmer,' 1924.
  The poet inherits a rose farm and asks the Persian whether he
should grow roses for their envanescent beauty or distill them
laboriously into attar, as the nearby Parsee does. The Persian
advises the poet to enjoy his sequence of passing blooms, which
he can also sell and give to friends, and not try for high-priced
attar.
  The Parsee, the Persian.

'Running the Batteries, as Observed from the Anchorage above
  Vicksburgh (April, 1863),' 1866.
  Hugh, Lot, Ned [Commodore David D.] Porter,
  [Admiral David T.] Porter.

'The Rusty Man (by a Soured One),' 1924.
  [Don Quixote].

'The Scout toward Aldie,' 1866.

Relates how the Colonel pursues Mosby and his men, captures a few Confederate prisoners—one of them evidently Mosby himself—and detains a Southern girl and her Negro servant Garry Cuff (really a Confederate soldier in disguise), only to be caught in an ambush, during which the Colonel is killed and several of his men wounded.

> Archy, Belisant, Blake, the Chaplain, Corporal Chew, Captain Cloud, the Colonel, Garry Cuff, the Guide, Hair-Brains, [General Robert E.] Lee, Luke, the Major, Mink, Captain Morn, [Colonel John S.] Mosby, Reb, Pansy, Sergeant, Sir Slyboots, Steward, the Surgeon.

'Shadow at the Feast: Mrs. B——,' 1924.
> Mrs. B——.

'Shelley's Vision,' 1891.
> [Percy Bysshe] Shelley.

'Sheridan at Cedar Creek (October, 1864),' 1866.
> [General Jubal A.] Early, [General] Philip [H.] Sheridan.

'Stockings in the Farm-House Chimney,' 1924.
> May, Nellie, Rob, Willie.

'Stonewall Jackson (Ascribed to a Virginian),' 1866.
> [General Thomas J.] Stonewall Jackson.

'Stonewall Jackson, Mortally Wounded at Chancellorsville (May, 1863),' 1866.
> [General Thomas J.] Stonewall Jackson.

"Story of Daniel Orme" [first draft], 1948.
> (For plot, see "Story of Daniel Orme" [revised text].)
> Asaph Blood, [Jean] Lafitte, Daniel Orme.

"Story of Daniel Orme" [revised text], 1948.

Daniel Orme, a burly, reticent old sailor, once captain of a topmast crew, has retired to a rooming house ashore. Curious fellow roomers drug him one night and examine his chest, finding there the tatoo of a crucifix and a scar through it. On an Easter Day he is found dead on an armed height overlooking the sea, sitting and leaning against a rusty old gun.

[Jean] Lafitte, Daniel Orme.

'Suggested by the Ruins of a Mountain-Temple in Arcadia, One Built by the Architect of the Parthenon,' 1947.

[Ictinus].

'The Surrender at Appomattox (April, 1865),' 1866.

[General Ulysses S.] Grant, [General Robert E.] Lee.

'Syra (a Transmitted Reminiscence),' 1891.

Pericles.

'The Temeraire,' 1866.

Admiral [Viscount Horatio Nelson].

'Time's Betrayal,' 1924.

Explains thaat when young maples are ruthlessly tapped for syrup, their leaves turn splendidly red earlier in autumn.

King.

'Timoleon (394 B.C.),' 1891.

Timoleon rescues his older brother, Timophanes, when Corinth is attacked. But their mother continues to favor Timophanes, who becomes a tyrannical prince. Timoleon, who loves Corinth, tries to reason with his brother but fails and therefore permits the tyrant to be killed. His mother and the scorn of the citizens drive him into exile, until, needing him, Corinth calls upon him to fight for it in Sicily, which he does. Now he is a hero but, refusing to return home, stays in Sicily.

Phocian, Plato, Timoleon, Timophanes.

'Tom Deadlight,' 1888.

Tom Deadlight says goodbye, when dying aboard the British *Dreadnaught*, to his messmates Matt and Jock.

Tom Deadlight, Holy Joe, Jock, Matt.

"To Major John Gentian, Dean of the Burgundy Club," 1924.

Gentian is praised for his quiet valor in the Civil War, is encouraged to reminisce, and is asked to write "Afternoon in Naples" about his experiences as consul there (appointed by Grant).

> Jerry Bland, Gentian, Major John Gentian, Marquis de Grandvin, [President Ulysses S.] Grant, Judge Mynhert van Groot, Nathaniel Hawthorne, Charlie Fenno Hoffman, [General Robert E.] Lee, [General Antonio Lopez de] Santa Anna, Charles Sumner.

'To Ned,' 1888.

> Adam, Ned Bunn, Paul Pry.

'To the Master of the "Meteor," ' 1888.

> [Captain Thomas Melville].

'To Tom,' 1947.

> Tom [Melville].

"The Two Temples," 1924.

One Sunday morning the narrator tramps from the Battery [in New York] three miles to a new-fashioned Gothic church, only to be turned away by a fat-paunched, beadle-faced man who says that there are no galleries. The rich-looking carriages standing outside attest to the wealth of the sinners within. Prayer book in hand, the narrator enters through a small side door leading to the tower, up which he climbs along stone steps and then wooden ones, until he is standing at a hot ventilator which permits him to look down—through a gauzy wirework, to be sure—at the opulent congregation a hundred feet below and glittering in warm lights from the stained-glass windows. What he next sees resembles a show, with the white-robed priest first intoning the hymn and then reappearing, clad in black, to deliver the eloquent if inaudible sermon. His text is "Ye are the salt of the earth." After benediction, the listeners flow out in three gilded freshets. When the narrator tries to leave, he finds the door locked. Finally, in desperation, he pulls some bell ropes hanging down from his narrow tower. In no time the beadle-faced man unlocks the door, collars him, and delivers him to three policemen as a lawless violator of a place of public worship. He is fined and violently reprimanded by the judge.

Next, the narrator finds himself temporarily penniless in London one Saturday night. After his experience in the church tower, he went to Philadelphia, got a job accompanying two women to England as their physician, but was then discharged. The tide of humanity now carries him between Fleet Street and Holborn, and then to a theater off the Strand. A placard announces Macready as Cardinal Richelieu. The lonely narrator longs to rest and refresh his spirits at the play, but he has no money. Suddenly a man gives him a ticket, explaining that he has been called home and cannot use it. The narrator easily rationalizes that since we all live interdependently on charity anyway, he might as well go in. Up, up he wanders, to the topmost gallery, reminded as he does so of the church tower back home. The orchestra reminds him of the church organ. A hundred feet below, glittering like coral through a sea of smoke, are jeweled ladies. A ragged but handsome young boy offers him a mug of ale, in which he gratefully drinks to the health of the lad's father, in America seeking his fortune. Macready is stately on stage and reminds the narrator of the robed priest back home. Finally the narrator rolls out with the others borne on billows of music from the orchestra. Strange, he muses in his lonely lodging, how he was treated charitably in one temple in a strange land but at home was thrust from another.

Macready.

Typee, 1846.

After six months at sea, the narrator reports, their ship the *Dolly* is a shambles and their fresh food is gone—including Captain Vangs's pig and all the chickens except Pedro the rooster. So they plan to shift their course for the Marquesas. Mowanna is now king of Nukuheva there. His gay wife once startled the Frenchmen present in the harbor by pulling up her skirts to compare her tatoos with those of a sailor. After a lazy while, during which the narrator observes various fish and seafowls, the *Dolly* approaches Nukuheva, which was discovered in 1791. French warships are now in port, and the lovely island seems a reproach to their guns. Natives bring coconuts out to the ship, accompanied by beautiful maidens who swim alongside and climb aboard, where many acts of debauchery then occur. The white man's civilization is uniformly corrupting. The natives fear and hate the French, with their resplendent troops, their curious forge, and their strange horses. In 1842, a few weeks before the *Dolly* arrived, the French under Admiral Du Petit Thouars named Mowanna king of the whole island, to stir unfriendly Typee natives and Happar natives to rebellion which the French could then step in and quell. Queen Pomare of nearby Tahiti, unable to resist French firepower, deserted her throne.

Soon the narrator decides to jump ship. The captain is tyrannical, the crew pusillanimous, the food bad, and the future aboard a slow whaler uncertain. So he learns what he can about the island—its harbor, native houses, inlets, mountains, valleys, and reputedly cannibalistic inhabitants. White occupation has been cruel, and the natives are often fiercely antagonistic. The narrator goes ashore with a landing party and plunges into the blessedly cool glen of Tior, where he sees a meeting between the king of Tior and Admiral Thouars. What a contrast! Surely the savage is the happier of the two.

The narrator returns to the ship and asks Toby, a slight, quick-tempered, handsome, intelligent, likable fellow sailor, to be his companion in the escape. Toby instantly agrees. So when the captain is unsuccessful in his attempt to warn the crew members not to avail themselves of permitted liberty ashore, the two go with their mates, who soon fall asleep in a canoe house. The escapees plunge into a dank grove and push through dense canes toward a mountain ridge, from which they hope to watch their ship leave in due time. At sunset they come to rest three thousand feet above sea level and gaze down at a scene of matchless beauty. Soon a series of ridges and valleys puzzles them, but they refuse to retreat. When they examine their supplies, they find bits of tobacco mixed with sweat- and rain-soaked bread, which they cut into rations for six days. Then they follow a path-like track until it stops at the edge of a ravine, where they build a hut which proves ineffective against returning rain. They spend a wretched night. In the morning the narrator suffers chills and fever, and develops a mysteriously swollen leg. But a paradise of lush green unfolds beneath them, dotted with native huts. Toby thinks that they contain friendly Happars, but the narrator fears that they house Typee cannibals. To play safe, they try to traverse some rocky gorges toward the valley ahead, in the hope that it will be both fertile and unoccupied. The narrator is burning with thirst, then is icy cold. After a fruitless day, they give up that route, have a bite of food, build a new shelter, and rest. The narrator's leg still hurts, but Toby arises refreshed and finds some soft bark to eat. He suggests that they follow the streams down to the huts, presumbly in the Happar valley. So they wade and crawl, then build another hut that night. Next day they encounter a cataract a hundred feet down, beside which they descend—with brave, lithe Toby in the lead—by swinging on roots in rock fissures. Then they make another descent along sloping ledges until their path ends, after which they rashly jump into palm trees and slide down their tall trunks. Another hut, another long day, yet another hut, and finally they are safe in the gorgeous valley.

They decide to stay here openly and risk the natives. While they are sampling the fruit of some rather poor annue trees, they see a naked boy and girl. The white men approach the pair, give them some cloth, and are soon led to a village of handsome bamboo buildings. By now it is evening, and several chiefs surround them. When it becomes clear that the natives are Typees, the narrator boldly says, "Typee mortarkee" (Typees are good). Instantly, all is friendly. The narrator is quickly named Tommo. The leading chief, Mehevi, stares fixedly at his guests, whose curious white limbs all the natives feel and smell. Then they all eat some coconuts and poee-poee, which is a breadfruit porridge. They smoke, try to communicate their common hatred of the French, and then go to sleep.

After a night made restless by his leg and fears, Tommo is aroused by a troupe of curious young girls and then a bunch of boys. Next, tall Mehevi enters in war dress: head plumes, tusk necklace, whale teeth in his ears, dark tappa loincloth, anklets and bracelets of human hair, gigantic paddle-spear, and pipe. He talks for many minutes, trying apparently to gain information about the French, and then noticing Tommo's swollen leg calls for a medicine man, who pounds it mercilessly and then covers it with wet herbs. Tommo surveys the commodious, well-ventilated hut in which he is staying, then carefully notes the hideous features of Kory-Kory, the tall, strong young native assigned as his valet to feed him and carry him to the stream to bathe. Tommo is also delighted with Marheyo, Kory-Kory's senile father, and Tinor, his bustling mother. But best of all is glorious Fayaway, an olive-skinned, brown-haired, blue-eyed, slightly tatooed native girl—usually naked but for flowers in her ears—who becomes his favorite.

One day, Tommo and Toby are taken to the taboo groves, where they examine a narrow temple—called the Ti—two hundred feet in length, some old muskets, and a few terribly old men with tatoos turning green, and where that night they see flames and are fed tender pork. At first Tommo thinks that they are being fattened for the kill, but soon they march back to Marheyo's home. Uncertain of their future, Toby persuades Marheyo to lead him to the edge of Happar territory, which he hopes to cross to Nukuheva for medicine for his friend's worsening leg. But soon Toby is attacked by three Happars, is badly wounded in the temple, and is carried back to his friends nearly dead. The white men become despondent, in spite of Kory-Kory's lectures on the delights of Typee life and in spite of Fayaway's tender ministrations. So when boats are reported in the harbor nearby, Toby, promising to return with medicine within three days, nonchalantly wanders to the beach under cover of the hubbub of natives carting coconuts to sell to the strange mariners there. Soon, conflicting stories come back: Toby will return, he is missing, he has deserted. At any rate, Tommo never sees him again in the lovely valley of the Typees, who now redouble their efforts to please the melancholy invalid.

Dismal Tommo watches the natives as they prepare their breadfruit in a variety of ways. About three weeks pass. He dresses in native tappa robes, shows the savages how he can sew, and shaves the head of Narmonee, a heroic-looking warrior. When his leg suddenly improves, Tommo feels better and favorably compares his island paradise with civilization and all of its executions, wars, prisons, debts, strife, and sickness. Suddenly word comes of a Happar attack, which, however, his allies under Mehevi are able to repulse. Tommo enjoys swimming with shoals of girls in a lake about a hundred yards across. He is even permitted to break a long-standing taboo and take Fayaway with him in a little boat. Once, she stands in it, converting herself into a fetching mast, and spreads her robe for a sail.

Suddenly Marnoo enters. He is a handsome, curly-haired, bright-eyed young native who is a sacred wanderer along all shores and through all valleys of the island. The Typees crowd around him, and his eloquence thrills them. He astonishes Tommo by suddenly speaking English to him; but when Tommo persuades him to ask Mehevi to let him go back to Nukuheva, a violent refusal results in the attractive stranger's precipitate departure.

Sad again, Tommo determines not to flinch from his fate. He has now spent about two months in the valley of happy natives, for whom he next whittles toy popguns out of bamboo sticks. He gives his worn-out shoes to Marheyo, who wears them proudly around his neck. Tommo watches the tappa-manufacturing process, samples horrible-tasting medicinal water, inspects curious ancient terraced masonry and also house foundations—called pi-pis—and watches the slaughter and baking of wild hogs and other preparations for a gigantic feast. The celebration takes place not far from the Ti, and it lasts three noisy days and nights. Tommo dresses in a native way much appreciated by his hosts, who feed him poee-poee and pork, share their soporific tobacco with him, and treat him to a narcotic beverage called arva, which is also useful in curing a certain disease introduced by white men. Tommo is puzzled by a group of nude old women dancing stiffly, until Kory-Kory explains that they are bereaved widows of warriors slain in battle. The pounding of sharkskin drums also provides entertainment. Tommo is convinced that the feast has religious significance. He then dilates on the subject of native beliefs. They are mysterious. In a hut near the lake, there is a curious effigy of a warrior perpetually paddling a canoe toward eternity. Natives offer food to their gods; and one imposing priest, named Kolory, has a tiny religious doll which he whispers to and cuffs into giving proper answers.

Tommo next discusses the appearance of the natives, their complexions and teeth, their customs regarding property, and their sexual, familial, working (or non-working), and burial habits. Civilization has brought many Polynesians dread diseases, and missionaries have made some natives—for example, those in Honolulu—beasts of burden. The islanders whom Tommo has seen seem more virtuous than their so-called superiors. They are cooperative and gay, without strife. Next he discusses the animals, insects, and birds of Typee; then taboos and tatoos (he resists the art of Karky, the master tatooer of Typee), the climbing and swimming propensities of the natives, and such varied topics as the weather, singing, hair oil, and cannibalism.

One day Tommo sees three human heads, one that of a white man (not Toby), swung down from the ridgepole of Marheyo's hut. The inmates seem embarrassed and quickly hustle the packages out of sight again. His leg beginning to hurt again, Tommo now fears that he will eventually be beheaded and the rest of him eaten. Soon thereafter, he watches a group of fierce warriors, including one-eyed Mow-Mow, return from battle with the Happars and bring with them what seem to be three pole-slung bodies of the defeated enemy. Tommo is now denied access to the Ti area, where a feast—to the beat of drums—is held for chiefs and priests only. By the next noon he is allowed to return to the taboo groves, where he sees a huge wooden vessel with a lid. Kory-Kory hustles him away again, but not before he has glimpsed a fresh, flesh-garnished human skeleton. Kory-Kory calls it pig, and Tommo pretends to believe him.

Some ten days later, Marnoo suddenly returns but refuses to intercede for Tommo, although he does tell the hapless white man to try to follow his path to Pueearka, his native valley. But

Tommo is intercepted by Kory-Kory, although at about this time Marheyo, Kory-Kory's father, seems to sympathize with their gloomy guest. After what seem to be about four months in all on the island, Tommo hears a rumor from the natives that Toby has returned. Reluctantly, Mehevi permits Tommo to be carried to a hut near the beach, but Toby is definitely not there. Tommo pretends, however, to believe that he is there, so that his enthusiasm will disarm the suspicious native guards while he tries to approach the water. Fayaway weeps at the mere possibility of his departure; Kory-Kory is sad; but Marheyo pronounces the two English words he knows, "Home" and "Mother," and seems to understand. Karakoee, a tabooed renegade Oahu shanghaier of seamen, appears and tries to bribe the Typees with a musket, some powder, and some cloth to release Tommo to a tabooed crew waiting just beyond the surf in a whaleboat. But most of the Typees shake their javelins in anger. As Karakoee returns to the boat, Tommo—after a last embrace with Fayaway—rushes into the water and is rescued. The boat pulls away. Several natives swim after it; but Tommo jabs Mow-Mow with a boat hook in the throat and an oarsman slashes another native's wrists at the gunwales. Soon the narrator tumbles aboard the *Julia*, an Australian vessel in need of additional crew members. But it is three months before he is healthy again.

Appendix.

Melville briefly explains the circumstances surrounding the arrival from England of Lord George Paulet at Oahu. Captain Charlton, British consul-general, abused by anti-British authorities in the Hawaiian Islands, appealed to Admiral Thomas, who sent Paulet. This straightforward man accepted at face value a native subterfuge, the surrender of the island, designed to arouse world opinion against England. The first thing Paulet did when he was governing the islands was to prohibit customary licentiousness. Five months later, Thomas landed at Honolulu, took down the British flag, and restored the islands to native rule, at which still more riotous local rejoicing occurred, for which Paulet was again blamed, wrongly. He deserved and received British and Hawaiian plaudits for his conduct.

Sequel.

Here Melville tells what happened to Toby. Leaving Tommo, he went to the beach under the shadow of Happar mountains; promised money to an irresponsible, tabooed old sailor named Jimmy, in the household of King Mowanna of Nukuheva, to lead him through Happar territory to Nukuheva; and there signed as a sailor aboard a vessel, in order to obtain money to pay Jimmy. Toby also urged that an armed boat be sent to Typee for his friend. But only Jimmy and some tabooed natives were allowed to go. And they returned without Tommo. After waiting in anguish for some days, Toby had to ship out of the Marquesas Islands for New Zealand. In 1846 he and the author met again.

> Captain Charlton, the Commodore, Fayaway, Dr. Judd, Jimmy, Queen Kaahumanu, Kalow, King Kammahammaha, King Kammahamaha III, Karakoee, Karky, Karluna, Karnoonoo, General Kekuanoa, Kolory, Kory-Kory, Jack Lewis, Marheyo, Marnoo, Mehevi, Monoo, Moonoony, King Mowanna, Mow-Mow, Mungo, Narmonee, Narnee, Ned, Lord George Poulet, Queen Pomare, Pritchard, Mrs. Pritchard, Ruaruga, Admiral [Frederick J.] Thomas, Admiral Du Petit Thouars, Tinor, the King of Tior, Toby, Tommo, Too-Too, Captain Vangs, Wormoonoo.

'Under the Ground,' 1924.

Master.

"Under the Rose," 1924.

Geoffry, the servant of My Lord the Ambassador from England to the Azem of Persia, narrates a curious little happening. One day the Azem's servant drops roses of various hues into a delicate amber vase for the Ambassador to enjoy. A couple of days later, Geoffry examines the vase relievos, which were formerly covered by the overhanging roses, and tells the covetous Ambassador about them. The tiny carvings in amber are of angels, with a spade, a wine jar, walking, and squatting Job-like. But stranger still are the dead little insects frozen in the amber of which the vase with its tiny relievos was fashioned. When the officials meet again and sit on green cushions and smoke pleasantly, the Ambassador praises the vase so much that the Azem, alarmed lest he be asked it as a gift, says that it is worth more than a villa to him and shows his guest a poem by [S]ugar-Lips which was inspired by the anatomies in that same amber. The Ambassador later plies a Greek with wine and thus gets him to translate the poem, which explains that amber walls are like windows revealing skeletons, that we are Death's open secret, and that the angel with the jar is coming. The Ambassador grows gloomy, because he thinks that perhaps his death is near, since he is now sixty-three years old, the age at which both his father and his grandfather died.

My Lord the Ambassador, the Azem, Geoffry, Goldbeak, the Great Duke, My lady, [S]ugar-Lips.

'The Vial of Attar,' 1924.
Lesbia.

'The Victory of Antietam (1862),' 1866.
[General Thomas J.] Stonewall [Jackson], [General Robert E.] Lee, [General George B.] McClellan, [General John] Pope

White-Jacket, 1850.
Lying in Callao, on the coast of Peru, in a man-of-war called the *Neversink*, the narrator is in need of a jacket; so he awkwardly fashions one out of white duck. He is thereafter called White Jacket. Suddenly all hands are ordered to up anchor, since they are homeward bound. And where is White Jacket? Aloft at the main royal. But first a description of the groups into which the crew of five hundred men are divided. There are two watches—starboard and larboard. There are three decks. There are old sheet-anchor men, dainty after-guardsmen, and waisters. Far below are the holders. White Jacket recalls having had trouble remembering his various assigned numbers. His noble first captain of the top is Jack Chase, tall, handsome, brown-bearded; he is

well-read and can recite parts of the *Lusiads* of Camoens, is somewhat dictatorial and hates all whalers, and once deserted his ship to fight for Peruvian independence and was so valuable a sailor that Captain Claret, when he found him, returned him to duty with no more punishment than a scolding. Next a little essay regarding ranks, from commodore and captain down through the chief executive officer and other wardroom officers, to forward officers and so to the useless little middies. The people, as the common seamen are called, eat at eight in the morning, at noon, and at four in the afternoon, and then go with no food for the sixteen hours which follow. The quarter-deck officers, Selvagee and Mad Jack, are entirely different sorts of men: the first is dainty and languid, and never should have shipped; the second, tyrannical but loved by his men, drinks heavily, loves wild weather, and knows his job. White Jacket stuffs all manner of things into the capacious pockets of his jacket until he learns that even aboard a man-of-war gangs of pickpockets rove; so now he keeps only his mittens with him.

White Jacket makes a few friends aboard the ship. Among them are Lemsford, a nervous, undiscouraged poet whose little casket of verse was once found by a wild little quarter-gunner named Quoin in one of his precious guns (later the verse is "published" when the gun is fired); Nord, a lonely, hermit-like sailor who is incredibly erudite; Williams, a former Yankee peddler and teacher whose gay philosophy is pleasant; and Old Coffee, the dignified Negro cook whose assistants include colorful Sunshine, Rose-Water, and May-Day. White Jacket cooks so badly for his mess when his turn comes that he is forced out but soon happily joins Jack Chase's rousing mess, called the Forty-two-pounder Club and cooked for permanently by a skinny varlet named Shanks. The narrator discusses first the effect on the crew of the announcement that through terrible oversight the ship's supply of grog is all depleted, then the foolishness of rehearsing various military maneuvers at sea—it is one thing to be killed or injured in naval combat but quite another to be ordered to sweat furiously during play-battles—then life buoys which are useless because leaky, next the thousand talents which a crew en masse possesses, then how hammocks are slung and taken down and scrubbed, and finally the habit of certain cruel lieutenants to order the sailors to holy-stone decks in bitter weather as punishment. Since there is no grog to celebrate with, Captain Claret graciously permits a Fourth of July theatrical to be presented; it is called *The Old Wagon Paid Off*, stars histrionic Jack Chase as Percy Royal-Mast, but is interrupted by a sudden storm. The officers who amicably attend are sour again soon thereafter.

The ship approaches Cape Horn cautiously. The weather turns colder, and all hands are ordered on deck to skylark, in order to keep warm. Then they are becalmed. Soon they meet a foolish ship with too much sail, which is stripped off in tatters as a howling gale suddenly springs up. Mad Jack daringly counter-mands pallid Claret's inept orders. Fifty men are required to furl the mainsail. They are too busy to feel any fear. Northeast of the Cape they run into snow, which blankets the upper deck and must be broomed off every gun station. Wooloo, the Com-modore's Polynesian servant, mistakes the snow for fine flour. The sailors pelt Mr. Pert, a hated midshipman, with snowballs. It is terribly difficult to haul the braces in the snowy, bitter-cold weather. But suddenly the *Neversink* is in balmy latitudes.

Next, White Jacket takes us on a tour down into the bowels of the ship, where the yeoman's storeroom is. Among other items, it contains pikes, cutlasses, and pistols, which the arms yeoman, called Old Revolver, keeps shining, and also contains barrels of deadly gunpowder, presided over the Old Combustibles. Suddenly all hands are summoned on deck to witness punishment of four seamen. John, a leering bully, started a fight; and instead of reporting it, Peter, Mark, and Antone got involved and must now be flogged at the mainmast under the glaring eye of remorseless Captain Claret, who tells piteous young Peter that he would not forgive God Almighty. This dreadful incident leads Melville into an essay against the abominable practice of flogging, which, he contends, puts a scourge into the hands of fools and which the best English and American naval commanders have long avoided using. The past is filled with instances of tyranny; America should look generously and optimistically to the future.

One day the ship steers into some barrels of excellent port

wine floating loose. Captain Claret commandeers the entire find but next day doles it out honestly to the happy crew. Melville next digresses on the subject of chaplains at sea—an anomaly because they often preach above the tars' heads and also because they share in bounties paid for dead enemy sailors.

Soon the *Neversink* enters the splendid harbor of Rio de Janeiro, where Claret and the Commodore dress up in their lush uniforms and look more august than the democracy-loving President of the United States, and where the narrator whiles away his time sampling the curious books in the ship's library. Other diversions useful for passing the time include tatooing, polishing brass, walking on deck, playing checkers, daydreaming, and napping. Smuggling liquor is a terrible temptation to many ingenious sailors while their ship is in harbor. One, the sergeant-at-arms Bland, does so by shipping bottles in chests marked to the purser and then ordering the boxes stored in his mess, where his assistant, a squint-eyed old marine named Scriggs, hides the contraband and then sells it at outrageous prices. Bland even flogs his own customers when they are caught tipsy by the officers, until one agonized culprit confesses as to his source of supply. Captain Claret then breaks Bland and assigns him as a waister; but the man conducts himself so courageously among his bitter enemies that he is not harmed and soon thereafter is reinstated as sergeant-at-arms. (Sneak temporarily replaces Bland and ferrets out illicit gamblers most diligently, with the assistance of Leggs and Pounce.) Bland is luckier than some hated sergeants-at-arms, whom their disgusted crews have been known to fall upon and castrate.

The various ships in the squadron occasionally compete to see which crew can furl its sails fastest. Baldy, a likable little Scot, is being ordered by a deck lieutenant to try harder and faster when he falls and cripples himself for life by smashing through a stout oak platform on deck. Next, the narrator digresses on the subject of auctions held at sea by pursers. Poor White Jacket still cannot get rid of his jacket, however, even though he asks the purser to try to sell it and plants Williams among the men to stimulate bidding. Rumors of war circulate at this time, with the men aghast at the prospect of being maimed or killed, but with some of the officers hoping for promotion in the fray. Suddenly Jack Chase eloquently asks Captain Claret for liberty in Rio for the men; when the Commodore strolls by in his glittering epaulets, he is amused and hints that the captain should grant leave. Next Melville digresses on the subject of vicious little midshipmen, most of whom are spoiled brats demanding obedience and obtaining it because they have the power to order floggings. Only occasionally does a pleasant one come along—for example, kind little Boat Plug.

When the sailors get liberty, they go wild, get drunk and worse, and come back or are hauled back to the ship looking dreadfully worn out. Then one day, while still in the harbor at Rio, the ship is favored by a visit from Don Pedro II, King of Brazil, resplendent in green dress coat, jewels, white pantaloons, and feathered chapeau. After a brief inspection, the royal entourage departs. Soon a man named Mandeville, once an officer but now broken for repeated drunkenness, is transferred from a sloop to the *Neversink*; within a week his former roommate, Lieutenant Bridewell, has him flogged for being drunk. A handsome sailor named Frank is in consternation when he reads that a store ship on which his brother, an officer, serves will be making contact with the *Neversink*; Frank averts his face and eyes to avoid being recognized, so conscious is he of what difference in rank can do in the navy. Next, a foretopman, anxious for liberty, violates orders and tries to swim ashore, only to be shot high in the thigh by an alert sentry on deck. Here is a chance for Dr. Cadwallader Cuticle, surgeon of the *Neversink* and ranking physician of the fleet, to parade his skill; so he confers with other medical officers and then decides to operate. The amputation is a swift and brilliant performance, but the once-brawny seaman dies and is quickly buried ashore.

Suddenly the men are ordered to up anchor, and the *Neversink* gracefully glides out of the bay of musky Rio de Janeiro. She races with an English frigate and a French ship, but in the night, as the American man-of-war slips behind, they lose sight of one another. Meanwhile, Jack Chase recites the *Lusiads* and reminisces eloquently, concluding that but for fate he might have been another Homer. Within a few days, they are in fair weather, and sports such as single-stick, boxing, and head-butting are permitted. Then one day the captain suddenly accuses White Jacket of being absent from his assigned post during tactics, arraigns him at the masthead, and is about to order him flogged when Colbrook and Jack Chase daringly speak in his defense. Fated somehow to release him, Claret carelessly turns him loose. The people are regularly ordered to attend worship, which procedure the narrator treats contemptuously. On the first Sunday of each month the dreadful Articles of War are read: offenders against them "shall suffer death." Melville traces the history of these terrible laws, argues that they are viciously cruel and are violated frequently by officers, and while admitting that the average sailor is wild concludes that the Articles are debasing.

The narrator repeats some of the gory stories of Tawney, a fine old Negro sailor who was impressed off a New England merchantman during the War of 1812 and forced at gunpoint to fire the guns of the British frigate the *Macedonian*, commanded by Cardan, who once engaged the *Neversink*. Then the narrator and other sailors query Jack Chase about his bloody adventures during the Battle of Navarino on October 20, 1827. To get away from gun-deck tumult, White Jacket occasionally lolls in the tranquil chains, on a small platform outside the hull, where he once overhead a venerable sheet-anchor man reverently praying.

When seamen aboard the *Neversink* are ailing, they report to the ill-ventilated, noisy sick bay far below the deck, where they are attended by Dr. Cuticle and his assistant, Pelican, and the cadaverous steward (who is called Pills by the men). Shenly, a formerly handsome sailor from Portsmouth, New Hampshire, now lies dying in the foul area, attended by his devoted messmates, including Priming and White Jacket. When the man finally dies, Pierre affectionately arranges his clothing, Bland stands over the group joking about death, Ringrope and Thrummings sew canvas about the corpse, and it is committed to the deep. Meanwhile, the Professor continues to instruct his class of midshipmen in mathematics, navigation, ballistics, and naval tactics. Suddenly, when not too far from home, Claret orders all beards shaved off or at least trimmed closely. After mutterings of mutiny, quelled by Mad Jack's customary exemplary tact, all beards disappear—even Jack Chase's chestnut treasure—except for the Neptune-like streamers of John Ushant, the brave captain of the forecastle. Claret orders the tarry old philosopher thrown into the brig overnight and then reluctantly causes the sixty-year-old man flogged and chained again. But the beard survives.

Reminded by the captain's inhumane act, the narrator returns to the subject of flogging at the gratings and then describes other horrible acts of punishment, including keel-hauling and flogging through the fleet. Then he discusses the lazy Irish marines aboard and the fact that discipline is maintained because sailors hate marines, men hate officers, and vice versa. Next he considers such topics as impressment, Negro slaves at sea, foreigners in the American navy, and smoking and gossiping aboard ship.

When the *Neversink* is off the coast of Virginia, White Jacket is ordered aloft at midnight to reeve the halyards, falls into the whelming sea, cuts himself out of his oppressive jacket to stay afloat, and is saved. He kisses noble Jack Chase's hand at Norfolk, and the crew soon scatters ashore. Melville prefers to remember the ship still at sea, surging through the brooding darkness. Life is like a voyage in a frigate with sealed orders; we are all homeward bound.

> Antone, Baldy, Dr. Bandage, Bill, Bill, Black Bet, Bland, Lieutenant Blink, Blue-Skin, Boat Plug, Bob, Bob, Baron de Bodisco, Boombolt, Ned Brace, Lieutenant Bridewell, Broadbit, Tom Brown, Ben Browns, Brush, Bungs, Joe Bunk, Candy, Captain [John S.] Cardan [Carden], Jack Chase, Chase, Claret, Claret, Captain Claret, Lord [Sir Alexander] Cochrane, Admiral [Sir Edward] Codrington, Coffin, Corporal Colbrook, Coleman, the Commodore, Dr. Cadwallader Cuticle, Cylinder, Marquis d'Acarty, Dick Dash, Adolphus Dashman, Captain Decatur, Dick, Dobs, Patrick Flinegan, Flute, Frank, Gammon, Grummet, Guinea, Joe Hardy, Hodnose, Jack Jewel,

Jim, King John I, John, Jonathan, Frank Jones, Ned Knowles, "Happy Jack" Landless, Leggs, Lemsford, Long-locks, Lieutenant Mad Jack, Mandeville, Mark, Queen Maria, May-Day, William Julius Mickle, Montgomery, Nord, Old Coffee, Old Combustibles, Old Revolver, Old Yarn, Chief Osceola, Paper Jack, Dr. Patella, Don Pedro II, the Pelican, Pert, Peter, Peter the Wild Boy, Pierre, Pills, Pounce, Priming, the Professor, Quoin, Captain Rash, Raveling, Red Hot Coal, Ringbolt, Ringrope, Rose-Water, Dr. Sawyer, Scriggs, Scrimmage, Seafull, Seignior Seignioroni, Lieutenant Selvagee, Don Sereno, Shakings, Shanks, Shenly, Mrs. Shenly, Shenly, Shenly, Shippy, the Marquis of Silva, Slim, Sneak, Stetson, Stribbles, Sunshine, Tawney, Thrummings, Tom, Tomasita, Tubbs, John Ushant, Dr. Wedge, White Jacket, Williams, Wooloo, Yellow Torch.

CHARACTERS

A. *Mardi.* One of the three vain daughters of Nimni, on the isle of Pimminee. The other daughters are I and O.

Abdon, "The Black Jew." *Clarel.* The host of the inn where Clarel stays in Jerusalem. He is formerly from India and more recently Amsterdam.

Abos and Padilla, José de. "Benito Cereno." The royal notary, provincial register, and notary public for the Bishop of Lima.

Abrazza, King. *Mardi.* The bachelor monarch of the island of Bonovona, who pities the fallen, aids none, and hates the sight of anything unpleasant. Babbalanja lectures him on Lombardo and his masterpiece, called *Koztanza.*

Adam. 'To Ned.' A general name for business-like modern man.

Adeea. *Omoo.* A chief on the island of Imeeo who wonders about the ability of the natives to resist the encroachments of the French.

Admiral. 'The Temeraire.' See [Nelson], Admiral [Viscount Horatio].

Admiral of the White, The. 'The Haglets.' The admiral who after defeating the Plate Fleet of Spain orders his flagship home to report the victory, only to sink on treacherous reefs because some sword blades clash in a case under the ship's compass and thus turn it.

Admiral of the White, The. 'The Admiral of the White.' The commander of the British ship which has defeated a French foe, has stowed surrendered French swords too near the compass, and now finds his needle turned and his ship dashed and sunk on jagged rocks.

Adondo. *Mardi.* A famous chief whose death is recorded in one of the chronicles recited by Mohi as Taji's party leaves the island of Diranda.

Ady. *Mardi*. The lost love of Ozonna, in a story which Mohi tells at Queen Hautia's isle of Flozella a Nina in order to dissuade Taji from continuing his search for his lost Yillah. When Ozonna seeks Ady in Hautia's court, he finds only Rea, who resembles Ady.

Agar. *Clarel*. Nathan's American Jewish wife and Ruth's mother. After her husband's death, she and Ruth die of heart-break.

Agath, "the Timoneer." *Clarel*. An old Greek ship pilot staying at Mar Saba. He relates the story of the wreck of *The Peace of God* and accompanies Clarel and the others to Bethlehem.

Agrippina [the younger]. 'Marquis de Grandvin: Naples in the Time of Bomba.' Described as a "true" wife exiled from Rome to Naples.

Ahab, Captain; "Old Thunder," "Mogul." *Moby-Dick*. The ungodly, godlike captain of the *Pequod*. He has been to colleges and among the cannibals, and his monomaniacal hatred of Moby Dick, who deprived him of his leg, engenders a pride which proves fatal to him.

Aimata. *Omoo*. The original name of Pomaree Vahinee I (which see).

Akim. "Benito Cereno." An Ashantee slave who polishes hatchets during Delano's visit aboard the *San Dominick* and is killed during the attack led by Delano's chief mate.

Alanno. *Mardi*. A tall, gaunt warrior from Hio Hio, who fulminates in the Temple of Freedom in Vivenza against King Bello and Dominora.

Albert. "Billy Budd." Captain Vere's hammock-boy who is sent to bring Billy Budd to hear Claggart's charges against him.

Aldina. *Mardi*. A Mardian writer quoted by Babbalanja, who also cites Aldina's annotated transcript of Lombardo's *Koztanza* and his note therein about the prosodist Pollo.

Aleema. *Mardi*. An old priest from the island of Amma who is killed by the narrator to prevent him from taking Yillah as a human sacrifice to Tedaidee.

Alexander of Russia. "Poor Man's Pudding and Rich Man's

Crumbs." One of the aristocratic guests at the Guildhall Banquet in London following the Battle of Waterloo.

Alla Mal(l)olla. *Mardi.* A Mardian juridical authority quoted occasionally by Babbalanja.

All-a-Tanto, Commander. 'Bridegroom Dick.' An officer remembered by Dick.

Allen, Ethan; "Ticonderoga." *Israel Potter.* The gigantic, eloquent, courageous Green Mountain boy who is captured and taken in chains to Falmouth, England.

Alma. *Mardi.* A great prophet in whose biography, told by Mohi, is a story in which a man was raised from his tomb. Alma was also known as Brami and Manko, and his creed of love and charity is the basis of the religion on the island of Serenia.

Almanni. *Mardi.* A resolute kinsman of King Media and his regent during the king's absence.

Amabilia, Miss Angelica. *Pierre.* A young lady from Ambleside whose request that he write a poem in her album Pierre most graciously declines.

Ambassador, My Lord the. "Under the Rose." The sixty-three-year-old English ambassador to the Azem of Persia; the Ambassador gets a Greek to translate [S]ugar-Lips' poem which was inspired by the Azem's amber vase and which hints that we are death's open secret.

Amelia, Princess. *Israel Potter* The British princess in whose garden Sir John Millet obtains employment for Israel Potter for a short while.

Amigo. 'L'Envio.' The poet's term for his addressee.

Amor. 'After the Pleasure Party.' The god of love who warns Urania, the Mediterranean intellectual, that she can ignore him only at her peril.

Amoree. *Mardi.* A laughing philosopher cited by Babbalanja in a rare mood of gaiety.

Ampudia, General [Pedro de]. "Authentic Anecdotes of 'Old Zack.'" A Mexican officer who when visiting General Taylor at Monterey found him letting out his coat seams.

Andrea. 'Marquis de Grandvin: Naples in the Time of Bomba.'
Joanna's husband, strangled by a cord of silk and gold.
[Probably Andrew, son of Charles Robert; he was King of
Hungary and first husband of Joanna I, Queen of Naples,
who may have had a part in Andrew's murder.]

Angelico, Fra. 'Marquis de Grandvin: At the Hostelry.' A painter
who sympathizes with henpecked Durer.

Anna. "I and My Chimney." One of the narrator's daughters, who
with her mother and her sister Julia unsuccessfully tries to
persuade the narrator to tear down his chimney.

Anna. "The Apple-Tree Table." The narrator's timid daughter,
sister of Julia, both of whom at first tearfully blame the
ticking in the table on spirits but later are thrilled by the
appearance of the bug.

Annatoo. *Mardi.* The shrewish wife of Samoa aboard the *Parki.*
She is from an anonymous Pacific island, survives the Cholo
attack on the *Parki,* troubles the narrator later because of
her pilfering, and is washed overboard during a storm.

Anselm. *Clarel.* A youthful monk whose approach Derwent uses
as an excuse for stopping his conversation on faith with
Clarel at Mar Saba.

Antone. *Omoo.* A Portuguese sailor aboard the *Julia.* He signs the
round robin.

Antone. *White-Jacket.* A Portuguese sailor who is involved with
Peter and Mark in a fight started by John. When flogged by
order of Claret, he curses violently.

Antonine [Antoninus Pius]. 'The Age of the Antonines.' A
Roman emperor [succeeded by Antonine (Marcus
Aurelius)] during a well-governed, frank age.

Antonine [Marcus Aurelius]. 'The Age of the Antonines.' A
Roman emperor [preceded by Antonine (Antoninus Pius)]
during a well-governed, frank age.

Ap [ap] Catesby. 'Bridegroom Dick.' See [Jones, Commodore
Thomas] Ap [ap] Catesby.

Apollo. 'Marquis de Grandvin: Naples in the Time of Bomba.' A
handsome, dirty-faced Neapolitan street-singer.

Apostle, An. *Pierre.* Any of a group of lawyers, artists, and other professionals living in rattletrap offices in the lower part of the city. Pierre joins them.

Aquaviva, Don Hannibal Rohon Del. *Clarel.* See Hannibal, Rohon Del Aquaviva, Don.

Aquella, Queen. *Mardi.* Donjalolo's first-night queen.

Aquovi. *Mardi.* A chemist and an authority on ambergris cited by Mohi.

Arabella. "Jimmy Rose." A charming New York lady complimented graciously by indigent Jimmy Rose.

Aramboalaza, Marques de. "Benito Cereno." See Joaquin, Marques de Aramboalaza, Don.

Aranda, Alexandro. "Benito Cereno." The owner from Mendoza of the slaves aboard Cereno's *San Dominick.* After their revolt succeeds, the slaves, led by Babo, murder Aranda and use his skeleton as a warning figurehead. His bones are ultimately interred at St. Bartholomew's church in Lima.

Architect of the Parthenon, The. 'Suggested by the Ruins of a Mountain-Temple in Arcadia, One Built by the Architect of the Parthenon.' See Ictinus.

Archy. *Moby-Dick.* A sailor who tells his friend Cabaco, a Cholo, that he hears men in the after-hold. They turn out to be Fedallah and his crew.

Archy. 'The Scout toward Aldie.' A Confederate soldier (under Mosby) who sings Pansy's song, beginning "Spring is come; she shows her pass." The soldier has been captured by the men of the Colonel during their ill-fated pursuit of Mosby.

Arfretee. *Omoo.* The native hostess of the narrator and Long Ghost during their stay at Partoowye. She is somewhat over forty years of age, has been Christianized, and is the wife of Po-Po and the mother of Loo, a dandified son, and also twins.

Arheetoo. *Omoo.* An intelligent native of the island of Motoo-Otoo who asks the narrator to forge some papers for him.

Arhinoo. *Mardi.* The husband of Nina, who when he was away moaned that she was a widow, according to Yoomy.

Aristippus. 'Ditty of Aristippus.' The singer of a hedonistic ditty, irresponsible but excusable.

Arnaut, The; "The Epirot," "The Illyrian." *Clarel.* An Albanian soldier living at Mar Saba. He is enormous, picturesque, hearty, but carnal.

Arrian. *The Confidence-Man.* The stoic philosopher. Metempsychotic Mark Winsome says that he was Arrian in a previous existence.

Asbestos. *Pierre.* The publisher who, with partners Steel and Flint, rejects Pierre's book. They intend to sue Pierre for costs and advances.

Ashby, [General Turner]. 'The Released Rebel Prisoner.' A dead Confederate leader thought of by the released Rebel prisoner.

Aspasia. 'The Parthenon.' Pericles's mistress. She is mentioned.

Aster, China. *The Confidence-Man.* The candlemaker who in Egbert's illustrative story was persuaded to accept a gift—later called a loan—to improve his business; but his expanded business failed, he could not repay, and he lost everything and died.

Aster, Mrs. China. *The Confidence-Man.* China Aster's uncomplaining wife, who died shortly after her husband did.

Aster, "Old Honesty." *The Confidence-Man.* China Aster's indigent father, now deceased.

Astor, John Jacob. "Bartleby." The Wall Street lawyer's rich employer, who pronounced the lawyer prudent and methodical.

Atahalpa. *Mardi.* Mentioned by Babbalanja as a friend, and an astrologer and alchemist.

Atama, Prince. *Mardi.* A Juam prince who refused to become king because he would also have had to give up roving.

Atee Poee. *Omoo.* The native nickname—meaning "Pudding Head"—of a pompous captain of a man-of-war.

Atufal. "Benito Cereno." A gigantic African king, now a slave owned by Alexandro Aranda. Atufal aided Babo in the revolt aboard Cereno's *San Dominick* and is shot and killed during the attack led by Delano's chief mate.

Azem, The. "Under the Rose." The Persian ruler whose beautifully carved amber vase sometimes contains roses which conceal relievos of angels—including an angel of death—and who does not allow the Ambassador to talk him out of his vase but instead lets him read [S]ugar-Lips' poem about it.

Azore Sailor. *Moby-Dick.* A *Pequod* sailor who dances during the midnight festivities in the forecastle.

Azzageddi. *Mardi.* The devilish spirit in Babbalanja (which see), as he himself explains.

Azzolino, Queen. *Mardi.* Donjalolo's second-night queen.

B–. "Bartleby." A lawyer who rents the Wall Street offices of Bartleby's employer once they are vacated.

B–, Mrs. 'Shadow at the Feast.' A bride in May, a widow in June. She shadowily attends a Christmas dinner.

Babbalanja. *Mardi.* The long-winded philosopher from the isle of Odo who accompanies Taji, along with King Media of Odo, Mohi, and Yoomy, on his long and fruitless search for Yillah. Babbalanja is so moved by his vision of heaven which he has on the isle of Serenia that he remains there. He explains that at times he is inspired by the devilish spirit of Azzageddi within himself.

Babo. "Benito Cereno." The thirty-year-old Senegalese slave who with the aid of Atufal and other Negroes revolts against his master Alexandro Aranda while aboard Cereno's ship the *San Dominick* between Valparaiso and Callao, orders the atrocious murder of most of the whites aboard, and plots to commandeer the *Bachelor's Delight*, commanded by Amasa Delano. When the plan fails, Babo is captured, turns silent, and is hanged.

Baby. 'The Chipmunk.' Mentioned as leaving the poet's hearth as though startled like a chipmunk.

Bach, Old. "The Paradise of Bachelors and the Tartarus of Maids." The dark-complexioned boss of the paper-making maids.

Baldy. *White-Jacket.* A likable little Scot who is captain of the mizen-top, is a messmate of White Jacket's, falls while furling a topsail under orders to do it excessively fast, and cripples himself for life by smashing through an oak platform on deck.

Baldy. 'Donelson.' A newspaper employee who posts war reports on a bulletin board for the crowds to read.

Ballad, Ned. *Mardi.* A song-singing sailor aboard the *Arcturion.*

Baltimore. *Omoo.* The old Negro cook aboard the *Julia.*

Bandage, Dr. *White-Jacket.* The *Mohawk* surgeon, who with others confers with Dr. Cuticle when that cold expert operates on the fatally wounded foretopman.

Banford, Isabel; "Bell." *Pierre.* Supposedly the illegitimate daughter of Pierre Glendinning's father and hence Pierre's half-sister, for whom he gives up his fiancée Lucy Tartan and argues with his haughty mother. Isabel spins a strange story of her childhood, appeals to Pierre, and accompanies him to the city, where they live together (with Delly Ulver) pretending to be man and wife. After Lucy joins them and thus indirectly causes Pierre to kill Glendinning Stanly and be imprisoned for murder, Isabel reveals that she is Pierre's sister and poisons herself in prison immediately after Pierre has taken poison himself.

Banker, The; "Mammon," "Mynheer," "the Thessalonian." *Clarel.* A banker of Greek and English background, fat and luxury-loving, materialistic, and afraid of death. He and Glaucon, his prospective son-in-law, are members of the pilgrimage only from Jerusalem to the Dead Sea, where they leave it.

Bannadonna. "The Bell-Tower." The proud, capable caster of the huge bell and the maker of Haman the bell striker which kills its creator at the stroke of one.

Bardianna. *Mardi.* An old Mardian authority from the island of Vamba. He is often quoted by Babbalanja.

Bargas, Lorenzo. "Benito Cereno." One of Aranda's young clerks from Cadiz and a *San Dominick* passenger.

Barlo, Bartholomew. "Benito Cereno." A Spanish sailor from the *San Dominick* who is prevented from killing a shackled Negro with a dagger.

Barnum, P. T.; "Peter Tamerlane B—m." "Authentic Anecdotes

of 'Old Zack.' " The Museum owner who seeks to exhibit the Mexican mortar shell which General Taylor defused, also the General's pants which were torn by a tack put in his saddle, and even his tobacco box. As Peter Tamerlane B—m, he is reportedly doing business with Sambo, General Taylor's servant, and is trying to buy General Santa Anna as well.

Bartleby. "Bartleby." The pale, passive, cadaverous scrivener who one day decides that he prefers to copy no longer, stands staring at the wall, is subsequently arrested for vagrancy, and dies in prison.

[Bartlett, Colonel William Francis.] 'The College Colonel.' See the Colonel.

"Bashaw with Two Tails, The." *Omoo*. The nickname of the narrator, also called Typee (which see). It is briefly bestowed on him by Long Ghost because of a turban the narrator makes out of a shirt.

Batho. *Mardi*. A jealous critic who, according to Babbalanja, denounced Lombardo's *Koztanza;* Lombardo ignored him.

Beatrice, "Bice." *Clarel*. A girl who Celio once erroneously thought might love him.

Beauty, "Chips." *Omoo*. The ugly carpenter aboard the *Julia*. He signs the round robin.

Belex, "The Spahi." *Clarel.* The European Turkish leader of the six Arab Bethlehemites guarding the pilgrims. As a Turkish cavalryman he was once almost massacred by Mahmoud [II, Sultan of Turkey] but escaped and became a toll gatherer at the Church of the Holy Sepulcher. He is friendly with Djalea and rides a fine bay named Solomon.

Belfast Sailor. *Moby-Dick*. A Pequod sailor who becomes gleeful when Daggoo and the Spanish sailor begin to fight during the midnight festivities in the forecastle.

Belisant. 'The Scout toward Aldie.' The cousin of a Confederate soldier who is captured by the Colonel's men as they vainly pursue Mosby.

Bell. *Omoo*. The white man who owns and runs the sugar plantation at Taloo.

Bell, Mrs. *Omoo.* The surpassingly beautiful Australian wife of the owner of the sugar plantation at Taloo.

Bello, King. *Mardi.* A Mardian king whose warriors have a paddle chant and who is mentioned in a manuscript book of voyages in Oh Oh's museum. Bello is the ambitious, imperialistic, basically good king of the important island of Dominora, defeated by brave but boastful Vivenza.

Beltha. *Clarel.* A wrinkled Bethlehemite, a member of Djalea's guard, who sings a "salt-song" beside the Dead Sea.

Bembo, "The Mowree." *Omoo.* The short, shaggy, tatooed savage who is second mate aboard the *Julia.* He tries to run her aground and is locked up and not seen again. He is still in irons when she leaves Papeetee.

Ben. *Omoo.* See Sydney Ben.

Beneventano. "Cock-a-Doodle-Doo!" A majestic opera singer after whom the narrator names Merrymusk's noble rooster.

Benignus Muscatel. *Clarel.* A friar from St. John's Convent [in Syria] who gave Rolfe a vellum-bound hymnbook.

Berzilli. *Mardi.* An authority on amber cited by Mohi.

Bet. *White-Jacket.* See Black Bet.

Bettie. *Pierre.* A pretty girl in the Miss Pennies' sewing circle.

Betty. *Omoo.* A waitress fondly recalled by Rope Yarn.

Betty. *Redburn.* A servant girl at Handsome Mary Danby's Baltimore Clipper in Liverpool.

Betty. *Moby-Dick.* Mrs. Hussey's chambermaid at the Try Pots Inn on the island of Nantucket.

Betty, Master. "The Fiddler." A British child prodigy of some time ago whose name Standard enigmatically links with that of Hautboy (which see).

Bey, The. *Clarel.* The militant [Turkish] friend of the Emir in the Arnaut's song during the wine revelry at Mar Saba.

"Bice." *Clarel.* See Beatrice.

Biddy. "Jimmy Rose." The maid of the narrator William Ford's family.

Biddy. "I and My Chimney." The maid of the narrator and his wife.

Biddy. "The Apple-Tree Table." The squeamish Irish maid of the narrator, his wife, and their daughters Julia and Anna. Biddy throws the first emergent bug into the fire.

Bidi Bidie. *Mardi.* One of the twelve aristocratic Taparian families on the isle of Pimminee, entertained by Nimni.

Bidiri. *Mardi.* An honest legatee mentioned in Bardianna's will.

Bildad, Captain. *Moby-Dick.* A tall, gaunt, parsimonious, well-to-do, pious, retired whaleman—once a chief mate—now one of the principal owners of the *Pequod.* Like Captain Peleg, another part-owner, he is a Quaker.

Bill. *Redburn.* A sailor aboard the *Highlander* whose politeness to the second mate astonishes Redburn when he is new to nautical etiquette.

Bill. *White-Jacket.* A sailor who mistakes White Jacket aloft for the ghost of drowned Bungs and helps lower the halyards to test its corporeality. Later he smokes and talks politics with a group in a recess between the guns.

Bill. *Israel Potter.* One of the two named shanghaiers of Israel Potter at Dover. The other is Jim.

Billy. *Redburn.* A tailor who is a steerage passenger aboard the *Highlander* from Liverpool to America. The coquettishness of his pretty wife infuriates him.

Billy [Budd]. '[Fragment of poem].' See [Budd], Billy.

Bishop, The. *Pierre.* The superior of the Rev. Mr. Falsgrave and, four years earlier, the consecrator of his little marble church, financed by Mrs. Mary Glendinning.

B. L. *Clarel.* See L., B.

Black Bet. *White-Jacket.* A Negress in Philadelphia, in whose honor White Jacket's Negro gun captain names their gun.

Black Dan. *Omoo.* A sarcastic sailor aboard the *Julia.* He signs the round robin.

Black Guinea, "Ebony." *The Confidence-Man.* A crippled Negro beggar whose authenticity is doubted by a wooden-legged man but supported by a Methodist army chaplain and an Episcopal clergyman.

Black Jew, The. *Clarel.* See Abdon.

Bland. *White-Jacket.* The sergeant-at-arms who smuggles liquor aboard the *Neversink,* sells it at outrageous prices through an assistant named Scriggs, and flogs his customers when they are caught drunk by the officers. When discovered and broken to the rank of a waister by Claret, Brand behaves so bravely among his enemies that he remains unharmed and is soon restored to his former position. Leggs and Pounce serve under him. In the presence of Shenly's corpse, he jokes about death.

Bland, Jerry. "To Major John Gentian, Dean of the Burgundy Club." A friend of the Marquis de Grandvin.

Blandmour. "Poor Man's Pudding and Rich Man's Crumbs." The narrator's poet friend who rhapsodizes on the fact that Nature bestows gifts upon the poor.

Blandmour. "Poor Man's Pudding and Rich Man's Crumbs." One of the poetic Blandmour's ruddy little children.

Blandmour. "Poor Man's Pudding and Rich Man's Crumbs." One of the poetic Blandmour's ruddy little children.

Blandoo. *Mardi*. A dead subject whose discretion King Peepi has inherited.

Blake. 'The Scout toward Aldie.' A Union soldier whose body was found earlier by the pursuers of Mosby.

Blink, Lieutenant. *White-Jacket*. The officer whom Claret dispatched to the Peruvian sloop-of-war to arrest Jack Chase.

Bliss, Major [William W. S.]. "Authentic Anecdotes of 'Old Zack.' " General Taylor's aide who gallops away from the Mexican mortar shell which the General offers to bet will not explode, who offers a reward for the arrest of the person who put a tack in the General's saddle and thus tore his pants, and who certifies as genuine the pants subsequently exhibited at Barnum's Museum.

Blood, Asaph. "Story of Daniel Orme" [first draft]. Evidently the original name of the hero, later renamed Daniel Orme.

Blue-Skin. *White-Jacket*. A mercilessly rasping barber.

Blumacher, Tuenis Van der; "Van." 'A Dutch Christmas . . .' A Christmas caller.

Blunt, Bill; "Liverpool." *Omoo*. A sailor aboard the *Julia*. He signs the round robin. (See also William.)

Blunt, Jack. *Redburn*. An ugly, ill-formed, twenty-five-year-old

Irish Cockney sailor aboard the *Highlander*. He consults a dream book, later attributes the bad weather which the ship experiences on the voyage back to America to the fact that Mrs. O'Brien reads the Bible to her triplet sons, and finally heads the group of men who insultingly bid farewell to Riga.

B—m, Peter Tamerlane. "Authentic Anecdotes of 'Old Zack.' " See Barnum, P. T.

Boat Plug. *White-Jacket*. A kind midshipman who is frequently blessed by the grateful sailors under him. He is rebuked by the Professor in class.

Bob. *Omoo*. See Captain Bob and also Navy Bob.

Bob. *White-Jacket*. A messmate with whom White Jacket tries without success to swap jackets.

Bob. *White-Jacket*. A deceased quarter-gunner whose boots the purser's steward auctions.

Bob, Orlop. 'Bridegroom Dick.' See Orlop Bob.

Boddo. *Mardi*. An erroneous old authority, cited by Babbalanja.

Bodisco, Baron de. *White-Jacket*. The Russian Minister, at whose ball in Washington White Jacket happens to meet the Commodore and becomes chatty with him.

Boldo. *Mardi*. A materialistic Mardian mentioned by Babbalanja.

Bolton, Harry; "Bury." *Redburn*. The mysterious, dapper, handsome little man from Bury St. Edmunds who evidently gambled much of his inheritance away and then ships aboard the *Highlander* on its trip to America. He seems to have lied about his experience as a midshipman on a vessel in the East India trade, because he is unable to climb the rigging of the *Highlander*. He and Redburn become close friends. Years later Bolton is crushed to death between a whale and a vessel off Brazil.

Bomba, [King]. 'Pausilippo.' "Bomba," cruel King Ferdinand II of the Two Sicilies, mentioned as ruling at the time of the poem. 'Marquis de Grandvin: At the Hostelry.' Mentioned as the father and royal predecessor of King Fanny [Francis II]. 'Marquis de Grandvin: Naples in the Time of Bomba.' Described slurringly as "The Bomb-King."

"Bomb-King, The." 'Marquis de Grandvin: Naples in the Time of Bomba.' See Bomba.

Bomblum. *Mardi*. A legatee mentioned in Bardianna's will.

Bondo. *Mardi*. Noojoomo's Valapee enemy who swears by his own teeth to be avenged.

Bonja. *Mardi*. A Mardian poet, according to Yoomy.

Bonny Blue, "Sweet Wrinkles." 'Bridegroom Dick.' The devoted, sentimental wife of Bridegroom Dick, who reminisces to her about his experiences at sea.

Boombolt. *White-Jacket.* A forecastle man who during an animated conversation as the *Neversink* is nearing home vows never to go to sea again.

Boomer, Captain. *Moby-Dick.* The captain of the *Samuel Enderby*. He lost his right arm while chasing Moby Dick with his mate Mounttop and was later attended by his surgeon Dr. Jack Bunger.

Boone, Daniel. *The Confidence-Man*. Mentioned in the story of Indian-haters as having lost his sons to Indians.

B[ooth]., E[dwin]. ' "The Coming Storm." ' The owner of the painting "The Coming Storm" [and noted Shakespearean actor and brother of assassin John Wilkes Booth].

Boots. *Redburn*. See Redburn, Wellingborough.

Borabolla, King. *Mardi*. A fat, jolly king who is King Donjalolo's guest at a huge banquet. On his island of Mondoldo he is wonderfully hospitable to Taji and his group. He calls King Media cousin.

Borhavo. *Mardi*. An authority of amber cited by Mohi.

Botargo. *Mardi*. A Mardian poet mentioned by Babbalanja.

Boteman. "The Encantadas." See Ferryman.

Bountiful, Lord. "The Marquis de Grandvin." A laudatory nickname for the Marquis de Grandvin (which see).

Bourbon-Draco. 'Marquis de Grandvin: Naples in the Time of Bomba.' The glittering, puffed-up drum major of Bomba's troops.

Bowser. *Israel Potter*. A sailor's name invented by Israel Potter (which see) for himself when aboard the British frigate which he alone boards from the *Ariel*.

Boy, The. 'The College Colonel.' See the Colonel.

Boy, The. 'At the Cannon's Mouth.' See Cushing, [Lieutenant William B.].

Boy. 'On the Slain Collegians.' The general name for a brave collegian slain in battle.

Brace, Ned. *White-Jacket.* The after-guardsman who plays the part of Captain Spyglass in the Fourth of July theatrical.

Brade. *The Confidence-Man.* The senior partner of Brade Brothers and Company who, according to John Ringman, introduced him to Henry Roberts.

Brade. *The Confidence-Man.* The brother of the senior Brade (which see).

Bragg, General [Captain Braxton]. "Authentic Anecdotes of 'Old Zack.'" A distinguished officer who certifies the genuineness of General Taylor's pants, which Barnum is exhibiting in his Museum.

Braid Beard. *Mardi.* See Mohi.

Brami. *Mardi.* An alias of the prophet Alma (which see).

Brandt. *Pierre.* A murderous half-breed Indian who fought against General Pierre Glendinning but who later dined with him.

Brandy-Nan. *Redburn.* Handsome Mary Danby's cook, a Welshwoman, at the Baltimore Clipper in Liverpool.

Breckinridge, [General John C.]. 'Battle of Stone River, Tennessee.' The Confederate commander defeated by Rosecrans at the Battle of Stone River.

Bridegroom Dick. 'Bridegroom Dick.' The retired sailor who reminisces to his devoted wife Bonny Blue about his experiences at sea long ago.

Bridenstoke. *Redburn.* An old family friend whom Redburn fondly remembers one gloomy Sunday off Newfoundland bound east for Liverpool.

Bridewell, Lieutenant; "First Luff." *White-Jacket.* The grayhaired first lieutenant aboard the *Neversink* mentioned in an order emanating from the Commodore and dispatched by Adolphus Dashman. Bridewell assigns White Jacket a mysterious set of numbers, for mess, watch roll, hammock, gun, and so on. Bridewell orders his former roommate

Mandeville, now broken in rank to common sailor, to be flogged for drinking, and fails to speak in defense of White Jacket when he is about to be flogged.

Bridges, James. *Israel Potter.* A pro-American Britisher who with The Rev. Mr. Horne Tooke and Squire John Woodcock plots to employ Israel Potter as a courier to Dr. Franklin in Paris.

Bridges, Molly. *Israel Potter.* Mentioned as living in Bridewell and as being the only person named Bridges known by the farmer to whom Israel Potter appeals for information concerning James Bridges.

Bright Future. *The Confidence-Man.* An angel with a cornucopia of gold about whom China Aster dreams.

Brinvilliers, The Marchioness of. 'The Marchioness of Brinvilliers.' [Marie Madeleine Marguerite d'Aubray], Marquise de Brinvilliers, a mild-looking woman [executed for being a poisoner, 1676].

Bristol, The Marquis of. *Redburn.* Supposedly a friend of Harry Bolton, who says that he knows Ickworth, the marquis's seat in Suffolk.

Bristol Molly. "Billy Budd." Billy's girl friend, according to his shipmate's poem "Billy in the Darbies."

Broadbit. *White-Jacket.* An old sheet-anchor man from whom White Jacket borrows a book.

Brooks. "Authentic Anecdotes of 'Old Zack.'" A New York clothier, who with his son in the firm of Brooks & Son might be appropriately asked to send General Taylor a new roundabout.

Brooks. "Authentic Anecdotes of 'Old Zack.'" A New York clothier, who with his father in the firm of Brooks & Son might be appropriately asked to send General Taylor a new roundabout.

Brouwer, Adrian. 'Marquis de Grandvin: At the Hostelry.' A wine-bibbing painter who discusses the picturesque with Dolci, is snortingly pleased by Veronese, and is critical of Michelangelo's withdrawn posture.

Brown, B. Hobbema. "The Marquis de Grandvin." A landscape

painter who voices words of tremendous praise for the Marquis de Grandvin.

Brown, John. 'The Portent.' Described as veiled, hanged, and portentous like a meteor.

Brown, Tom. *White-Jacket*. A shipmate, reported killed in an imaginary sea fight. A sailor of the same name later plays the part of Captain Bougee in the Fourth of July theatrical.

Brown. 'Bridegroom Dick.' The sailor told to tie the Finn before his ordered flogging.

Brown, Mrs. "The Apple-Tree Table." Evidently the owner of an establishment in which the narrator has ice cream.

Browns, Ben. *White-Jacket*. Mentioned in an anecdote as a painter on the Mississippi River. He painted hands on Red Hot Coal's blanket as symbols of the murderous Indian's victories.

Bruat, [Admiral Armand J.]. *Omoo*. A hated Frenchman left behind by Admiral Thouars as the governor of Tahiti.

Brush. *White-Jacket*. The captain of the paint room of the *Neversink*. He twice refuses to give White Jacket any paint with which to waterproof his jacket.

[Budd], Billy. '[Fragment of poem].' A sailor to be hanged.

Budd, William; "Billy," "Baby," "Beauty." "Billy Budd." The tall, handsome, naive, stammering twenty-one-year-old foretop-man impressed from the *Rights-of-Man* to the *Bellipotent* under Captain Vere. When Claggart lies to Vere that Billy is fomenting mutiny, Billy strikes and kills his accuser without premeditation, and is hanged for the capital offense.

Buddha. 'Buddha . . .' Depicted as expressing a hope for nirvana. 'Rammon.' The religious teacher whose beliefs the Princess of Sheba is [fictitiously] said to bring to Solomon's Palestine.

Bulkington. *Moby-Dick*. A tall, noble-shouldered, big-chested seaman, perhaps from Virginia, who after disembarking at New Bedford from a four-year voyage aboard the *Grampus* signs in a matter of days aboard the *Pequod*. He is popular but aloof and seems unable to remain ashore for very long.

Bunger, Dr. Jack. *Moby-Dick*. The surgeon aboard the *Samuel Enderby*, whose captain, Boomer, lost his right arm while chasing Moby Dick.

Bungs. *Omoo*. The perpetually half-drunk old cooper aboard the *Julia*. Although he signs the round robin, he stays behind on the *Julia* and therefore does not go to the French ship nor, later, to the Calabooza.

Bungs. *White-Jacket*. A cooper with whom Scrimmage argues about buoys. Bungs later drowns, not saved by any of his leaky buoys.

Bunk, Joe. *White-Jacket*. The sailor of the launch who plays the part of the Commodore's cockswain in the Fourth of July theatrical.

Bunkum, Colonel Josiah. "Major Jack Gentian and Colonel J. Bunkum." A valiant, muscular, rash Union officer who during the Civil War distributed spelling books throughout the South while McClellen delayed his attack. Later Bunkum criticizes the Bourbons for their anti-democratic ways. "The Cincinnati." The Burgundy Club member whose comments on the ribbon of the Society of the Cincinnati another member queries pleasantly.

Bunn, Ned. 'To Ned.' The poet's companion long ago in vividly remembered adventures in the Marquesas Islands.

Bury. *Redburn*. See Bolton, Harry.

Buttons. *Redburn*. See Redburn, Wellingborough.

Cabaco. *Moby-Dick*. A Cholo sailor, whose friend Archy tells him that he hears men in the after-hold (they turn out to be Fedallah and his crew).

Cabin Boy, The. *Omoo*. See Guy, Captain.

Calends, Queen. *Mardi*. Donjalolo's twenty-eighth-night queen.

Calvert, [George]. *Clarel*. Mentioned as a friend of one of Ungar's ancestors. The ancestor helped settle Maryland and married an Indian.

Camoens, [Luiz de]. 'Camoens.' Depicted as aspiring, noble, and

idealistic before embarking on his quest, and as dis-
illusioned and critical in the hospital afterwards.

Candy. *White-Jacket*. A good-natured foretopman who correctly
predicts that he will be flogged because when he was
imitating Priming the captain thought he was imitating him.

Canny, Walter. *Moby-Dick*. A sailor lost with five others from the
Eliza in 1839. Their shipmates placed a marble in their
memory in the Whaleman's Chapel in New Bedford.

Captain. ''The Death Craft.'' The commander of the vessel
dreamed about by the narrator.

Captain. *Moby-Dick*. Jonah's mercenary captain in Father
Mapple's sermon at the Whaleman's Chapel in New Bedford.

Captain. *Moby-Dick*. The commander of a merchant ship who
once visited Queequeg's father, the King of Kokovoko,
ignorantly washed his hands in the punchbowl, but was not
laughed at by the tolerant natives.

Captain. *Moby-Dick*. The captain of the *Moss*, which transports
Ishmael and Queequeg from New Bedford to Nantucket
and aboard which Queequeg wrestles a mimicking bumpkin.
Queequeg then saves the bumpkin when he is knocked
overboard by a swinging boom.

Captain. *Moby-Dick*. The captain of the *Town-Ho* who resists the
temptation to flog mutinous Steelkilt, whereupon his mate
Radney does so and is soon thereafter killed by Moby Dick.

Captain. 'Marquis de Grandvin: Naples in the Time of Bomba.' A
fat, nervous captain of the guard in Naples, whose citizens
hate all the soldiers.

Captain Bob. *Omoo*. The fat, hearty Tahitian who acts as the
relaxed guard of the white prisoners at the Calabooza.

Captains. 'The Admiral of the White.' French sea captains who
surrendered their flags and swords to the Admiral of the
White.

Cardan [Carden], Captain [John S.]. *White-Jacket*. The captain
of the British frigate the *Macedonian* who during the War of
1812 ordered an impressed American Negro seaman named

Tawney to fire at the American man-of-war the *Neversink*. Cardan later surrendered to Decatur.

Carlo. *Redburn.* A fifteen-year-old Sicilian who comes to Liverpool and pays for his passage aboard the *Highlander* to America by playing his hand organ with incredible charm.

Carlo, "a Triton." *Mardi.* Naples in the Time of Bomba.' A Levantine youth who sings about the hubbub of Naples, partly in time with Bomba's troops, whom he then dangerously criticizes.

Carpegna. *Omoo.* A French assistant with Reine to Bruat, governor of Tahiti.

Casks. *Pierre.* The old Black Swan innkeeper at Saddle Meadows. He is saddened when he hears that Pierre, whom he taught to shoot, is married and is moving certain possessions out of his mother's mansion.

Catesby, Ap. 'Bridegroom Dick.' See [Jones], Commodore Thomas] Ap [ap] Catesby.

Cavour, [Count Camillo]. 'Marquis de Grandvin: At the Hostelry.' Described as the crafty guard to Garibaldi's sword.

Celibate, The. *Clarel.* An innocent Greek monk at Mar Saba.

Celio, "The Unknown." *Clarel.* A facially attractive, hunchbacked Italian who resides at the Franciscan Terra Santa monastery. He is a bitter Catholic doubter and dies shortly after Clarel meets and is impressed by him.

Cereno, Captain Benito. "Benito Cereno." The Spanish captain, aged twenty-nine, of the *San Dominick*, whose cargo of slaves, owned by his friend Alexandro Aranda, revolt between Valparaiso and Callao, murder most of the whites, and unsuccessfully plot to commandeer Amasa Delano's American sealer the *Bachelor's Delight* in the harbor of Santa Maria. Cereno is so completely unnerved by the conduct of Babo, leader of the revolt, that he dies three months after his rescue.

Chaplain, The. 'The Scout toward Aldie.' The young chaplain with the Colonel's men during their ill-fated pursuit of

Mosby. The chaplain tends a Confederate prisoner, evidently Mosby himself, who feigns injury from a fall.

Charity, Aunt. *Moby-Dick.* Captain Bildad's thin old sister, who supplies the *Pequod* with ginger-jub, a mild and therefore unwanted drink.

Charlement. *The Confidence-Man.* The hero of a story told by Frank Goodman. Wealthy Charlemont of St. Louis hints that when twenty-nine years old he ruined himself financially to aid a needy friend. He then supposedly made another fortune after nine years in Marseilles.

Charlie. *The Confidence-Man.* The fictitious name taken in his dialogue with Frank Goodman by Egbert (which see).

Charlton, Captain. *Typee.* An abused British authority in Hawaii in 1843. He reports to Admiral Thomas at Valparaiso.

Chartres, Duke de. *Israel Potter.* A pro-American French aristocrat through whom and the Count D'Estang Dr. Franklin obtains a commission for John Paul Jones.

Chase, Jack; "Don John." *White-Jacket.* The tall, handsome, brown-bearded first captain of the top, whom White Jacket worships almost like a god. Chase fought under Admiral Codrington at the Battle of Navarino and lost a finger fighting for Peruvian independence. He plays the role of Percy Royal-Mast in the Fourth of July theatrical *The Old Wagon Paid Off.* He is bold enough to ask Captain Claret and the Commodore for liberty to see Rio de Janeiro. He and Colbrook defend the reputation of White Jacket and thus protect him from an unmerited flogging. On Claret's general order, Chase reluctantly trims his fine beard. White Jacket kisses Chase's hand in Norfolk, Virginia, when the two part forever.

Chase. *White-Jacket.* Jack Chase's father, who sailed aboard the man-of-war *Romney* with William Julius Mickle, translator of Camoens's *Lusiads.*

Cherry. "Hawthorne and His Mosses." The Virginian's country cousin who in Vermont recommends Hawthorne's *Mosses from an Old Manse.*

Chew, Corporal. 'The Scout toward Aldie.' The soldier who leads in some supposed civilians—a Southern girl and her Negro servant Garry Cuff—to his Colonel, who is vainly attempting to capture Mosby.

Chief. 'The Scout toward Aldie.' See the Colonel.

Chief, The. 'Lee in the Capitol.' The name which the Senators silently assign to Lee (which also see) when they see him approach after the Civil War to answer their summons to testify.

China Aster. *The Confidence-Man.* See Aster, China.

China Sailor. *Moby-Dick.* A *Pequod* sailor critical of the dancing during the midnight festivities in the forecastle.

Chips. *Omoo.* See Beauty.

Chock-a-Block, Lieutenant. 'Bridegroom Dick.' A quarter-deck officer under whom Bridegroom Dick once sailed.

Chris, Cousin. 'A Dutch Christmas . . .' A girl who dances with Hans.

Christodolus. *Clarel.* The authoritative, blind, sleepy old abbot of Mar Saba who shows unctuous Derwent jeweled relics and saintly bones.

Christopher. *Pierre.* A servant of the Glendinnings who drives the vehicles and handles odd jobs.

Claggart, John; "Jemmy Legs." "Billy Budd." The tall, thin, pallid, thirty-five-year-old master-at-arms who through envy of the handsomeness and innocence of Billy and because of innate depravity falsely accuses him of fomenting mutiny, at which Billy strikes and kills him without premeditation and is hanged for the capital offense.

Clara. *Pierre.* A small, vivacious brunette with whom Glendinning Stanly is talking about statuary at his party when Pierre bursts in.

Clarel. *Clarel.* An American theological student assailed by religious doubts. He meets and likes Nehemiah, Rolfe, Vine, Derwent, and Ungar; falls in love with Ruth; journeys with the other pilgrims to Jericho, the Dead Sea, Mar Saba, and Bethlehem; and is ravaged by sorrow at the death of Ruth, which he learns about when he returns to Jerusalem.

Claret. *White-Jacket*. A veteran of the Battle of the Brandywine, and the father of Captain Claret of the *Neversink* and also the father of the former commander of the frigate *Brandywine*.

Claret. *White-Jacket*. The son of the veteran of the Battle of the Brandywine and brother of Captain Claret of the *Neversink*. Claret was once the commander of the frigate *Brandywine*.

Claret, Captain. *White-Jacket*. The son of a veteran of the Battle of the Brandywine and now the large, portly captain of the American frigate *Neversink*. He permits the crew to present a Fourth of July theatrical and, at the eloquent request of Jack Chase, allows the men liberty at Rio de Janeiro. He sets May-Day and Rose-Water at head-butting and then flogs them for fighting. He almost has White Jacket flogged but is dissuaded by Jack Chase and Colbrook. He orders Ushant flogged for refusing to shave his splendid beard.

Clarissa. *Pierre*. Pierre's nurse, now dead and hence unfortunately not available for consultation by his biographers.

Claude. "I and My Chimney." The pseudonym of the writer of a note published in the local paper criticizing the narrator's chimneyed house for blemishing the view. The real author may be the narrator's wife.

Claude [Lorraine]. 'Marquis de Grandvin: At the Hostelry.' See [Lorraine], Claude.

Cleothemes the Argive. "The Fiddler." A character in the narrator Helmstone's unwanted poetic masterpiece.

Cloud, Captain. 'The Scout toward Aldie.' A compassionate officer under the Colonel, who leads his men in a vain pursuit of Mosby.

Cochrane, Lord [Admiral Sir Alexander]. *White-Jacket*. Mentioned by Dr. Cuticle as the fleet admiral under whom he served some twenty years earlier.

Cockney, The. *Omoo*. See Shorty.

Codrington, Admiral [Sir Edward]. *White-Jacket*. The commanding officer of the British flagship the *Asia*, aboard which Jack Chase was captain of one of the main-deck guns during the Battle of Navarino, October 20, 1827.

Coffin, Johnny. *Moby-Dick*. The younger son of Peter and Sal Coffin.

Coffin, Peter. *Moby-Dick*. The landlord at the Spouter-Inn, New Bedford. He assigns Ishmael to be the roommate of Queequeg there. Coffin and his wife Sal have two sons, Sam and Johnny. Peter Coffin and Hosea Hussey are cousins.

Coffin, Mrs. Sal. *Moby-Dick*. Peter Coffin's wife. The Coffins have two sons, Sam and Johnny.

Coffin, Sam. *Moby-Dick*. The older son of Peter and Sal Coffin.

Coffin. *White-Jacket*. The quartermaster who plays the part of Old Luff in the Fourth of July theatrical.

Colbrook, Corporal. *White-Jacket*. The handsome, gentlemanly, lady's man of a marine corporal. He and Jack Chase defend the reputation of White Jacket before Claret and thus protect him from an unmerited scourging.

Coleman, Deacon Deuteronomy. *Moby-Dick*. The deacon of the First Congregational Church, on the island of Nantucket. Ishmael tells Peleg and Bildad that Queequeg is a member of "the First Congregational Church"—meaning the congregation of mankind.

Coleman, Nathan. *Omoo*. Named by Melville as a Nantucket whaling captain who, because of a dispute with some natives, vindictively introduced mosquitoes on the island of Imeeo.

Coleman, Nathan. *Moby-Dick*. A sailor lost with five others from the *Eliza* in 1839. Their shipmates placed a marble tablet in their memory in the Whaleman's Chapel in New Bedford.

Coleman. *White-Jacket*. Evidently an official at the New York Astor House, where Old Coffee once worked.

C[oleridge, Samuel Taylor]. 'C—'s Lament.' One who laments the passing of youth.

Colonel, The; "the Boy" 'The College Colonel.' A maimed, experienced young colonel who leads the remnant of his regiment home after two years of combat in the Civil War. [In real life, Colonel William Francis Bartlett.]

Colonel, The; "the Leader," "the Young Man," "the Youth," "Chief," "the Soldier." 'The Scout toward Aldie.' The

recently married commanding officer of the party ordered to pursue Mosby. The Colonel is killed from ambush, and his body is brought back to his bride, who is waiting in his tent.

Colonel. 'Iris (1865).' Depicted as one of three bearded puritans accompanying Iris (Peace) north after Sherman's March.

Colonel. 'Iris (1865).' Depicted as one of three bearded puritans accompanying Iris (Peace) north after Sherman's March.

Colonel. 'Iris (1865).' Depicted as one of three bearded puritans accompanying Iris (Peace) north after Sherman's March.

Commodore, The. *Typee.* The commander of the naval vessel aboard which the narrator later served when she entered the bay of Nukuheva. Mowanna's tatooed wife comes aboard.

Commodore. 'Donelson.' The commander of gunboats damaged during the siege of Donelson.

Commodore. *White-Jacket.* The silent senior captain who is in command of several ships and whose presence aboard Claret's *Neversink* has a numbing effect on everyone about him. He is old, small, skinny, and supposedly virtuous.

Constable, [John]. 'Marquis de Grandvin: At the Hostelry.' A painter mentioned very briefly by Veronese in conversation with Watteau.

Constantine, Emperor. 'The Apparition.' Mentioned as smitten by the Cross.

Coonskins. *The Confidence-Man.* The nickname by which Charlie Noble refers to Pitch (which see).

Corps Commander. 'On the Photograph of a Corps Commander.' See [Hancock, General Winfield Scott].

Coulter, Mrs. Martha. "Poor Man's Pudding and Rich Man's Crumbs." William Coulter's pregnant, sick, uncomplaining wife. She serves the narrator Poor Man's Pudding made of rice, milk, and salt.

Coulter, Martha. "Poor Man's Pudding and Rich Man's Crumbs." The daughter of William and Martha Coulter who died in infancy.

Coulter, William. "Poor Man's Pudding and Rich Man's Crumbs." The poor wood cutter who works hard for Squire Teamster and whose pregnant wife Martha is weak though uncomplaining like himself.

Coulter, William. 'Poor Man's Pudding and Rich Man's Crumbs.'' The son of William and Martha Coulter who died at the age of six.

Count. *Pierre.* A rich foreign scholar who sends a package of excellent books to Plotinus Plinlimmon, who, however, refuses the books and says that he would prefer a few jugs of Curaçoa.

Crab, Sir. *Clarel.* A name by which Rolfe refers to the Elder (which see).

Cranz. *Pierre.* A stable slave of General Pierre Glendinning, Pierre's grandfather.

Crash, Captain. *Omoo.* A sailor convicted by a local court at Taloo of seducing a native girl and hence banished.

Cream, William. *The Confidence-Man.* The barber aboard the *Fidèle* who removes his "No Trust" sign when Frank Goodman guarantees the barber in writing against loss. Goodman then walks out owing Cream for a shave.

Creole, The. "The Encantadas." A Cuban adventurer who fought for Peruvian independence from Spain and was rewarded by being given Charles's Isle, which neither he nor his dogs could hold when his deserter-recruits mutinied.

C., R. F. "The Paradise of Bachelors and the Tartarus of Maids." The narrator's bachelor host at the sumptuous dinner of the latter-day Templars in London.

Crokarky, The Laird of. *Israel Potter.* The Scottich laird whose men want to buy powder and balls from John Paul Jones, who gives them a barrel of pickles instead.

Croesus, A. "Jack Gentian (omitted from the final sketch of him)." A rosy young traveler who gossips about old Gentian.

Crowfoot, Widow. "Cock-a-Doodle-Doo!" One of the narrator's rural neighbors. She does not own the lusty rooster.

Cuff, Garry. 'A Scout toward Aldie.' Supposedly a Southern girl's Negro servant, led by Corporal Chew to his Colonel, who is vainly attempting to capture Mosby. Cuff is really one of Mosby's men, disguised.

Cupid. "The Paradise of Bachelors and the Tartarus of Maids." The impudent young lad who takes the narrator on a tour through the paper mill.

Cushing, [Lieutenant William B.]; "the Boy." 'At the Cannon's Mouth.' A death-defying Union officer who with several other men used a torpedo launch to sink the Confederate ram the *Albemarle*.

Cuticle, Dr. Cadwallader. *White-Jacket*. The *Neversink* physician, the ranking surgeon of the fleet. In the presence of Drs. Bandage, Wedge, Sawyer, and Patella, this sixty-year-old, scrawny, bewigged, false-toothed, glass-eyed butcher amputates the wounded foretopman's leg and thus hastens the man's death.

Cylinder. *White-Jacket*. A stuttering, club-footed gunner's mate.

Cypriote, The. *Clarel*. A good-looking youth who meets the pilgrims between the Dead Sea and Mar Saba. He likes wine and love songs.

Cyril. *Clarel*. A shrouded, apparitional figure who guards a rocky grotto full of skulls at Mar Saba. He was formerly a soldier.

D'Abrantes, Duchess. *Israel Potter*. An aristocratic French woman presumably interested in Dr. Franklin's scientific inventions.

d'Acarty, Marquis. *White-Jacket*. An old Brazilian nobleman who deferentially attends King Pedro II of Brazil when the monarch condescends to visit the *Neversink*.

Dacres, Captain Julian. "I and My Chimney." The rich late kinsman of the narrator, a former shipmaster and merchant in the Indian trade thought momentarily by the narrator to have hidden a treasure in the chimney of the house while he lived there.

Daggoo. *Moby-Dick*. A gigantic Negro from Africa and then Nantucket. He is little Flask's harpooneer.

Dago. "Benito Cereno." An intelligent slave, aged forty-six, who digs graves for the Spaniards.

Dainty Dave. 'Bridegroom Dick.' A skinny sailing master under whom Bridegroom Dick one studied.

Dallabdoolmans. *Redburn*. A Lascar sailor from the Indian vessel the *Irrawaddy*. Redburn learns much by talking with him on the Liverpool docks.

Dan. *Omoo*. See Black Dan.

Danby, Mrs. Handsome Mary. *Redburn*. The attractive, forty-year-old English wife of a brutal, dissolute Yankee named Danby. She efficiently manages their Liverpool boarding-house the Baltimore Clipper.

Danby. *Redburn*. The brutal, dissolute Yankee husband of Handsome Mary, who efficiently manages their Liverpool boardinghouse the Baltimore Clipper.

Danish Sailor. *Moby-Dick*. A *Pequod* sailor who is indifferent to the approaching storm during the midnight festivities in the forecastle.

Dansker, The; "Board-Her-in-the-Smoke." "Billy Budd." A grim, scarred old mainmastman, an *Agamemnon* veteran, who laconically tells worried Billy that Claggart has it in for him.

Darby. *Omoo*. The nickname given by Long Ghost to an old lover on the beach at Imeeo. His wife is called Joan.

Darfi. *Mardi*. The proud and ambitious uncle of Donjalolo, who decides to become king of Juam to prevent Darfi from being king.

Dash, Dick. *White-Jacket*. A chivalric midshipman from Virginia who plays the part of Gin and Sugar Sal in the Fourth of July theatrical. He is later rebuked by the Professor in class.

Dashman, Adolphus. *White-Jacket*. The Commodore's urbane, polished, graceful secretary.

Dates, "Sergeant." *Pierre*. The impeccable servant of Mrs. Mary Glendinning and Pierre at Saddle Meadows.

Dave. 'Bridegroom Dick.' See Dainty Dave.

[Da Vinci], Leonardo. 'Marquis de Grandvin: At the Hostelry.' An artist pictured as lost in dreamy and subtle thought.

Deacon. *The Confidence-Man*. The man in Frank Goodman's digression whose wife is cured of sickness by getting drunk.

Deadlight, Tom. 'Tom Deadlight.' A grizzled petty officer who when dying aboard the British *Dreadnought* says goodbye to his messmates Matt and Jock.

Dead Man, The. *Clarel*. The name by which Rolfe (which see) refers to himself when he says that he would like to be buried by a grassy road in the Holy Land.

Dean. "The Cincinnati." See Gentian, Major Jack, Dean of the Burgundy Club.

Decatur, Captain [Stephen]. *White-Jacket*. The former captain of the American man-of-war the *Neversink*, who during the War of 1812 captured the British frigate the *Macedonian*, commanded by Cardan. 'Bridegroom Dick.' A famous naval officer with whom Ap Catesby Jones served.

Dedidum. *Mardi*. One of the twelve aristocratic Taparian families on the isle of Pimminee, entertained by Nimni.

Deer, Derick De. *Moby-Dick*. The German captain of the *Jungfrau* of Bremen. She is devoid of sperm oil.

De Grasse. "Billy Budd." See Grasse, de.

Delano, Captain Amasa. "Benito Cereno." The naive but resolute captain of the *Bachelor's Delight*, a sealer and trader from Duxbury, Massachusetts. When he boards Cereno's slave-controlled *San Dominick*, he misjudges the situation and suspects the Spaniard of plotting against him.

Delano. "Benito Cereno." Amasa Delano's brother who died and had to be coldly buried at sea.

Del Fonca. "The Bell-Tower." The Florentine painter whose picture of Deborah is said to resemble Una's face.

Democritus, Mrs. "The Apple-Tree Table." The narrator's humorous nickname for his wife. It is chosen because of her energetic, level-headed practicality.

Demorkriti. *Mardi*. A laughing philosopher cited by Babbalanja in a rare mood of gaiety.

De Nesle, The Sire. 'L'Envoi: The Return of the Sire de Nesle. A.D. 16—.' See Nesle, The Sire de.

Denton, Lord Jack. "Billy Budd." A relative of Vere who congratulates Vere for his gallant part in the West Indian cruise under Rodney. He nicknames Vere "Starry."

De Reyter, [Admiral]. 'Marquis de Grandvin: At the Hostelry.' See Reyter, De.

Dermoddi, Chief. *Mardi*. A Kaleedoni leader who when his

subjects became seditious fled to King Bello of Dominora for protection, according to Media.

Derwent. *Clarel*. An Anglican priest who is affable and professionally somewhat irresponsible though quite learned.

Despairer, The. *Mardi*. A famous warrior of the island of Diranda who at the end of the war games held there by Kings Hello and Piko wanders over the Field of Glory in anguish because five of his sons were killed in previous games.

De Squak. *Redburn*. An old Negro woman fortuneteller whose house in Liverpool was much frequented by sailors, according to Jack Blunt.

D'Estang, Count. *Israel Potter*. A pro-American French aristocrat through whom and the Duke de Chartres Dr. Franklin obtains a commission for John Paul Jones.

Devonshire, The Duchess of. "Poor Man's Pudding and Rich Man's Crumbs." One of the aristocratic guests at the Guildhall Banquet in London following the Battle of Waterloo.

Diamelo. "Benito Cereno." The calker slave Mure's slave son who is killed during the attack on the *San Dominick* led by Delano's chief mate.

Dick. *Omoo*. A sailor aboard the *Leviathan* at Taloo.

Dick. *White-Jacket*. An assistant surgeon who witnesses Dr. Cuticle's amputation operation.

Dick. 'Bridegroom Dick.' See Bridegroom Dick.

Diddledee. *Mardi*. One of the twelve aristocratic Taparian families on the isle of Pimminee, entertained by Nimni.

Diddler, Jeremy. *The Confidence-Man*. The name by which Pitch derisively refers in conversation with Frank Goodman to the herb doctor (see "The Happy Man"), to the Philosophical Intelligence Office man, and to Goodman himself.

Dididi. *Mardi*. Mentioned by Babbalanja as a digger of trenches.

Didymus. *Clarel*. A person who visits Hafiz in a garden in the song sung by Derwent during the wine party at Mar Saba.

Digby, Colonel. *Redburn*. A person at whose home in Liverpool Redburn's father left his card back in 1808.

Diloro. *Mardi*. An authority quoted once by Babbalanja.

Diogenes. 'The Apparition.' Mentioned as one who would have been less cynical if he had seen the Parthenon.

Dives. "The Piazza." The name assigned by the narrator to his neighbor, who laughs at the idea of a piazza on the north side of a house.

Divino. *Mardi*. A wealthy pilgrim to Ofo on the isle of Maramma who refuses to pay Pani the blind guide.

Djalea; "The Druze," "Lord Djalea," "The Emir." *Clarel*. A Lebanese Emir's exiled son, the guide and leader of the pilgrimage guards. He is noble, self-possessed, serene, dignified, and thoughtful, and expertly rides a beautiful mare named Zar.

Dobs. *White-Jacket*. A sailor who with Hodnose is accused by a Down Easter sailor of stealing his dunderfunk.

Doc. *Pierre*. Glendinning Stanly's loyal Negro servant.

Doc. 'The Scout toward Aldie.' See the Surgeon.

Doctor, The. *Redburn*. See Thompson.

Dods, Daniel. *Redburn*. An old friend of Jonathan Jones. In 1798 he gave Jones a copy of Adam Smith's *Wealth of Nations*, which Jones's son gives to Redburn.

Dolce [Dolci], Carlo. 'Marquis de Grandvin: At the Hostelry.' A fastidious painter who discusses the picturesque with Brouwer.

Doleful Dumps. *The Confidence-Man*. The nickname of Orchis (which see) before he won a big sum of money in a lottery.

Dominican, The. *Clarel*. A French Catholic priest who beside the Jordan River tells the pilgrims about his religious beliefs.

Don, The. 'Marquis de Grandvin: At the Hostelry.' See Spagnoletto.

Don Hannibal Rohon Del Aquaviva. *Clarel*. See Hannibal, Don, Rohon Del Aquaviva.

Don Pedro II. *White-Jacket*. See Pedro II, Don.

Donald. "Billy Budd." Billy's shipmate who, according to another shipmate's poem "Billy in the Darbies," promised Billy to stand by his plank at burial.

Donjalolo, King; "Fonoo." *Mardi*. The effeminate, twenty-five-year-old king of the island of Juam. His nickname "Fonoo" means "the Girl."

Donna. 'Marquis de Grandvin: Naples in the Time of Bomba.' A fictitious girl with a sweet voice in an unaging region.

Donno. *Mardi*. One of Karrolono's retainers, who envies his master and is envied by Flavona.

Doldrum. *Mardi*. A lachrymose legatee mentioned in Bardianna's will.

Dough-Boy. *Moby-Dick*. The pale-faced steward of the *Pequod* whom Tashtego terrifies with a scalping knife. Dough-Boy times the spouting of whales and is rebuked for offering ginger-jub to Queequeg.

Douw. *Pierre*. A stable slave of General Pierre Glendinning, Pierre's grandfather.

Douw, Gerard [Gerrit]. 'Marquis de Grandvin: At the Hostelry.' The painter who joshes Van der Velde by saying that he prefers old oak in furniture rather than in ships. Douw then describes Phillis as picturesquely plucking a pheasant.

Doxodox. *Mardi*. An incomprehensibly verbose, so-called wise man who inhabits an island west of Hamora.

Dragoni, Prince. *Mardi*. A person in a manuscript chronicle in Oh Oh's museum.

Drinker, Tobias. *Redburn*. The name on a Liverpool tombstone, upon which Redburn observes a drunkard asleep.

Drouon, Clement. 'The Devotion of the Flowers to Their Lady.' An eleventh-century Provençal troubadour turned monk.

Drouth, Daniel. 'A Grave near Petersburg, Virginia.' The name supposedly of a Confederate soldier buried near Petersburg, Virginia, by retreating soldiers. In reality a heavy gun is buried beneath the headboard against the hoped-for return of the Rebels.

Druze, The. *Clarel*. See Djalea.

Dua. "The Bell-Tower." The garlanded hour of two, which holds Una's hand on the clock bell.

Duke, The. *Redburn*. The white-whiskered old master of the lush establishment, called Aladdin's Palace, which Redburn visits with Harry Bolton in London.

Duke of Wellington, The. *Redburn*. See Wellington, The Duke of. "Poor Man's Pudding and Rich Man's Crumbs." See Wellington, The Duke of.

Dumdi. *Mardi*. A philosopher, cited by Babbalanja, who defined life as mere vibration. This philosophy was opposed by Bardianna.

Dundonald, Donald. *Pierre*. The chairman of the lecture committee of the Urquhartian Club for the Extension of Knowledge, who invited Pierre to lecture in Zadockprattsville. Pierre respectfully declined.

Dunk. *Omoo*. A Danish sailor aboard the *Julia*. He continues to serve aboard her.

Dunker, Mrs. *Pierre*. A fictitious dead dowager in a German prince's proclamation imagined by Pierre.

Dupont, [Commodore Samuel Francis]. 'Dupont's Round Fight.' A Union blockade commander who sails down a river to bomb a fort on one side and then returns upstream to bomb another fort on the other side.

Durer, Agnes. 'Marquis de Grandvin: At the Hostelry.' Albert Durer's henpecking wife, who evidently dislikes gaiety.

Durer, Albert [Albrecht]. 'Marquis de Grandvin: At the Hostelry.' A henpecked painter described as melancholy and sad in appearance.

Dutcher, Tom. "Jack Gentian (omitted from the final sketch of him)." A Newport vacationer who gossips about old Gentian.

Dutch Sailor. *Moby-Dick*. A *Pequod* sailor who sings and talks during the midnight festivities in the forecastle.

Early, [General Jubal A.] 'Sheridan at Cedar Creek.' The Confederate general belatedly forced by the arrival of General Sheridan to retreat.

Ebony. *Moby-Dick*. Another name for the Negro cook Fleece (which see).

Ebony. *The Confidence-Man.* A nickname of Black Guinea (which see).

Edgar. *Pierre.* The subject of an anagram by Pierre.

Edwards, Monroe. "Bartleby." A forger who died in Sing Sing. Mentioned by the grub-man in the prison where Bartleby dies.

Egbert, "Charlie." *The Confidence-Man.* The mystical philosopher Mark Winsome's practical follower. Egbert is neat, commercial-looking, and about thirty years old. In a dialogue with Frank Goodman he refuses him a loan on the grounds that everyone should be self-reliant. He also tells the illustrative story of China Aster, the man ruined by his friend Orchis's loan to him.

Eld. 'The New Ancient of Days: The Man of the Cave of Engihoul.' Mentioned as the drooling companion of the man in the cave.

Elder, The; "Sir Crab." *Clarel.* A fiery-tongued, perpetually hatted Scotch Presbyterian who argues with the other pilgrims and soon turns back and thus leaves the party.

Eld of Mexico, The. *Clarel.* See Hannibal, Don, Rohon Del Aquaviva.

Elijah. *Moby-Dick.* A tattered prophet on the wharf at Nantucket who hints to Ishmael and Queequeg at an adverse fate in store for Ahab and his crew.

Ellery, Willis. *Moby-Dick.* A sailor lost with five others from the *Eliza* in 1839. Their shipmates placed a marble tablet in their memory in the Whaleman's Chapel in New Bedford.

Elsie. 'A Dutch Christmas . . .' A girl whom the poet asks to give crumbs to the snow-birds.

Emir, The. *Clarel.* The militant [Arabian] friend of the Bey in the Arnaut's song during the wine revelry at Mar Saba.

Emir, The. *Clarel.* Mentioned as noble Djalea's father.

Emir, The. *Clarel.* A complimentary nickname for Djalea (which see).

Emmons, Pop. "Hawthorne and His Mosses." The imaginary American author of an epic called the *Fredoniad.*

Enderby, Samuel. *Moby-Dick.* The merchant leader of a family in

London which fitted out many whaling vessels, including the *Samuel Enderby*, commanded by Captain Boomer.

Engihoul, The Man of the Cave of. 'The New Ancient of Days: The Man of the Cave of Engihoul.' A cave man whose skeleton when discovered upsets traditions.

English Sailor. *Moby-Dick*. A *Pequod* sailor who during the midnight festivities in the forecastle praises Ahab and then insists that the fight between Daggoo and the Spanish sailor be a fair one.

Epirot, The. *Clarel*. See the Arnaut.

Ethelward. *Clarel*. A man whom Rolfe knew long ago and whose grave he visits in the Latin and English Cemeteries at Zion hill, south of Jerusalem.

Eve. 'The Lover and the Syringa Bush.' Mentioned as a truant whom the poet waits to meet.

Excellency, His. 'Marquis de Grandvin: Naples in the Time of Bomba.' A tumbler in the streets of Naples.

Excellenza. "The Bell-Tower." The chief magistrate, who suspects Haman of being endowed with almost human powers of locomotion. After the killing of Bannadonna, he orders cloaked Haman sunk at sea.

Falcone, [Agniello]. 'Marquis de Grandvin: Naples in the Time of Bomba.' Mentioned as linked with patriotic Neapolitan brigands. [A Neapolitan battle-painter.]

Falconer, [William]. 'Off Cape Colonna.' [A British poet and sailor, whose poem "The Shipwreck" describes a wreck off Cape Colonna.]

Falsgrave. *Pierre*. The dainty Rev. Mr. Falsgrave's father, a poor Northern farmer.

Falsgrave, Mrs. *Pierre*. The dainty Rev. Mr. Falsgrave's mother, formerly a pretty seamstress.

Falsgrave, Rev. Mr. *Pierre*. The gracious, gentlemanly leader of the Saddle Meadows congregation. He greatly admires his benefactress Mrs. Mary Glendinning.

Falstaff, Jack; "Fat Jack," "Honest Jack." 'Falstaff's Lament

over Prince Hal Become Henry V.' Depicted as sad that Hal
has snubbed him.

Fanfum. *Mardi*. One of the twelve aristocratic Taparian families
on the isle of Pimminee, entertained by Nimni.

Fanna. *Mardi*. A healthy pilgrim to Ofo on the isle of Maramma
who pays Pani the blind guide before he is asked to pay.

Fanny, King. 'Marquis de Grandvin: Naples in the Time of
Bomba.' See [Francis II, King].

Farnoopoo, "Night," "Night-born." *Omoo*. A lovely maiden
encountered by the narrator and Long Ghost on the beach
at Imeeo.

Farnow. *Omoo*. A retired footman of Queen Pomaree. He now
lives near Captain Bob in Papeetee.

Farnowar, "Morning," "Day-born." *Omoo*. A lovely maiden
encountered by the narrator and Long Ghost on the beach
at Imeeo.

Farragut, [Admiral David G.]. 'The Battle for the Mississippi.'
The Union admiral ordered to bombard St. Philip and
Jackson, two forts on the Mississippi River above New
Orleans, and then to capture that city. 'The Battle for the
Bay.' The Union admiral who bravely commanded from his
flagship the *Hartford* the attack on Mobile Bay. 'Bride-
groom Dick.' A famous naval officer under whom Bride-
groom Dick served at Vicksburg and later in the Battle of
Mobile Bay.

Fathers. "The Cincinnati." A general term for the founding
fathers of the United States. They were mostly Revolutionary Army officers and hence members of the Society of
the Cincinnati.

Fat Jack. 'Falstaff's Lament over Prince Hal Become Henry V.'
See Falstaff, Jack.

Fayaway. *Typee*. The beautiful, olive-hued native girl who
evidently loves and is loved by Tommo. She is slightly
tatooed, eats raw fish, and weeps at his departure.

Fedallah. *Moby-Dick*. The Parsee whom, with four fellow
Orientals, Ahab smuggles aboard the *Pequod*. Fedallah gives
Ahab specious comfort with equivocal prophecies but

precedes his master to death because of the seeming malice of Moby Dick.

Fee. *Mardi.* One of the twelve aristocratic Taparian families on the isle of Pimminee, entertained by Nimni.

Felipe. "The Encantadas." The pure-blooded Castilian husband of Hunilla, who when he and his brother-in-law Truxill drowned while fishing became the wretched Chola widow of Norfolk Isle.

Fergus, Major. *Omoo.* A Polish-born officer in the employe with Lafevre of Bruat, the hated French governor of Tahiti.

Fernandez, Juan. "The Encantadas." The famous pilot who discovered Juan Fernandez Island, procured a deed to it, and lived there for some years.

Ferryman, "Boteman." "The Encantadas." The ferryman or boatman of the dreary Wandering Isles.

Fiddlefie. *Mardi.* One of the twelve aristocratic Taparian families on the isle of Pimminee, entertained by Nimni.

Fidi. *Mardi.* Bardianna's body servant, mentioned in the philosopher's will.

Fifth Nantucket Sailor. *Moby-Dick.* A *Pequod* sailor who sees lightning during the midnight festivities in the forecastle.

Finfi. *Mardi.* A vivacious guest who tells Taji about Nimni's other Taparian guests at his party on the isle of Pimminee. According to Gaddi, Finfi is a parvenu.

Finn, The; "Man." 'Bridegroom Dick.' A gigantic sailor recalled by Bridegroom Dick as once ordered flogged by Captain Turret but then let go.

First Luff. *White-Jacket.* See Bridewell, Lieutenant.

First Nantucket Sailor. *Moby-Dick.* A *Pequod* sailor who sings during the midnight festivities in the forecastle.

Flagstaff, Lord George. *Redburn.* A British officer reported as advertising in Liverpool to obtain a crew for his frigate *Thetis.*

Flash Jack, "Flashy." *Omoo.* A sailor aboard the *Julia.* He signs the round robin.

Flask, "King-Post." *Moby-Dick.* The short, stout, ruddy, pugnacious third mate of the *Pequod.* He is a native of Tisbury, in Martha's Vineyard. Daggoo is his harpooneer. Flask sees no symbolism in the doubloon nailed to the mainmast.

Flavona. *Mardi.* One of Donno's servitors, who envies his master and is envied by Manta.

Fleece, "Ebony." *Moby-Dick.* The *Pequod's* old Negro cook, who preaches to the noisy sharks as they gobble whale blubber and whom Stubb queries on religion and lectures on how to cook whale steak.

Fletz. *Pierre.* A fictitious bankrupt baker, partner of Flitz, in a German prince's proclamation imagined by Pierre.

Flinegan, Patrick. *White-Jacket.* The captain of the head. A storm prevents his singing "The True Yankee Sailor" in costume in the Fourth of July theatrical.

Flinnigan, Patrick. *Redburn.* Mentioned as the Irish ostler of Redburn's uncle.

Flint. *Pierre.* The publisher who, with partners Steel and Asbestos, rejects Pierre's book. They intend to sue Pierre for costs and advances.

Flitz. *Pierre.* A fictitious bankrupt baker, partner of Fletz, in a German prince's proclamation imagined by Pierre.

Florence, The Grand Duke of. 'Marquis de Grandvin: At the Hostelry.' See Grand Duke of Florence, The.

Flute. *White-Jacket.* A boatswain's mate who warns White Jacket that Captain Claret may flog him.

Fofi. *Mardi.* A wounded man from King Piko's island of Diranda. Nimni on the isle of Pimminee sponsors him as a famous captain, but, according to King Media, he is a cunning braggart whom King Piko exiled.

Fonca, Del. "The Bell-Tower." See Del Fonca.

Foni. *Mardi.* An upstart rebel against the god Doleema, in a story by Mohi concerning the isle of Maramma. Once handsome, he was last seen old and miserable, eating food sacrificed to the god in his sacred forest, where Foni was finally killed.

Fonoo. *Mardi.* A nickname, meaning "the Girl," of King Donjalolo (which see).

Foofoo. *Mardi.* The name of a dynasty in a manuscript chronicle in Oh Oh's museum.

Ford, William. "Jimmy Rose." The conservative narrator who has inherited a home in New York once owned by his friend Jimmy Rose. Ford tries without success to help Jimmy when he is swept to financial ruin.

Ford, Mrs. William. "Jimmy Rose." The young, relatively less conservative wife of the narrator. She wants to modernize their New York home, which was once owned by Jimmy Rose.

Ford, Miss. "Jimmy Rose." One of the daughters of William Ford, the narrator.

Ford, Miss. "Jimmy Rose." One of the daughters of William Ford, the narrator.

"The Forgiver." 'The Martyr.' See [Lincoln, Abraham].

Fourth Nantucket Sailor. *Moby-Dick*. A *Pequod* sailor who during the midnight festivities in the forecastle reports that Ahab told Starbuck to steer the ship straight into the approaching storm.

France, King [Louis XVI] of. *Israel Potter*. The monarch who rewards John Paul Jones for his exploits.

Frances. "Jimmy Rose." A charming New York lady complimented graciously by indigent Jimmy Rose.

Francesco. "Benito Cereno." A mulatto slave, aged about thirty-five years, who was Aranda's cabin-steward and a leading plotter during the revolt of the slaves aboard Cereno's *San Dominick*. He wanted to poison Amasa Delano during lunch.

[Francis II, King of the Two Sicilies]; "King Fanny." 'Marquis de Grandvin: At the Hostelry.' Mentioned as Bomba's frightened son and heir who flees Naples on receipt of news concerning Garibaldi's advance. 'Marquis de Grandvin: Naples in the Time of Bomba.' Mentioned as endangered by the Red Shirt, Garibaldi.

Frank. *White-Jacket*. A handsome common sailor about sixteen years of age who because of the difference in their ranks avoids speaking to or even looking straight at his brother, who is an officer aboard a store ship which supplies the *Neversink* off Rio de Janeiro. He may be Frank Jones (which see).

Franklin, Dr. [Benjamin]. *Israel Potter*. The canny, unsympathetically portrayed American "man of wisdom" in Paris for whom Israel Potter acts as a courier. Through him, Israel meets John Paul Jones.

Frederic William, King of Prussia. "Poor Man's Pudding and Rich Man's Crumbs." One of the aristocratic guests at the Guildhall Banquet in London following the Battle of Waterloo.

French Sailor. *Moby-Dick*. A *Pequod* sailor who dances during the midnight festivities in the forecastle.

Fry, Thomas; "Happy Tom." *The Confidence-Man*. A man on crutches, who first says that he became crippled in the legs through being held in jail as an innocent witness to a murder but who later professes to be a Mexican War casualty. The herb doctor tries to comfort him.

Fry, Mrs. *The Confidence-Man*. A woman named by the herb doctor as a friend of his who corresponds with him on the subject of prisons. Thomas Fry denies having any knowledge of her.

Fulvi. *Mardi*. A Mardian writer quoted by Babbalanja.

G—, General. "Jimmy Rose." A hero to whom Jimmy Rose graciously gives a brace of pistols decorated with turquoise.

Gabriel. *Moby-Dick*. The mad prophet of the *Jeroboam*. He came from the Neskyeuna Shakers and predicted the death of Macey when that man sought to kill Moby Dick.

Gaddi. *Mardi*. An informative guest who tells Taji about Nimni's other Taparian guests at his party on the isle of Pimminee. According to Finfi, Gaddi is a parvenu.

Galgo, Luys. "Benito Cereno." A sixty-year-old Spanish sailor who tries to warn Delano by signals but is seen by the Negroes and murdered.

Gamboge. *Omoo*. See Old Gamboge.

Gammon. *White-Jacket*. The name assigned to a sailor who is impertinent to Pert.

Gandix, Hermenegildo. "Benito Cereno." One of Aranda's young clerks from Cadiz and a *San Dominick* passenger. He is accidentally killed during the attack led by Delano's chief mate.

Gan[sevoort], Guert. 'Bridegroom Dick.' A brave naval officer whom Bridegroom Dick remembers from Vera Cruz days.

Gardiner, Captain. *Moby-Dick*. The Nantucket commander of the *Rachel*. Ahab refuses to join in the search for Gardiner's son, who is or was in a missing whaleboat tugged out of sight or destroyed by Moby Dick. After the *Pequod* is sunk by Moby Dick, Gardiner happens to sail back and rescues Ishmael.

Gardiner. *Moby-Dick*. A son of Captain Gardiner of the *Rachel*. The lad was rescued from one of three whaleboats which pursued Moby Dick, but his twelve-year-old brother is missing in a fourth whaleboat.

Gardiner. *Moby-Dick*. The twelve-year-old son of Captain Gardiner of the *Rachel*. The boy is or was in a missing whaleboat tugged out of sight or destroyed by Moby Dick.

Garibaldi, [Giuseppe]. 'Marquis de Grandvin: At the Hostelry.' Mentioned as taking Naples by railroad train, and later compared to the Cid. 'Marquis de Grandvin: Naples in the Time of Bomba.' Mentioned as signaling danger to Bomba's son [later King Francis II]. Garibaldi is referred to as the Red Shirt.

Gayete, Juan Bautista. "Benito Cereno." Cereno's *San Dominick* carpenter, who is severely wounded during the revolt of the slaves.

Gay-Head Indian. *Moby-Dick*. See Old Gay-Head Indian.

Genteel, Jack; "Genteel Jack." 'Bridegroom Dick.' A shaggy, amorous sailor remembered by Bridegroom Dick.

Gentian. "To Major John Gentian, Dean of the Burgundy Club." Major John Gentian's father, also a member of the Society of the Cincinnati.

Gentian, Major John; "Jack," Dean of the Burgundy Club, "Milor." "The Marquis de Grandvin." Mentioned as the Marquis de Grandvin's foremost disciple. "Portrait of a Gentleman." Described as Dean of the Burgundians, a gentlemanly, outspoken Northerner of South Carolina

stock who since 1865 has led a calm life. "To Major John
Gentian, Dean of the Burgundy Club." Described as brave
and now full of reminiscence. He lost an arm fighting in the
Wilderness during the Civil War under Grant, who later
appointed him American consul in Naples. "Jack Gentian
(omitted from the final sketch of him)." Described as now
becoming infirm in mind and body, but ever loving and
kind. "Major Gentian and Colonel J. Bunkum." Described
as proud of his Cincinnati badge in his old age. "The
Cincinnati." Mentioned as a rightly proud member of the
Society of the Cincinnati. 'Marquis de Grandvin: At the
Hostelry.' Mentioned by the Marquis de Grandvin as about
to tell a story about an afternoon in Naples. 'Marquis de
Grandvin: Naples in the Time of Bomba.' The Marquis de
Grandvin's friend who describes the crowds and activities in
the streets and scenes nearby—fortresses, troops, singers, a
dancing girl, Vesuvius, jugglers, tumblers, an urchin, and a
canopied priest in a procession—and then thinks of
Garibaldi and the future of Italy.

Geoffry. "Under the Rose." The servant of My Lord the
	Ambassador. Geoffry narrates the events concerning his
	master's coveting of the Azem's amber vase.

George III, King of England. *Israel Potter*. The British monarch in
	whose Kew Gardens Israel Potter works briefly. The two
	talk there once.

George, the Prince Regent of England. "Poor Man's Pudding and
	Rich Man's Crumbs." The host at the Guildhall Banquet in
	London following the Battle of Waterloo.

Georgiana Theresa, Lady. *Redburn*. Presumably an acquaintance
	of Harry Bolton in London. She is said to be the daughter
	of an anonymous earl.

Ghofan. "Benito Cereno." An African-born slave, a calker by
	trade, between sixty and seventy years old.

Ghost. *Omoo*. See Long Ghost, Dr.

Gifford, S[anford]. R[obinson]. ' "The Coming Storm." ' An
	American landscape painter of "The Coming Storm," which
	shows a demon-cloud bursting on a lake and which is now
	owned by E.B.

Ginger Nut. "Bartleby." The Wall Street lawyer's twelve-year-old office boy.

Glaucon, "The Smyrniote." *Clarel*. A Smyrna family scion who is traveling with the Greek Banker, his prospective father-in-law. Glaucon is gay, irreverent, and happy-go-lucky.

Gleig, Samuel. *Moby-Dick*. A sailor lost with five others from the *Eliza* in 1839. Their shipmates placed a marble tablet in their memory in the Whaleman's Chapel in New Bedford.

Glen. 'Bridegroom Dick.' A gun-room sailor remembered by Bridegroom Dick as loving scotch.

Glendinning, Dorothea. *Pierre*. The lonely, city-dwelling, maiden sister of Pierre's deceased father. She gave Pierre, when he was fifteen years old, the smaller, more youthful portrait of his father.

Glendinning, Mrs. Mary. *Pierre*. The mother, almost fifty years of age, of Pierre, who calls her "Sister Mary." She is so proud and righteous that her son cannot tell her anything about his supposed half-sister Isabel Banford. When he breaks his engagement to Lucy Tartan and leaves Saddle Meadows for the city with Isabel, Mrs. Glendinning curses him, makes out her will in favor of Glendinning Stanly, goes insane, and dies.

Glendinning, General Pierre. *Pierre*. Pierre's huge, robust grandfather, a heroic Revolutionary War general who defended a stockaded fort against Indians—including Brandt—Tories, and Regulars and who greatly loved horses. He died in 1812.

Glendinning, Pierre. *Pierre*. Pierre's well-read, gentle father, who died when the boy was twelve years old. Knowledge that the man had an illegitimate daughter, Isabel Banford, sours Pierre's memory of his father and ultimately ruins his life.

Glendinning, Pierre. *Pierre*. The heroic young scion of the Glendinning family of Saddle Meadows, just emerging from his teens. He is engaged to Lucy Tartan until his supposed half-sister Isabel Banford appeals to him for help, at which he abandons Lucy, argues with his haughty mother Mrs. Mary Glendinning, and goes with Isabel—pretending that she is his wife—and with Delly Ulver to the city. There he argues with his cousin Glendinning Stanly, who has inherited his estates (following the death of Mary Glendinning), argues with Lucy's brother Frederic Tartan, kills Stanly, and poisons himself in prison to avoid death by hanging.

Glendinning. *Pierre.* Pierre Glendinning's great-grandfather, who was mortally wounded in an Indian battle at Saddle Meadows.

Gola, Martinez. "Benito Cereno." A Spanish sailor from the *San Dominick* who is prevented by Delano from killing a shackled Negro slave with a razor.

Golconda, The Prince of. "Marquis de Grandvin." An extravagant pseudonym for the Marquis de Grandvin (which see).

Gold-beak. "Under the Rose." The Shaz at Shiraz at whose palace, during a bridal festival, [S]ugar-Lips was inspired to write a poem about the rose-filled amber vase.

Goneril. *The Confidence-Man.* The vicious, straight-bodied, cactus-like wife of John Ringman. Her vicious conduct causes him to leave her for a wandering life until he learns of her death.

Goodman, Francis; "Frank," "Popinjay-of-the-world," "Philanthropos." *The Confidence-Man.* The colorfully dressed, self-styled cosmopolitan whose conciliatory words Pitch mistakenly regards as acceptably misanthropic. Goodman hears Charlie Noble's story of the Indian-hater Colonel John Moredock, drinks convivially with Noble, and tells him about unselfish Charlemont. Goodman talks with the mystic Mark Winsome and his practical follower Egbert, whose story about China Aster he deplores. He agrees in writing to guarantee William Cream the barber against loss if he removes his "No Trust" sign and then walks out owing him for a shave. Finally Goodman talks with an old man and leads him to his stateroom.

Goodwell. *Redburn.* A kind clerk in a forwarding house in New York. Redburn, who knows him, asks him to help Harry Bolton find employment.

Graceman, Mark. *Pierre.* A minister whose obituary Pierre writes.

Grand Duke of Florence, The. 'Marquis de Grandvin: At the Hostelry.' Mentioned as a gouty loser.

Grandissimo, King. *Mardi.* A person in a manuscript memoir in Oh Oh's museum.

Grando. *Mardi.* A philosopher who hated his own body. He is cited by Babbalanja.

Grandvin, Marquis de, The; "The Prince of Goloconda," "Lord Bountiful." "The Marquis de Grandvin." Praised extravagantly as a generous and eloquent Frenchman, and a valued visitor to New York and a member of various Fifth Avenue clubs, including the Burgundy Club. "To Major John Gentian, Dean of the Burgundy Club." Mentioned. 'Marquis de Grandvin: At the Hostelry.' A genial Frenchman who at the hostelry speaks about Italian politics, then summons shades of famous artists to debate on the nature of the picturesque, and finally recommends a story to be told by his friend Jack Gentian.

Grant, General [Ulysses S.]. 'Donelson.' The Union general who captured Donelson. 'Chattanooga.' Described as watching his men charge in advance of his own plans for the capture of Chattanooga. 'The Armies of the Wilderness.' Described here as silent, meek, and grim, and called the Man. 'The March to the Sea.' Mentioned as having a Union gamecock named after him. 'The Fall of Richmond.' The three-star general praised for his bravery and faith. 'The Surrender at Appomattox.' Described as receiving Lee's sword. 'Rebel Color-Bearers at Shiloh.' Mentioned. 'Lee in the Capitol.' The Union general remembered by Lee as victorious in Washington at the close of the Civil War. Lee is now going to the Senate to testify. "To Major John Gentian, Dean of the Burgundy Club." Mentioned as the commander in the Wilderness, where Gentian lost an arm. Grant later appointed Gentian to be American consul in Naples.

Grasse, [Francois Joseph Paul, Marquis de Grassetilly, Comte] de. "Billy Budd." The enemy naval officer defeated by the British fleet under Rodney, after which Vere, who served under Rodney, was promoted to post captain.

Graveairs, Don. *Clarel*. Mentioned as glum in a song during the masque presented at Mar Saba.

Graveling, Captain. "Billy Budd." The fat, cheerful, fifty-year-old captain of the *Rights-of-Man* who is sad but necessarily passive when Lieutenant Ratcliffe impresses Billy from her to the *Bellipotent*.

Gray-back. 'The Armies of the Wilderness.' A Confederate prisoner who refuses to tell his Union captors what the enemy earthworks across the valley mean.

Great Duke, The. "Under the Rose." The duke in whose Florentine museum the Ambassador once saw rare amber in which insects were congealed.

Green, Dr. *The Confidence-Man*. An herb doctor mentioned by Pitch as hospitalized in Mobile in spite of his herbs.

Greenlander, The. *Redburn*. A handsome lady's man of a sailor aboard the *Highlander*. He helps Redburn's initial seasickness by giving the youth a dose of rum. The Greenlander later leads a party of sailors who extort drinking money from one of the passengers bound for Liverpool.

Groot, Judge Myndert Van. "To Major John Gentian, Dean of the Burgundy Club." A New Yorker whom Gentian knew. Groot as a boy liked firecrackers.

Grummet. *White-Jacket*. A tobacco-chewing quarter-gunner who refuses to bid at auction on White Jacket's jacket.

Guernseyman, The. *Moby-Dick*. The ignorant chief mate of the French whaler the *Bouton de Rose*. Stubb talks him out of a precious, unsuspected treasure of ambergris within a diseased whale's corpse.

Guide. 'The Scout toward Aldie.' A fat, wheezing guide for the Union forces pursuing Mosby. The guide's son fights on Mosby's side, and his wife has left him also.

Guinea. *White-Jacket*. The purser's Virginia slave, who ships as a seaman aboard the *Neversink* and attends his indulgent master, who collects the Negro's wages. Guinea is sleek and gay, and is regularly excused from witnessing any flogging at the gangway.

Guinea. *The Confidence-Man*. See Black Guinea.

Gun-Deck. *Redburn*. A little sailor aboard the *Highlander* who is full of stories.

Guy, Captain; "The Cabin Boy," "Paper Jack," "Miss Guy." *Omoo*. The despised, sickly captain of the *Julia*. He turns over all command of his ship to John Jermin, the first mate, lounges ashore at Papeetee with his friend the consul Wilson, and leaves Tahiti when he is unable to force his rebellious sailors to continue working under him.

Habbibi, "Habbi." *Clarel*. A Greek monk, now dead, who formerly lived in a grotto at Mar Saba.

Hafiz. *Clarel*. A person in a garden, visited by Didymus, in the song sung by Derwent during the wine party at Mar Saba.

Hair-Brains. 'The Scout toward Aldie.' The name by which one Union soldier refers to himself during the Colonel's ill-fated pursuit of Mosby.

Hal, Prince. 'Falstaff's Lament over Prince Hal Become Henry V.' See Henry V.

Hal. 'Bridegroom Dick.' A sailor recalled by Bridegroom Dick. The *Merrimac*, which Hal was aboard, sank the *Cumberland*, which his former shipmate Will was aboard.

Hall, Judge James. *The Confidence-Man*. Charlie Noble's father's friend and the source of Noble's story about Colonel John Moredock the Indian-hater.

Hals, Franz. 'Marquis de Grandvin: At the Hostelry.' A painter who discusses the picturesque and also English patronage with Van Dyke.

Haman. "The Bell-Tower." The grotesque mechanical monster— also called Talus—designed and built by Bannadonna as a bell striker. It clubs its creator to death at the stroke of one.

Hancock, John. "Major Gentian and Colonel J. Bunkum." Mentioned as resisting King George's tea tax but not for democracy.

[Hancock, General Winfield Scott]. 'On the Photograph of a Corps Commander.' Highly praised as a manly leader.

Handsome Mary. *Redburn*. See Danby, Mrs. Handsome Mary.

Handsome Sailor. "Billy Budd." A typically tall, handsome sailor whose shipmates walk with him on shore. Billy Budd is such a type.

Hannibal, Rohon Del Aquaviva, Don; "The Eld of Mexico." *Clarel*. A one-armed, one-legged veteran fighter for Mexican freedom. Now skeptical of progress and reform, he is a friend of Derwent.

Hans. 'A Dutch Christmas . . .' A boy who dances with Cousin Chris.

Hanto. *Mardi*. A reader who told Lombardo that his *Koztanza* was rather good, according to Babbalanja.

Happy Bone-setter, The. *The Confidence-Man*. See the Happy Man.

Happy Man, The; "The Happy Bone-setter," "Mr. Palaverer." *The Confidence-Man*. The reported nickname of the herb doctor, who sells Omni-Balsamic Reinvigorator and Samaritan Pain Dissuader to a sick man, a cripple named Thomas Fry, and a senile miser. However, a shaggy backwoodsman refuses to buy any but slugs him instead. Nor does Pitch buy any.

Happy Tom. *Confidence-Man*. See Thomas Fry.

Hardy, Captain Ezekiel. *Moby-Dick*. A whaling captain killed by a sperm whale off Japan in 1833. His widow erected a tablet in his memory in the Whaleman's Chapel in New Bedford.

Hardy, Mrs. Ezekiel. *Moby-Dick*. Captain Ezekiel Hardy's widow, who erected a tablet in his memory in the Whaleman's Chapel in New Bedford.

Hardy, Joe. *White-Jacket*. A shipmate reported killed in an imaginary sea-fight.

Hardy, Lem; "Hardee-Hardee." *Omoo*. An English-born deserter at Hannamanoo who after ten years ashore has become the military leader, and even a war-god, of the island. He has married into the royal family.

Harry. *Moby-Dick*. A sailor who, with Jack and Joe, is suspicious of Jonah in Father Mapple's sermon at the Whaleman's Chapel in New Bedford.

Harry the Reefer. "The Death Craft." The narrator, a sailor who dreams that he is aboard an imperiled craft and then awakens to embrace his wife.

Harry, Top-Gallant. 'Bridegroom Dick.' See Top-Gallant Harry.

Hat, The. *Clarel*. A name for Nehemiah (which see), because he is hatted among turbaned Turks in Jerusalem.

Hautboy. "The Fiddler." The titular hero, a short, fat, ruddy-faced fiddler about forty years of age, whose emotional and intellectual balance the narrator Helmstone admires. Hautboy is a former touted child prodigy. (See also Betty, Master.)

Hautia, Queen. *Mardi*. The luscious queen of Flozella a Nina who as an incognito stares at Yillah on the isle of Odo, evidently spirits her away perhaps to a watery death, sends flower-bearing messengers to follow Taji on his quest for Yillah, and finally though only temporarily woos him on her delightful island, which he visits in the hope of learning news about Yillah.

Hawthorne, Nathaniel; "The Man of Mosses," "The Mossy Man." "Hawthorne and His Mosses." The author of *Mosses from an Old Manse*, which Melville praises tremendously. 'Monody.' The unnamed, deceased object of the poet's tender lament? "To Major John Gentian, Dean of the Burgundy Club." Mentioned as appreciating the past.

Hay-Seed. *Moby-Dick*. A typical green bumpkin who comes to New Bedford to ship aboard a whaler.

Hello, King. *Mardi*. The convivial ruler with King Piko of the island of Diranda. The two reduce their exploding population by holding war games on the Field of Glory.

Helmstone. "The Fiddler." The unsuccessful poet whose moroseness Hautboy the fiddler dissipates.

Henro. *Mardi*. Bello's father, who seized control of Kaleedoni, according to Media.

Henry V, [King]. 'Falstaff's Lament over Prince Hal Become Henry V.' The monarch whose snub Jack Falstaff laments.

Hevaneva. *Mardi*. A materialistic carver of religious icons and canoes on the isle of Maramma.

High Chief, A. *Moby-Dick*. The King of Kokovoko (which see), Queequeg's Polynesian father.

High Priest, A. *Moby-Dick*. Queequeg's noble Polynesian uncle and brother of the King of Kokovoko, Queequeg's father.

Hill, [General Ambrose P.]. 'The Released Rebel Prisoner.' A dead Confederate leader thought of by the released Rebel prisoner.

Hiram [I], King. 'Rammon.' The king of Tyre, who has a commercial alliance with Solomon which survives both monarchs and makes possible Zardi's visit with Rammon. Rammon knows that Hiram's sailors often tell of the Enviable Isles.

[. . .] Hivohitee MDCCCXLVIII. *Mardi*. The present pontiff of the isle of Maramma, who is the product of 1847 successive incestuous unions. During the lifetime of any Hivohitee pontiff his name may not be spoken, a ban resulting in linguistic confusion on Maramma.

Hodnose. *White-Jacket*. A sailor who with Dobs is accused by a Down Easter sailor of stealing his dunderfunk.

Hoffman, Charlie Fenno. "To Major John Gentian, Dean of the Burgundy Club." A poet whom Gentian knew personally.

Hohori. *Mardi*. King Media's attendant whose beautiful teeth King Peepi of Valapee and the beggar Jiji of Padulla unsuccessfully covet.

Holy Joe. 'Tom Deadlight.' Evidently the chaplain aboard the British *Dreadnought*.

Honest Jack. 'Falstaff's Lament over Prince Hal Become Henry V.' See Falstaff, Jack.

Horror, A. *Clarel*. See Toulib.

Howe, Lord General. *Israel Potter*. The British commander in America whose name Ethan Allen reviles during his captivity in Falmouth, England.

Hugh. 'Running the Batteries.' A Union sailor aboard a ship with Ned and Lot running past the Confederate batteries at Vicksburg.

Hughs, Sir Edward. *Israel Potter*. Mentioned as the commander of the fleet which the *Unprincipled*, onto which Israel Potter has been impressed from Dover, is sailing to join when he is sent from her to become part of the depleted crew of a revenue cutter.

Hull, [Captain Isaac]. 'Bridegroom Dick.' A famous naval officer with whom Ap Catesby [Jones] served.

Hull, General [William]. *The Confidence-Man*. An army officer whose act of apparent cowardice caused brave Colonel John Moredock to refuse once to sleep in a bed in which Hull once slept.

Hummee Hum. *Mardi*. One of the twelve aristocratic Taparian families on the isle of Pimminee, entertained by Nimni.

Hunilla. "The Encantadas." The Chola widow, a half-breed Indian woman of Payta, Peru, who went with her husband Felipe and her brother Truxill to collect tortoise oil on Norfolk Isle, and through terrible adversity was left there alone for three horrible years.

Hurta, Roderigo. "Benito Cereno." A boatswain's mate thrown alive overboard with Manuel Viscaya from the *San Dominick* during the slave revolt.

Hussey, Hosea. *Moby-Dick*. The proprietor of the Try Pots on the island of Nantucket. Ishmael and Queequeg stop there before signing aboard the *Pequod*. Hussey and Peter Coffin are cousins.

Hussey, Mrs. Hosea. *Moby-Dick*. The wife of the proprietor of the Try Pots on the island of Nantucket. She is famous for her clam chowder and cod chowder, which Ishmael and Queequeg enjoy.

Huysum, [Jan Van]. 'Marquis de Grandvin: At the Hostelry.' A flower painter mentioned by Dolci.

I. *Mardi*. One of the three vain daughters of Nimni, on the isle of Pimminee. The others are A and O.

Ibrahim, [Pasha]. *Clarel*. A tough military leader [and an Egyptian general] under whom Belex once fought in Lebanon.

Iceland Sailor. *Moby-Dick*. A *Pequod* sailor who refuses to dance during the midnight festivities in the forecastle.

Ictinus. 'The Parthenon.' The reputed architect of the Parthenon.

He is mentioned. 'Suggested by the Ruins of a Mountain-Temple in Arcadia, One Built by the Architect of the Parthenon.' The Architect.

Ideea. *Omoo.* The backsliding, semi-Christianized daughter of Farnow, at Tahiti.

Ides, Queen. *Mardi.* Donjalolo's thirtieth-night queen.

Illyrian, The. *Clarel.* See the Arnaut.

Inamorata. "Fragments from a Writing Desk. No. 2." The deaf and dumb beauty who writes L.A.V. asking him to come to her.

India, The King of. 'Honor.' The monarch who orders out the jeweled welcoming procession.

Inez. *Clarel.* The object of the Lyonese's love song, overheard by lonely Clarel at Bethlehem.

Infelez. "Benito Cereno." The Peruvian monk who attends litter-borne Cereno during the trial at Lima.

Invader, The. 'Lee in the Capitol.' See Lee.

Irving, Washington. 'Rip Van Winkle's Lilac.' Mentioned as the author of the original "Rip Van Winkle."

Ishmael. *Moby-Dick.* The narrator, who after four voyages in the merchant service signs aboard Ahab's *Pequod*, becomes the bosom friend of Queequeg, vows with the others to pursue Moby Dick, and uniquely escapes the ensuing wreck. He is called Skrimshander by Peter Coffin.

Isleman, The. *Clarel.* See the Lesbian.

Jack. *Omoo.* A Hawaiian sailor whom the narrator takes along as an interpreter when he attends the missionary cathedral of Papoar, near the Calabooza.

Jack. *Omoo.* The name, perhaps generically used, of a white man-of-war's man who acts as barber to a Tonga Island king.

Jack. *Omoo.* See Flash Jack.

Jack. *Redburn.* See Redburn, Wellingborough.

Jack. *White-Jacket.* See Mad Jack and also Paper Jack.

Jack. *Moby-Dick.* A sailor who, with Joe and Harry, is suspicious of Jonah in Father Mapple's at the Whaleman's Chapel in New Bedford.

Jack Jewboy. *Israel Potter.* See Jewboy, Jack.

[Jackson, Jane]. ' "Formerly a Slave." ' The subject of an idealized portrait of Elihu Vedder. She appears to be long-suffering but prophetic of a better future for her descendants.

Jackson, [General Thomas J.] Stonewall. 'The Victor of Antietam.' The Confederate general under Lee who was defeated at Antietam by McClellan. 'Stonewall Jackson, Mortally Wounded . . .' Praised as a fierce, earnest, true, and relentless enemy leader. 'Stonewall Jackson (Ascribed to a Virginian).' Praised as a calm, stoical, iron-willed, fatalistic warrior. 'The Armies of the Wilderness.' Mentioned as having led a charge in this area previously. 'Rebel Color-Bearers at Shiloh.' Mentioned. 'Lee in the Capitol.' The dead Confederate general remembered by Lee as he approaches the Capitol.

Jackson. *Redburn.* A physically weak but domineering sailor, anywhere between thirty and fifty years old, who bullies the *Highlander* crew and particularly hates Redburn because of his youth and handsomeness. On the return voyage Jackson grows sick, coughs blood while reefing a sail, and falls overboard to his death.

Jacobi, Cranz. *Pierre.* A fictitious name in a German prince's proclamation imagined by Pierre.

Jake. "Cock-a-Doodle-Doo!" The narrator's servant boy.

Jan o' the Inn. 'Marquis de Grandvin: At the Hostelry.' See Steen, Jan.

Jarl, "The Viking," "The Skyeman." *Mardi.* The sailor who deserts the *Arcturion* with the narrator and becomes his faithful follower as far as the island of Mondoldo, where the narrator leaves him with King Borabolla as a remembrance. Later the narrator while at the island of Maramma receives a message from Borabolla that Jarl has been killed by arrows, probably shot by Aleema's sons.

Jarmi. *Mardi.* A Mardian minstrel about whom Yoomy tells an anecdote.

Jefferson, [Joseph]. 'Rip Van Winkle's Lilac.' Mentioned as the star actor in a dramatic version of Washington Irving's "Rip Van Winkle."

Jehu. "Poor Man's Pudding and Rich Man's Crumbs." The London hack driver who takes the narrator from the Guildhall back to his rooms.

Jemmy Legs. "Billy Budd." See Claggart, John.

Jennie. *Pierre.* A pretty girl in the Miss Pennies' sewing circle.

Jennings, Betsy. *Redburn.* A starving woman who dies with her three children in a cellar under a Liverpool warehouse, in spite of Redburn's efforts to help her.

Jenny. *Moby-Dick.* A name in a song which is partly recited by Pip in front of the doubloon nailed to the mainmast.

Jermin, John. *Omoo.* The short, thick-set, curly-haired first officer of the *Julia,* whose command he has from Captain Guy by default. Jermin is often drunk, is an eager fighter, but is respected by his men for his expert seamanship. When the *Julia* leaves Papeetee, he is virtually in charge again.

Jeroboam. 'Rammon.' A valorous, mighty, and penitent man who unsuccessfully offers his allegiance to recently crowned, disdainful Rehoboam.

Jethro. 'Rammon.' Mentioned [erroneously] as the father of Solomon.

Jewboy, Jack. *Israel Potter.* A sailor aboard the British frigate which Israel Potter boards alone off the *Ariel.*

Jewel, Jack. *White-Jacket.* A shipmate, reported killed in an imaginary sea fight.

Jewsharp Jim. 'Bridegroom Dick.' A sailor remembered by Bridegroom Dick.

Jiji. *Mardi.* A hungry miser on the isle of Padulla who collects monetary teeth in pelican pouches but has to beg for food.

Jim. *Omoo.* The rich, officious, capable native pilot who takes the *Julia* into the harbor at Papeetee.

Jim. *Omoo.* See Long Jim.

Jim. *White-Jacket.* A sailor rebuked for putting his foot on a mess cloth in Mess No. 15.

Jim. *Israel Potter.* One of the two named shanghaiers of Israel Potter at Dover. The other is Bill.

Jim, Jewsharp. 'Bridegroom Dick.' See Jewsharp Jim.

Jimmy. *Typee.* An irresponsible, tabooed old sailor in the household of King Mowanna of Nukuheva. Jimmy helps Toby escape from Nukuheva but is unable, or unwilling, to try to effect the release of Tommo from Typee.

Jimmy Dux. *Redburn.* See Redburn, Wellingborough.

Jingling Joe. *Omoo.* A sailor aboard the *Julia* who pretends before Dr. Johnson to be sick. Jingling Joe signs the round robin.

Jiromo. *Mardi.* A rebellious plotter against King Media, who orders him beheaded.

Joan. *Omoo.* The nickname given by Long Ghost to an old woman seen cozily amorous with her Darby on the beach at Imeeo.

Joanna [I], Queen [of Naples]. 'Marquis de Grandvin: Naples in the Time of Bomba.' Described as joking with her husband Andrea [possibly Andrew, son of Charles Robert] about strangling him. That night he is hanged by a cord of silk and gold.

Joaquin, Marques de Aramboalaza, Don. "Benito Cereno." A *San Dominick* passenger, lately from Spain, accidentally killed during the attack led by Delano's chief mate. On his body is found a jewel meant for the shrine of Our Lady of Mercy in Lima.

Jock. 'Tom Deadlight.' One of dying Tom Deadlight's messmates.

Joe. *Omoo.* A wooden-legged Portuguese violinist who is part of the foreign rabble around King Tammahamaha III of Hawaii.

Joe. *Moby-Dick.* A sailor who, with Jack and Harry, is suspicious of Jonah in Father Mapple's sermon at the Whaleman's Chapel in New Bedford.

Joe, Holy. 'Tom Deadlight.' See Holy Joe.

Joe, Jingling. *Omoo.* See Jingling Joe.

Joe, Rigadoon. 'Bridegroom Dick.' See Rigadoon Joe.

John I, King. *White-Jacket.* Mentioned as the former king of

Portugal and the grandfather of Don Pedro II, the present king of Brazil, and of Maria, the present queen of Portugal.

John. *White-Jacket.* A bully who starts a fight with Peter, Mark, and Antone, is flogged by order of Claret, but only leers under the cat.

Johnson, Colonel Guy. *Israel Potter.* A Tory who sailed to England on the same ship which bore Ethan Allen there as a prisoner.

Johnson, Dr. *Omoo.* The British resident physician of Papeetee who is friendly with Captain Guy of the *Julia* and who interviews the supposedly sick members of the *Julia* crew both aboard ship and in the Calabooza. The men despise him.

Johnson, Professor. "The Apple-Tree Table." The cool, long-winded naturalist who explains to the narrator and his family that the emergent bug probably came from an egg laid in the living wood of the apple tree 170 years ago.

Jonah. *Moby-Dick.* The Biblical hero of Father's Mapple's sermon at the Whaleman's Chapel in New Bedford.

Jonah. *Moby-Dick.* The wrinkled little bartender at Peter Coffin's Spouter-Inn, New Bedford.

Jonathan. *White-Jacket.* A sailor from New England who from the relative security of the main-royal-yard flings insults down at Don Pedro II on deck until calmed down by Jack Chase.

Jones, Frank. *White-Jacket.* A sailor who plays the part of Toddy Moll in the Fourth of July theatrical. (See also Frank.)

Jones, Captain John Paul. *Israel Potter.* The daring, tawny-colored, tatooed Scottish-born American naval officer who terrorizes British waters in his *Ranger, Bon Homme Richard,* and *Ariel.* He reveres Israel Potter, calls him "Yellow-hair," and makes him his quartermaster.

Jones, Jonathan. *Redburn.* The father of Redburn's friend in New York.

[Jones, Commodore Thomas] Ap [ap] Catesby; "Ap." 'Bridegroom Dick.' A famous naval officer under whom Bridegroom Dick evidently once sailed. Ap Catesby served with Decatur, Perry, Hull, and Porter.

Jones. *Redburn.* A New York friend, aged about twenty-five years, of Redburn's older brother. Jones and his wife befriend Redburn, and Jones introduces the youth to Captain Riga of the *Highlander* and thus starts him on his first voyage.

Jones, Mrs. *Redburn.* The kind wife of the friend of Redburn's older brother. She feeds Redburn well during his brief stay in New York.

Jones III. 'The New Ancient of Days: The Man of the Cave of Engihoul.' A common man, dethroned by the new ancient.

Jones, Mrs. "Jack Gentian (omitted from the final sketch of him)." the hostess at a dinner where old Gentian was the subject of gossip.

Jos. 'The New Ancient of Days: The Man of the Cave of Engihoul.' A common man, opposed by the new ancient.

José. ""Benito Cereno." A Spanish-speaking slave, about eighteen years old, owned by Aranda, on whom he spied for Babo.

Josy. *Omoo.* The "man" of Old Mother Tot.

Juan Fernandez. "The Encantadas." See Fernandez, Juan.

Judd, Dr. *Typee.* A sanctimonious adventurer who irresponsibly advises the half-civilized king of Hawaii, King Kammahamaha III, in 1843, and who refuses to cooperate with either Captain Charlton or Lord George Paulet.

Judy. *Redburn.* A servant girl at Handsome Mary Danby's Baltimore Clipper in Liverpool.

Julia. "I and My Chimney." One of the narrator's daughters, who with her mother and her sister Anna unsuccessfully tries to persuade the narrator to tear down his chimney.

Julia. "The Apple-Tree Table." The narrator's timid daughter, who at first fearfully blames the ticking in the table on spirits but who later sees in the emergence of the bug from it a proof of man's ultimate spiritual resurrection. She is Anna's sister.

Kaahumanu, Queen. *Typee.* Mentioned as the four-hundred-pound dowager queen of Hawaii who used to break the spines of offending men.

Kalow. *Typee.* A Typee chief who attends the probably cannibalistic feast from which Tommo is barred.

Kamehameha III. *Omoo.* See Tammahamaha III.

Kammahammaha, King. *Typee.* Mentioned as the renowned conqueror and king of the Hawaiian Islands.

Kammahamaha III, King. *Typee.* The half-civilized king of Hawaii in 1843. He is foolishly persuaded by Dr. Judd to surrender Hawaii to the British. Admiral Thomas returns the islands to their king.

Kandidee, King of. *Mardi.* A person in a manuscript chronicle in Oh Oh's museum.

Karakoee. *Typee.* A tall, tabooed, renegade Oahu shanghaier through whose efforts, along with those of Marnoo, Tommo is able to leave the Marquesas Islands aboard the *Julia.*

Karhownoo. *Mardi.* One of King Borabolla's sea divers. He fractures his skull against a coral reef and dies, in spite of Samoa's skillful surgery. Karhownoo was Roi Mori's younger son.

Karkeke. *Mardi.* The man whose spirit after death misplaced its head in heaven, according to a story by Babbalanja.

Karkie. *Mardi.* One of the twelve aristocratic Taparian families on the isle of Pimminee, entertained by Nimni.

Karky. *Typee.* The master tatooer of Typee, whose arts Tommo resists.

Karluna. *Typee.* Mentioned as a native whose property, like that of all other Typees, is respected by all.

Karnoonoo. *Typee.* A Typee native whose javelin handle Tommo carves.

Karolus [I], King. *Mardi.* The beheaded king of Dominora, according to the anonymous manuscript read in northern Vivenza.

Karolus [II], King. *Mardi.* The second monarch named Karolus, who reigned in Dominora after the first Karolus was beheaded there.

Karrolono. *Mardi.* One of King Uhia's chieftains. He envies his monarch and is envied by Donno.

Katrina. 'A Dutch Christmas . . .' A girl working in the kitchen.

Kean, Captain Hosea. "The 'Gees." A Nantucket sea captain who examines 'Gees on the Isle of Fogo before hiring them as seamen aboard his ship, instead of relying on false descriptions of them from middlemen.

Keekee. *Omoo*. See Zeke.

Kekuanoa, General. *Typee*. The immoral governor of Oahu in 1843. He profiteers from prostitution.

Kemble, [Charles]. "The Fiddler." The famous Drury Lane actor reputedly ousted from the public eye by Master Betty.

Kemble, [John Philip]. "The Fiddler." The famous Drury Lane actor reputedly ousted from the public eye by Master Betty.

King. 'Time's Betrayal.' The poet, who is King of his maple orchard.

King of India, The. 'Honor.' See India, The King of.

King of France, The. *Israel Potter*. See France, King of.

King-Post. *Moby-Dick*. Stubb's nickname for Flask (which see).

Kilpatrick, [General Judson]. 'The March to the Sea.' The commander of some of Sherman's perplexing outriders.

Kit. *Pierre*. A stable slave of General Pierre Glendinning, Pierre's grandfather.

Kitoti. *Omoo*. One of the four recreant chiefs whom the French governor Bruat puts in charge of the four sections into which he divides Tahiti. The others are Tati, Utamai, and Paraita.

Klanko, King. *Mardi*. The slave-driving monarch of a gloomy land between Bobovona and Serenia. Media insists on avoiding Klanko's region of volcanic mines.

Kniphausen. *Israel Potter*. The Hessian commander in America whose name Ethan Allen reviles during his captivity in Falmouth, England.

Knowles, Ned. *White-Jacket*. Jack Chase's first loader at a main-deck gun of Admiral Codrington's flagship the *Asia*. Knowles was killed during the Battle of Navarino, October 20, 1827.

Kokovoko, The King of. *Moby-Dick*. Queequeg's Polynesian

father, a high chief. He may be dead by the time Ishmael and Queequeg meet.

Kolor. *Typee*. See Kolory.

Kolory (also Kolor), "Lord Primate." *Typee*. A Typee soldier-priest who cuffs Moa Artua, his religious doll, into providing acceptable answers to whispered questions.

Konno. *Mardi*. An ingenious man of Kaleedoni who cured the evils of his land by building a fire under a huge caldron and thus making the people believe that he was very busy, according to Babbalanja.

Kooloo. *Omoo*. A Tahitian native man who adopts the narrator as his friend but then spurns him for another. The narrator's other native friend, Poky, is more loyal.

Kory-Kory. *Typee*. The tall, athletic, gay son, aged about twenty-five years, of Marheyo and Tinor. Kory-Kory transports Tommo on his back, bathes him, and ministers to his needs as well as he can.

Krako. *Mardi*. Bardianna's disciple, mentioned in the philosopher's will.

Kravi. *Mardi*. A cunning man whose finger bones, made into a fishhook, are in Oh Oh's museum.

Kroko, King. *Mardi*. A character in a manuscript ballad in Oh Oh's museum.

Kubla. *Mardi*. A priest who gives Donjalolo the royal girdle which makes him king of Juam.

L—, Miss. *Redburn*. A person to whom Redburn's father presented a letter in Liverpool back in 1808.

L., B. *Clarel*. A devout pilgrim from St. Mary's Hall, Oxford, who some time earlier left an enigmatic anti-revolutionary poem on a wall in Clarel's room at the inn in Jerusalem.

Lacedaemonian Jim. *Omoo*. See Long Jim.

Laced Cap. 'Bridegroom Dick.' A general term used by Bridegroom Dick to refer to fancy naval officers.

Lafitte, [Jean]. "Story of Daniel Orme" [first draft and revised text]. A buccaneer reputed to have been Daniel Orme's leader at one time.

Lais. 'The Parthenon.' A beautiful Greek courtesan, whose beauty Spinoza thinks of when he also thinks of the architectural beauty of the Parthenon.

Lakreemo. *Mardi*. A legatee mentioned in Bardianna's will.

Lamia. 'Lamia's Song.' A singer who urges the mountaineer to come down.

Lanbranka Hohinna. *Mardi*. A spinster legatee mentioned in Bardianna's will.

Landless, "Happy Jack.' *White-Jacket*. A foretopman with ten years of service in the Navy. He is a typically immature, stupid, gay sailor, frequently flogged and caring for nothing but rum and tobacco. He advises Shippy.

Langsdorff, Captain [Georg H. von]. *Redburn*. A Russian friend of Redburn's old sea-captain uncle.

Larfee. *Mardi*. A witch, in Mohi's story, who falsely condemns the questing lover Ozonna for supposedly killing Rea, a maiden in Queen Hautia's court on the isle of Flozella a Nina. Mohi tells the story to dissuade Taji from continuing his search for his lost Yillah.

Larry. *Redburn*. A sailor aboard the *Highlander* who speaks of his experiences as a whaler and who rails against "snivilization."

Larry o' the Cannakin [*sic*]. 'Jack Roy.' A jovial singer of the praises of his mate Jack Roy.

Lascar Sailor. *Moby-Dick*. A *Pequod* sailor who interrupts the dancing during the midnight festivities in the forecastle by noting the approach of a storm.

L. A. V. "Fragments from a Writing Deck. No. 1." "Fragments from a Writing Desk. No. 2." See V., L. A.

Lavender. *Redburn*. The handsome mulatto steward of the *Highlander*. He is a former Broadway barber and likes Liverpool because he can step along freely there.

Lazarus. *Moby-Dick*. The name Ishmael assigns to a shivering beggar sleeping on the curb outside Peter Coffin's Spouter-Inn at New Bedford.

Lazarus. *Clarel*. The name taken by a count turned monk who came to Mar Saba and set up the carved marble shield in a porch of a minster there.

Leader, The. 'The Scout toward Aldie.' See the Colonel.

Lecbe. "Benito Cereno." A vicious Ashantee slave who polishes hatchets during Delano's visit aboard the *San Dominick*. He helped Matinqui mortally mutilate Aranda and also helped kill Francisco Masa.

Lee, [General Robert E.]. 'The Victor at Antietam.' The Confederate general defeated at Antietam by McClellan. 'The Armies of the Wilderness.' Lauded by a Confederate prisoner. 'The March to the Sea.' Has a Union gamecock named after him. 'The Surrender at Appomattox.' Gives his sword to Grant. 'Rebel Color-Bearers at Shiloh.' Mentioned. 'Presentation to the Authorities.' Mentioned as surrendering. 'The Scout toward Aldie.' Mentioned. 'Lee in the Capitol.' After the Civil War, Lee (called "the Invader" here) testifies before the Senate and is imagined as urging a policy of understanding and renewal of harmony under re-established law. "To Major John Gentian, Dean of the Burgundy Club." Mentioned.

Le Fan, Chaplain. 'Bridegroom Dick.' The chaplain whom Bridegroom Dick in his reminisces contrasts with Lieutenant Tom Tight.

Lefevre. *Omoo*. A scoundrel and spy in the employe with Major Fergus of Bruat, the hated French governor of Tahiti.

Legare, Tom. *Redburn*. The treasurer of the Juvenile Temperance Society, of which Redburn is a member.

Leggs. *White-Jacket*. With Pounce, one of the two ship's corporals under Bland. Leggs, formerly a prison turnkey in New York, ferrets out illicit gamblers aboard the *Neversink*.

Lemsford. *White-Jacket*. A nervous poet, whose acquaintance White Jacket cherishes. Lemsford hides his poetry in a little casket-like box. He wants to draw up the playbill for the Fourth of July theatrical and reveres the sea, at least in his talk.

Leonardo. 'Marquis de Grandvin: At the Hostelry.' See [Da Vinci], Leonardo.

Lesbia. 'The Vial of Attar.' Depicted as having a lover who is sad at her death.

Lesbian, The; "Lesbos," "The Mytilene," "The Isleman." *Clarel*. A middle-aged salesman from Mytilene, on the island of Lesbos, who does business at Mar Saba. He is a gay believer only in the happy here and now.

Lesbos. *Clarel*. See the Lesbian.

Levi, Max. *Clarel*. A friend of Margoth, who says that Levi traversed the traditionally impassable Seir, a region near the Dead Sea.

Lewis, Jack. *Typee*. A sailor aboard the *Dolly* whose ability to steer is unfairly criticized by Captain Vangs.

Limeno, The. *Clarel*. A close Peruvian friend, mentioned with a sigh by the Lyonese.

[Lincoln, President Abraham]; "The Forgiver." 'The Martyr.' Praised as a clement, calm, kind leader, whose assassination from behind will cause the avenger to replace the forgiver.

Lippi, Frater [Fra Filippo]. 'Marquis de Grandvin: At the Hostelry.' A wicked-eyed former monk, now an artist who discusses the picturesque with other artists.

Livella. *Mardi*. A Mardian historian, some of whose books have been lost. He is mentioned by Babbalanja.

Liverpool. *Omoo*. See Blunt, Bill.

Llanyllan, Mrs. *Pierre*. Lucy Tartan's childless, widowed aunt, whom the girl visits in the village of Saddle Meadows and thus can be near Pierre.

Logodora. *Mardi*. An aloof Mardian mentioned by Babbalanja.

Lol Lol. *Mardi*. One of the twelve aristocratic Taparian families on the isle of Pimminee, entertained by Nimni.

Lombardo. *Mardi*. The independent, long-suffering genius author of *Koztanza*, an ancient Mardian masterpiece revered by Babbalanja (who discusses Lombardo's career), much read by Media, known by Yoomy, and never read by Abrazza.

Long, Robert. *Moby-Dick*. A sailor lost with five others from the *Eliza* in 1839. Their shipmates placed a marble tablet in their memory in the Whaleman's Chapel in New Bedford.

Long Ghost, Dr.; "The Long Doctor." *Omoo*. The tall, colorless, fair-haired, gray-eyed ship's physician who shares all of the adventures of the narrator, as they rebel against Captain

Guy of the *Julia*, go to the Calabooza at Papeetee, and wander to Martair, Tamai, Imeeo, Loohooloo, Partoowye, and Taloo. At one point he calls himself Peter (which see).

Long Island Sailor. *Moby-Dick*. A *Pequod* sailor who dances during the festivities in the forecastle.

Long Jim, "Lacedaemonian Jim." *Omoo*. An eloquent, belligerent sailor aboard the *Julia*. He signs the round robin.

Long-locks. *White-Jacket*. The afterguardsman who plays the part of Mrs. Lovelorn in the Fourth of July theatrical.

Long Lumbago, Lieutenant. 'Bridegroom Dick.' An officer remembered by Bridegroom Dick as a crabbed, severe person aboard Captain Turret's ship.

Longstreet, [General James]. 'The Armies of the Wilderness.' Mentioned as slanting through the Wilderness.

Loo. *Ommo*. The voluptuous but cold fourteen-year-old daughter of Po-Po and Arfretee. She stabs Long Ghost with a thorn with he gets fresh.

Loon, Billy. *Omoo*. A shabbily dressed Negro who is part of the rabble around King Tammahamaha III of Hawaii.

Lord Bountiful. "The Marquis de Grandvin." A laudatory nickname for the Marquis de Grandvin (which see).

Lord Mayor of London, The. "Poor Man's Pudding and Rich Man's Crumbs." A host of the Guildhall Banquet in London following the Battle of Waterloo.

[Lorraine], Claude. 'Marquis de Grandvin: At the Hostelry.' A mild painter from Lorraine who declines to discuss the picturesque with other artists.

Lot. 'Running the Batteries.' A Union soldier aboard a ship with Ned and Hugh running past the Confederate batteries at Vicksburg.

Louis Philippe. *Omoo*. Mentioned as the French king to whom Queen Pomaree appeals in an effort to have hated Merenhout recalled.

[Louis XVI]. *Israel Potter*. See France, King of.

Love. 'Hearth Roses.' The poet's faithful love.

Lovely, Lord. *Redburn*. A doll-like, glossy little aristocratic friend whom Harry Bolton avoids in Liverpool.

Lucree. *Mardi.* A reader who asked Lombardo how much money he would make by his *Koztanza,* according to Babbalanja.

Ludwig, King. *Mardi.* A monarch whose Franko throne, according to Babbalanja, was burned. (See also Ludwig the Great, King.)

Ludwig the Debonair, King. *Mardi.* One of several Ludwigs mentioned by Babbalanja at Abrazza's banquet.

Ludwig the Do Nothing, King. *Mardi.* One of several Ludwigs mentioned by Babbalanja at Abrazza's banquet.

Ludwig the Fat, King. *Mardi.* One of several Ludwigs mentioned by Babbalanja at Abrazza's banquet.

Ludwig the Great. *Mardi.* One of several Ludwigs mentioned by Babbalanja at Abrazza's banquet. He may be the same as the Ludwig (which see) whose throne was burned.

Ludwig the Juvenile, King. *Mardi.* One of several Ludwigs mentioned by Babbalanja at Abrazza's banquet.

Ludwig the Pious, King. *Mardi.* One of several Ludwigs mentioned by Babbalanja at Abrazza's banquet.

Ludwig the Quarreler, King. *Mardi.* One of several Ludwigs mentioned by Babbalanja at Abrazza's banquet.

Ludwig the Stammerer, King. *Mardi.* One of several Ludwigs mentioned by Babbalanja at Abrazza's banquet.

Luff. *Omoo.* The nickname bestowed by the *Julia* crew on Wymontoo-Hee (which see).

Lugar-Lips. "Under the Rose." See [S]ugar-Lips.

Luke. 'The Scout toward Aldie.' Evidently a Union soldier concealed in the yard of a deserted house during the ill-fated pursuit of Mosby.

Lullee. *Omoo.* A native girl at Taloo loved vainly and from a distance by William, a runaway ship's carpenter.

Lumbago, Lieutenant Long. 'Bridegroom Dick.' See Long Lumbago, Lieutenant.

Lyon, [General Nathaniel]. 'Lyon.' A brave Union officer killed leading his men at the Battle of Springfield, Missouri, August, 1861.

Lyonese, The; "The Prodigal.' *Clarel.* A happy, sensual French Jewish salesman who has traveled from Jaffa to Bethlehem for flirtatious purposes and who spends a night at the Bethlehem inn with unquiet Clarel.

M—. "Fragments from a Writing Desk. No. 1." The recipient of a letter from L.A.V. (of the village of Lansingburgh [New York]), who describes three lovely girls.

Macey, Harry. *Moby-Dick.* The chief mate of the *Jeroboam*, the commander of which is Captain Mayhew. Macey defies the prediction of the mad prophet Gabriel and pursues Moby Dick, which kills him.

Macey, Mrs. Harry. *Moby-Dick.* The woman whose letter via the *Pequod* tardily reaches the *Jeroboam*, of which her husband was chief mate before Moby Dick killed him.

Mack, "Commodore." *Omoo.* A Scotsman who leads a gang of beachcombers at Papeetee.

Macready, [William Charles]. "The Two Temples." The brilliant actor whose performance in London as Cardinal Richelieu seems to the narrator almost priest-like.

Macy, Seth. *Moby-Dick.* A sailor lost with five others from the *Eliza* in 1839. Their shipmates placed a marble tablet in their memory in the Whaleman's Chapel in New Bedford.

Mad Jack, Lieutenant. *White-Jacket.* A tyrannical, lovable, alcoholic, bellicose quarter-deck officer. He is contrasted with Lieutenant Selvagee. Mad Jack's bravery, in the face of Captain Claret's ineptness, saves the *Neversink* during a storm off Cape Horn. By off-handed geniality, Mad Jack later stops an incipient mutiny of the crew over Claret's order that all beards be trimmed.

Mahinee. *Omoo.* An old Tahitian chief with whom John Jermin leaves the sea chests of the rebellious sailors from the *Julia.*

Mahmoud, [II, Sultan of Turkey]. *Clarel.* Mentioned as ordering the massacre of the Spahis, one of whom, Belex, escaped.

Mahone. 'The New Ancient of Days: The Man of the Cave of Engihoul.' A common man, opposed by the new ancient. escaped.

Mai-Mai. *Omoo.* A fat old native at Taloo who is a drinking crony of the captain of the *Leviathan.*

Major, The. "Fragments from a Writing Desk. No. 1." L.A.V.'s friend, who has courteously attended to a request.

Major, The; "The Senior." 'A Scout toward Aldie.' A grizzled, experienced officer under the young Colonel. The Major survives Mosby's ambush of the Colonel and his men.

Major. 'Bridegroom Dick.' The commanding officer of the marines ordered by Captain Turret to supervise the flogging of the Finn, according to Bridegroom Dick's reminiscence.

Maltese Sailor. *Moby-Dick.* A *Pequod* sailor who talks erotically while his mates dance during the midnight festivities in the forecastle.

Mammon. *Clarel.* A name by which Rolfe refers to the Banker (which see).

Man, The. 'The Armies of the Wilderness.' See Grant.

Man. 'Bridegroom Dick.' The name by which Captain Turret addresses the Finn (which see).

Mandeville. *White-Jacket.* A rakish-looking former officer, who after being broken in rank for excessive drinking is transferred aboard the *Neversink.* Within a week he is found drunk and is ordered flogged by Lieutenant Bridewell, formerly Mandeville's roommate aboard the *Macedonian.*

Manko. *Mardi.* An alias of the prophet Alma (which see).

Man of Mosses, The. "Hawthorne and His Mosses." See Hawthorne, Nathaniel.

Manta. *Mardi.* A bedridden person in Ohonoo who envies gadabout beggars and who is envied by King Uhia for being able to die unmolested.

Manxman, The; the Old Manx Sailor. *Moby-Dick.* An old nautical seer who the first time he sees Ahab says that he must be scarred from crown to sole. The old sailor is wearily critical of the wild crew during the midnight festivities in the forecastle.

Mapenda. "Benito Cereno." An Ashantee slave who polishes hatchets during Delano's visit aboard the *San Dominick* and is killed during the attack led by Delano's chief mate.

Mapple, Father. *Moby-Dick.* The rugged, venerable preacher at the Whaleman's Chapel in New Bedford. Since he was once

a sailor, his salty sermon on Jonah deeply moves Ishmael
and the other seamen in attendance.

Marbonna. *Omoo*. A large, muscular, proud Nukuhevan who is
the guardian of Queen Pomaree's children at Taloo. He
escorts the narrator and Long Ghost into the queen's court.

Marchioness of Brinvilliers, The. 'The Marchioness of Brinvilliers.'
See Brinvilliers, The Marchioness of.

Marcy, Secretary [of War William L.]. "Authentic Anecdotes of
'Old Zack.'" The Secretary of War who writes his
sympathy when General Taylor has his pants torn by a tack
put in his saddle.

Mardonna, Prince. *Mardi*. A Juam prince who refused to become
king because he would have had to give up roving.

Margoth. *Clarel*. A powerfully built, atheistic, materialistic Jewish
geologist.

Margrave, The. 'The Margrave's Birthnight.' The owner of the
castle, whose birthnight the peasants mechanically celebrate.

Marhar-Rarrar, "The Wakeful," "Bright-eyed." *Omoo*. An
especially lovely maiden encountered by the smitten
narrator and by Long Ghost on the beach at Imeeo.

Marharvai. *Omoo*. The old chief who is the host of the narrator
and Long Ghost at Loohooloo.

Marheyo. *Typee*. Kory-Kory's father, in whose hut Tommo stays
during his captivity among the Typees. Marheyo is senile,
spends much time tinkering with the construction of a
shed, but sympathetically understands his guest's desire to
return home.

Maria, Queen. *White-Jacket*. Mentioned as the present queen of
Portugal and the sister of Don Pedro II, king of Brazil.

Marianna. "The Piazza." The lonely girl who lives with her
hard-working brother in the mountain-side cottage, which is
thought by the romantic narrator to be theatrically
attractive. She in turn thinks that his house resembles
marble and must be the abode of a happy man.

Marie. *Pierre*. A pretty girl in the Miss Pennies' sewing circle.

Marjora, King. *Mardi*. The brother of King Teei of the island of

Juam. Marjora killed his brother and set up his own residence at Willamilla.

Mark. *Mardi.* A harpooneer aboard the *Arcturion.*

Mark. *White-Jacket.* A sailor suffering from a pulmonary complaint. When he becomes involved with Peter and Antone in a fight started by John, he is flogged by order of Claret and turns sullen.

Marko. *Mardi.* Bardianna's scribe, mentioned in the philosopher's will.

Marmonora. *Mardi.* A rich Taparian guest of Nimni on the isle of Pimminee. Marmonora is heartless, according to Gaddi.

Marnoo. *Typee.* The handsome, curly-haired native of Pueearka who is permitted to wander inviolate through all valleys. When Marnoo speaks English, Tommo decides to beg him—to no avail—to lead him back to Nukuheva. Later Marnoo is instrumental, however, in aiding Karakoee's management of Tommo's escape.

Marr, John. 'John Marr.' A wounded, retired sailor who about 1838 settles on the frontier in the prairies, marries, has a child, then loses both wife and child. Not especially esteemed by his farmer neighbors, he apostrophizes his former shipmates poignantly.

Marr, Mrs. John. 'John Marr.' John Marr's wife, who dies of a fever in the prairies.

Marr. 'John Marr.' John Marr's child, who dies with its mother of a fever in the prairies.

Marrot, Lieutenant. 'Bridegroom Dick.' The officer remembered by Bridegroom Dick as ordering his constables to imprison the drunken Finn.

Marten. *Pierre.* The servant of Pierre's aunt Dorothea Glendinning. He once served the boy some fruitcake.

Martha. *Pierre.* A pretty girl in the Miss Pennies' sewing circle.

Martha. *Pierre.* Lucy Tartan's chambermaid, who tends stricken Lucy when Pierre tells her that he is married.

Martindale, Captain. *Israel Potter.* The officer in command of the brigantine *Washington* from which Israel Potter is taken captive by the British ship *Foy.*

Marvel, Bill. *Mardi.* A yarn-spinning sailor aboard the *Arcturion.*

Mary. *Redburn.* The imagined girl friend of a typical Canadian soldier on cold sentry duty at Quebec.

Masa, Francisco. "Benito Cereno." Aranda's middle-aged cousin from Mendoza, wounded by Lecbe and thrown overboard alive off the *San Dominick.*

Masaniello. 'Marquis de Grandvin: Naples in the Time of Bomba.' Mentioned as a bridegroom, darling of the Neapolitan mob, and finally a beheaded martyr and patriot.

Master. 'Old Counsel.' The master of a wrecked clipper who warns sailors to beware when rounding the Horn out of the Golden Gate.

Master. 'Under the Ground.' The boyish gardener's master, who orders roses to be entombed.

Mate, The. "The Death Craft." In Harry the Reefer's dream, the officer of the Death Craft who throws himself overboard.

Matilda. *Redburn.* One of the three charming girls who live with their parents in a cottage outside Liverpool. Redburn has a memorable afternoon drinking tea and eating buttered muffins with them.

Matinqui. "Benito Cereno." An Ashantee slave who polishes hatchets during Delano's visit aboard the *San Dominick.* He helped Lecbe mortally mutilate Aranda and is killed during the attack led by Delano's chief mate.

Matt. 'Tom Deadlight.' One of dying Tom Deadlight's messmates. Matt fans his friend with a sou'wester.

Max the Dutchman, "Red Max." *Redburn.* A good-natured, red-haired sailor aboard the *Highlander,* with a wife named Meg in New York and another named Sally in Liverpool. He tosses Mrs. O'Brien's Bible overboard on the return trip, to America.

Maxwell, Mungo. *Israel Potter.* A mutinous sailor reportedly flogged to death by Captain John Paul Jones, who denies the charge.

May. 'Stockings in the Farm-House Chimney.' Depicted as waiting for Santa Claus.

May-Day. *White-Jacket.* An enormous Negro assistant of Old

Coffee, the ship's cook. May-Day is especially good at the sport of head-butting but after thus fighting Rose-Water he is flogged for it by Captain Claret.

Mayhew, Captain. *Moby-Dick*. The commander of the whaler *Jeroboam*, which has the mad Shaker prophet Gabriel aboard, is now swept by a malignant epidemic, and recently lost her chief mate Harry Macey to Moby Dick.

May Queen. *The Confidence-Man*. The name assigned by the herb doctor to the Creole or Comanche daughter who accompanies Pitch the shaggy backwoodsman, whose mysterious pain impels him to strike the herb doctor.

Mayor of London, The. "Poor Man's Pudding and Rich Man's Crumbs." See the Lord Mayor of London.

McClellan, [General George B.]. 'Malvern Hill.' The Union commander at Malvern Hill, the final engagement of the Seven Days' Battle. 'The Victor of Antietam.' The Union commander who after the Seven Days' Battle was discarded, only to be recalled, to improve the army after Pope, to rout Lee, to force Stonewall Jackson's retreat, and to win at Antietam. 'Rebel Color-Bearers at Shiloh.' Mentioned. "Major Gentian and Colonel J. Bunkum." Mentioned as delaying.

McCloud, Colonel. *Israel Potter*. The British commander at Montreal who mistreats his prisoner Ethan Allen there.

McGee. *Omoo*. See M'Gee.

McPherson, [General James B.]; "Sarpedon." 'A Dirge for McPherson.' Commemorated after being killed in front of Atlanta in July, 1864.

Media, King. *Mardi*. The father of Taji's friend King Media of Odo.

Media, King. *Mardi*. The initially materialistic monarch of the isle of Odo, who professes to be a demigod. Ordering Babbalanja, Mohi, and Yoomy along, he accompanies Taji on his long and fruitless search for Yillah as far as Serenia (the charitable religion of which moves him greatly), then returns to his kingdom, remaining there to try to quell sedition.

Meg. *Redburn*. The New York wife of Max the Dutchman, who has a wife named Sally in Liverpool.

Mehevi. *Typee*. The brave, noble-looking chief of the Typees among whom Tommo lives for about four months. Mehevi's damsel is Moonoony, and the chief does not want Tommo to leave.

[Melville, Captain Thomas]. 'To the Master of the "Meteor."' The captain of the *Meteor*, whom the poet thinks of fondly.

[Melville,] Tom. 'To Tom.' See Tom [Melville].

Merenhout [Moerenhaut, J. Antoine]. *Omoo*. The hated commissioner royal under the hated French governor Bruat of Tahiti.

Merry Andrews. 'Marquis de Grandvin: Naples in the Time of Bomba.' Happy people on the beach in Naples.

Merrymusk. "Cock-a-Doodle-Doo!" The indigent wood-sawyer who owns the noble rooster Trumpet (also called Shanghai, Beneventano, and Dr. Cock), which he refuses to sell to the narrator. Merrymusk, a Marylander and formerly a sailor, and all his family die.

Merrymusk, Mrs. "Cock-a-Doodle-Doo!" The mortally sick but uncomplaining wife of the indigent wood-sawyer who owns Trumpet, which he refuses to sell to the narrator.

Merrymusk. "Cock-a-Doodle-Doo!" One of the mortally sick children of the Merrymusks, who own Trumpet.

Merrymusk. "Cock-a-Doodle-Doo!" One of the mortally sick children of the Merrymusks, who own Trumpet.

Merrymusk. "Cock-a-Doodle-Doo!" One of the mortally sick children of the Merrymusks, who own Trumpet.

Merrymusk. "Cock-a-Doodle-Doo!" One of the mortally sick children of the Merrymusks, who own Trumpet.

Methodist, The. *The Confidence-Man*. A tall, Tennessee-born army chaplain who saw service in the Mexican War and who supports Black Guinea when he begs on the deck of the *Fidèle*.

Methodist. *Clarel*. The chaplain of the ship the *Apostles*.

According to Agath, he composed a poem about the evening star, steadfast even in times of war.

Metrodorus. 'The Garden of Metrodorus.' The owner of a secluded Athenian garden, in which may be found what— sadness, happiness, peace, sin?

M'Gee (also McGee). *Omoo*. An ugly sailor aboard the *Julia*, born in Ireland but transported to Australia, according to rumor. He signs the round robin. Father Murphy at Papeetee refuses to have anything to do with him.

Michael Angelo [Michelagniolo Buonarroti]. 'Marquis de Grandvin: At the Hostelry.' An artist described as sitting withdrawn. Brouwer is critical of him in conversation with Lippi.

[Michelangelo]. 'Marquis de Grandvin: At the Hostelry.' See Michael Angelo.

Mickle, William Julius. *White-Jacket*. The translator of Camoens's *Lusiads* and a fellow sailor with Jack Chase's father aboard the man-of-war *Romney*.

Midni. *Mardi*. An ontologist and entomologist, cited by Babbalanja.

Milk-and-Water. *White-Jacket*. A nickname for Pert (which see).

Millet, Sir John. *Israel Potter*. The kindly Britisher who befriends Israel Potter, although he knows that the wretched man is an escaped American, and even employs him as his gardener at Brentford for six months.

Millthorpe, Charles; "Charlie." *Pierre*. The refined, sweet-tempered son—aged twenty-two years—of tenant farmers on a small plot of Glendinning land. As a youth, he played with Pierre. Then, shortly after his father's death, Mill-thorpe sold out and took his mother and sisters to the city to support them by law and authorship among the Apostles. He aids Pierre in the city and offers to introduce him to Plotinus Plinlimmon. He tries to help Pierre in prison but arrives just after the fated youth has taken poison.

Millthorpe. *Pierre*. Charlie Millthorpe's father. Now deceased, he once was a handsome, poverty-stricken, melancholy old farmer who lived on a small plot of Glendinning land.

Millthorpe, Mrs. *Pierre.* Charlie Millthorpe's gentle, thin, retiring mother, whom Pierre remembers well.

Millthorpe, Miss. *Pierre.* One of Charlie Millthorpe's sadly inquisitive sisters.

Millthorpe, Miss. *Pierre.* One of Charlie Millthorpe's hopeless sisters.

Millthorpe, Miss. *Pierre.* One of Charlie Millthorpe's half-envious sisters.

Milor. 'Marquis de Grandvin: Naples in the Time of Bomba.' The term of respect which His Excellency the Neapolitan tumbler might have used in addressing Major Jack Gentian (which see).

Mink. 'The Scout toward Aldie.' A Union soldier wounded during the ambush set for the Colonel and his men by Mosby.

Minta the Cynic. *Mardi.* A legatee mentioned in Bardianna's will.

Miquel. "Benito Cereno." A Negro slave who strikes the hours aboard Cereno's *San Dominick.*

Miriam. 'Magian Wine.' Mentioned as prizing certain amulets.

Miss Guy. *Omoo.* See Guy, Captain.

Mocmohoc. *The Confidence-Man.* The perfidious Indian who treacherously killed the Wrights and the Weavers, who were migrants from Virginia to Kentucky.

Mogul. *Moby-Dick.* The crew's nickname for Captain Ahab (which see).

Mohi, "Braid Beard." *Mardi.* The bearded historian from the isle of Odo who accompanies Taji, along with King Media of Odo, Babbalanja, and Yoomy, on his long and fruitless search for Yillah. Mohi and Yoomy leave Taji on the isle of Flozella a Nina but return from Odo to try to rescue him from Queen Hautia of Flozella.

Moll. *Omoo.* See Mother Moll.

Molly. *Redburn.* A servant girl at Handsome Mary Danby's Baltimore Clipper in Liverpool.

Molly. "Billy Budd." See Bristol Molly.

Mondi. *Mardi.* A neighbor of Bardianna, mentioned in the philosopher's will.

Monee. *Omoo.* The grinning, paunchy, bald old man who acts as cook and butler for Po-Po at Partoowye.

Monoo. *Typee.* A Typee chief and warrior of long ago who, according to Kory-Kory, built in one day the foundation of the sacred Hoolah Hoolah ground.

Montaigne, [Michel de]. 'Montaigne and His Kitten.' A Frenchman who speaks to his kitten Blanche about immortality.

Moonoony. *Typee.* The damsel of Mehevi, who shares her affections with a fifteen-year-old lad.

Montgomery. *White-Jacket.* A midshipman who is ordered by his lieutenant to break open a chest mailed by the sergeant-at-arms Bland to the purser and containing contraband liquor.

Morairi, Jose. "Benito Cereno." One of Aranda's young clerks. He is from Cadiz and is a *San Dominick* passenger.

Mordant, Captain. "Billy Budd." Vere's captain of marines. He is a good-natured, obese, brave officer, serves on the drumhead court, and reluctantly votes to condemn Billy Budd to death.

Mordecai. *Omoo.* A villainous-looking juggler who is part of the rabble around King Tammahamaha III of Hawaii.

Moredock, Colonel John. *The Confidence-Man.* The celebrated Indian-hater whose life Frank Goodman summarizes in conversation with Charles Noble.

Moredock, Mrs. John. *The Confidence-Man.* Colonel John Moredock's wife, for whom the Indian-hater provided well.

Moredock. *The Confidence-Man.* Colonel John Moredock's father, who was massacred by Indians.

Moredock, Mrs. *The Confidence-Man.* Colonel John Moredock's mother, whose three husbands and eight of her nine children were massacred by Indians, thus causing her one surviving child to become a ruthless Indian-hater.

Moredock. *The Confidence-Man.* The family of Moredock Hall, in Northamptonshire, England, mentioned by Frank Goodman but not related to Colonel John Moredock.

Morille. *Redburn*. A person on whom Redburn's father called in Liverpool back in 1808.

Morn, Captain. 'The Scout toward Aldie.' The officer ordered by the Colonel to picket the roads and stop all travelers, during their ill-fated pursuit of Mosby.

Morrison, Colonel [William R.]. 'Donelson.' A Union officer killed during the siege of Donelson.

Mortmain, "the Swede." *Clarel*. An illegitimate Swede, formerly a revolutionary leader in Paris, now philosophically and spiritually a desperate masochist. He dies high in the rocks at Mar Saba.

Mosby, [Colonel John S.]. 'The Armies of the Wilderness.' Mentioned as having his men on the prowl. 'The Scout toward Aldie.' The elusive partisan leader who outwits his Union pursuers near Aldie. He may be the Confederate prisoner who after attempting to escape feigns injury from a fall (See also Sir Slyboots.)

Moss-Rose. 'Amoroso.' See Rosamond.

Mossy Man, The. "Hawthorne and His Mosses." See Hawthorne, Nathaniel.

Mother Moll. *Omoo*. A muffin expert fondly recalled by Rope Yarn.

Mounttop. *Moby-Dick*. The first mate of the *Samuel Enderby*, whose captain, Boomer, lost his right arm while chasing Moby Dick.

Mowanna, King. *Typee*. The ruler of Nukuheva, supported by the French in order to foment trouble involving Nukuheva, the Typees, and the Happars. He has a tatooed wife.

Mow-Mow (also Mow Mow). *Typee*. The fierce, one-eyed Typee chief who is wounded in a victorious engagement with some Happars. He later resists Tommo's successful attempt to escape to the Australian vessel in the harbor.

Mowree, The. *Omoo*. See Bembo.

Moyar. *Pierre*. The loyal Negro servant of General Pierre Glendinning, Pierre's grandfather.

Mungo. *Typee*. The Negro cook aboard the *Dolly*.

Mure. "Benito Cereno." An African-born slave, a calker by trade, between sixty and seventy years old, killed—as was his son Diamelo—during the attack on the *San Dominick* led by Delano's chief mate.

Murphy, Father. *Omoo.* An Irish-born, French-trained priest who visits the rebellious crew members when they are in the Calabooza. He ignores M'Gee but befriends Pat and the other prisoners.

Mustapha. *Clarel.* The old muezzin who tardily cries from the Omar minaret to announce the coming of dawn.

My Lady. "Under the Rose." The respectful term by which Geoffry refers to My Lord the Ambassador's wife, who has fine lace.

My Lord the Ambassador. "Under the Rose." See the Ambassador.

Mynheer. *Clarel.* A name with which Glaucon addresses the Banker (which see).

Mytilene, The. *Clarel.* See the Lesbian.

Nacta. "Benito Cereno." An African-born slave, a calker by trade, between sixty and seventy years of age, and aboard Cereno's *San Dominick*.

Nan. *Redburn.* See Brandy-Nan.

Napoleon [Bonaparte]. 'In the Desert.' Mentioned as having soldiers who defeated the Emirs but lost to the bayonet-like sun of the [Egyptian] desert.

Narmo-Nana Po-Po. *Omoo.* See Po-Po.

Narmonee. *Typee.* A brave Typee warrior, badly wounded in an engagement with the Happars which yields three Happar corpses for what is probably a cannibal feast.

Narnee. *Typee.* A clownish but expert coconut tree climber.

Nat. "Benito Cereno." A cousin with whom Amasa Delano used to go berry hunting on the beach when they were both children.

Nathan. *Clarel.* The husband of Agar and the father of Ruth. He is an American who moved from puritanism to doubt to deism and pantheism to espousal of the Jewish faith and

Zionism. He takes his family to Jerusalem, farms outside the walls, and is murdered by hostile Arabs.

Nature, Dame. "The Encantadas." The creator of the ugly island tortoises.

Navy Bob. *Omoo.* A sleepy old sailor aboard the *Julia.* He signs the round robin.

Ned. *Typee.* A sailor aboard the *Dolly* who points to the valley of Typee as the locale of cannibals.

Ned. *Redburn.* A sailor aboard the *Highlander* who offers cigars all around, shortly after the ship leaves port for Liverpool.

Ned. *Pierre.* One of Mrs. Mary Glendinning's servants, who though a husband and a father has evidently seduced Delly Ulver, another servant, and must therefore be dismissed.

Ned. 'Running the Batteries.' A Union sailor aboard a ship with Hugh and Lot running past the Confederate batteries at Vicksburg.

Ned, Rhyming. 'Bridegroom Dick.' See Rhyming Ned.

Ned. 'To Ned.' See Bunn, Ned.

Nehemiah, "the Hat." *Clarel.* A gentle, Bible-quoting old American millenialist. He talks with Clarel, takes him to the home of Nathan and Agar, introduces him to their daughter Ruth, accompanies the other pilgrims on their journey, rides along on a patient ass, and drowns in the Dead Sea.

Nellie. *Pierre.* A pretty girl in the Miss Pennies' sewing circle.

Nellie. 'Stockings in the Farm-House Chimney.' Depicted as waiting for Santa Claus.

[Nelson], Admiral [Viscount Horatio]. 'The Temeraire.' The admiral of the *Victory.*

Nesle, The Sire de. 'L'Envoi: The Return of the Sire de Nesle. A.D. 16—.' Described as happy to end his rovings and return to his towers and his good love.

Nestors. 'Marquis de Grandvin: Naples in the Time of Bomba.' The name assigned by the beach juggler to thralls.

Nimni. *Mardi.* The leading Taparian of the isle of Pimminee. He is married to Ohiro Moldona Fivona, is the father by her of three daughters—A, I, and O—and holds open house for Taji and his friends to show them the well-dressed Taparian aristocracy.

Nina. *Mardi.* Arhinoo's young wife, who when her husband was away moaned that she was a widow, according to Yoomy.

Nippers. "Bartleby." The Wall Street Lawyer's twenty-five-year-old scrivener. He is whiskered, sallow, impatient, possessed of a poor stomach, and—unlike his fellow-worker Turkey—irritable only until noon.

Noble, Charles Arnold; "Charlie." *The Confidence-Man.* The stranger who tells Frank Goodman about the Indian-hater Colonel John Moredock. Noble and Goodman then have a curious talk over some wine about misanthropy and generosity. Mark Winsome calls Noble a Mississippi operator and warns Goodman about him.

Nones, Queen. *Mardi.* Donjalolo's twenty-ninth-night queen.

Nonno. *Mardi.* A sour Taparian guest at Nimni's party on the isle of Pimminee.

Noojoomo. *Mardi.* A Valapee enemy of Bondo, who swears by his teeth to be avenged.

Noomai. *Omoo.* The King of Hannamanoo and a friend of Hardy.

Nord. *White-Jacket.* A tall, thin, upright, aloof after-guardsman. White Jacket becomes friendly with him through their interest in books. Nord is a saturnine hermit aboard the *Neversink* and refuses to be friendly with Williams. When the crew disembarks at Norfolk, Virginia, Nord stalks into the woods alone.

Normo, King. *Mardi.* A king in a story told by Babbalanja. Normo ordered his fool Willi to go to a tree, and Willi had to do so though whether by walking on his feet or on his hands he was free to decide for himself.

Nulli. *Mardi.* The cadaverous, gray-haired, bright-eyed advocate of slavery in southern Vivenza.

O. *Mardi.* One of the three vain daughters of Nimni, on the isle of Pimminee. The others are A and I.

Oberlus. "The Encantadas." A Caliban-like farmer on Hood's Isle who used to sell his potatoes and pumpkins to passing ships. When discomfited in a kidnapping attempt, he grew misanthropic and criminal, later escaped to Payta, Peru, and was finally imprisoned.

O'Brien, Mrs. *Redburn.* A widowed Irish woman who is a passenger, along with her mild triplet sons, aboard the *Highlander* bound for America. Her widowed sister, Mrs. O'Regan, and her wild triplet sons are also aboard.

O'Brien. *Redburn.* One of Mrs. O'Brien's triplet sons.

O'Brien. *Redburn.* One of Mrs. O'Brien's triplet sons.

O'Brien. *Redburn.* One of Mrs. O'Brien's triplet sons.

Ohiro Moldona Fivona. *Mardi.* The wife of Nimni, the leading Taparian on the isle of Pimminee.

Oh Oh. *Mardi.* A hump-backed, large-nosed antiquarian on the isle of Padulla. The manuscripts in his museum intrigue Babbalanja.

Old Bach. "The Paradise of Bachelors and the Tartarus of Maids." See Bach, Old.

Old Coffee. *White-Jacket.* The ship's cook, a dignified Negro who claims to have worked at the New York Astor House. His assistants are Sunshine, Rose-Water, and May-Day.

Old Combustibles. *White-Jacket.* A short, grim, grizzled gunner, with a frightful scar on his left cheek and forehead.

Old Conscience. *The Confidence-Man.* A friend—along with Plain Old Talk and Old Prudence—of China Aster's now deceased father.

Old Gamboge. *Omoo.* A lieutenant aboard the French frigate in the harbor at Papeetee. He is old, bald, and all moustache and stick-thin little legs.

Old Gay-Head Indian. *Moby-Dick.* A member of the *Pequod* crew who explains that Ahab lost his leg off Japan.

Old Hemlock. 'Bridegroom Dick.' See Turret, Captain.

Old Honesty. *The Confidence-Man.* See Aster.

Old Manx Sailor. *Moby-Dick.* See the Manxman.

Old Mother Tot. *Omoo.* A notorious English woman who runs one disreputable house after another all over the South Seas and whose "man" is Josy. When she is ferreted out by Wilson in Tahiti, she spits on him.

Old Plain Talk. *The Confidence-Man.* One of the conservative friends of China Aster who try to talk him out of accepting Orchis's money.

Old Prudence. *The Confidence-Man.* One of the conservative friends of China Aster who try to talk him out of accepting Orchis's money.

Old Revolver. *White-Jacket.* The tiny, bald, bespectacled arms yeoman of the *Neversink.* He fails in his efforts to make White Jacket his subaltern.

Old Rough and Ready. "Authentic Anecdotes of 'Old Zack.' " See Taylor, General Zachary.

Old Thunder. *Moby-Dick.* The name that the mad prophet Elijah gives Captain Ahab (which see).

Old Yarn, "Yarn," "Pipes." *White-Jacket.* The boatswain who is an expert smuggler of liquor. He is once robbed of some brandy but flogs the culprit when the thief is found drunk.

Old Zack. "Authentic Anecdotes of 'Old Zack.' " See Taylor, General Zachary.

Ononna. *Mardi.* A valiant warrior begotten through the efficacy of the marzilla wine treasured by King Donjalolo of the island of Juam.

Oram. *Mardi.* Bardianna's servant, mentioned in the philosopher's will.

Orchis, "Doleful Dumps." *The Confidence-Man.* China Aster's friend who after winning a huge sum of money in a lottery induced China Aster to borrow a thousand fatal dollars from him, then married and demanded repayment.

Orchis, Mrs. *The Confidence-Man.* The wife of Orchis, who after marrying her changed his generous ways and demanded repayment of his loan of a thousand dollars to China Aster.

O'Regan, Mike. *Redburn.* One of the triplet sons of Mrs. O'Regan.

O'Regan, Pat. *Redburn.* One of the triplet sons of Mrs. O'Regan.

O'Regan, Teddy. *Redburn.* One of the triplet sons of Mrs. O'Regan.

O'Regan, Mrs. *Redburn.* A widowed Irish woman who is a passenger, along with her wild triplet sons, Pat, Teddy, and Mike, aboard the *Highlander* bound for America. Her widowed sister, Mrs. O'Brien, and her mild triplet sons are also aboard.

Orlop Bob. 'Bridegroom Dick.' A sailor remembered by Bridegroom Dick.

Orme, Daniel. "Story of Daniel Orme" [first draft and revised text]. A burly, reticent, crucifix-tatooed old sailor, once captain of a maintop crew, who retires to a rooming house ashore and then dies one fine Easter Day on an armed height overlooking the sea.

Osceola, Chief. *White-Jacket.* A Florida Indian against whom a marine now aboard the *Neversink* once fought, he boasts, from daybreak to breakfast.

Otoo. *Omoo.* The original name of Pomaree [I] (which see).

Ottimo, Prince. *Mardi.* A foolishly fame-thirsty man, in one of Mohi's stories.

Ozonna. *Mardi.* A young lover in Mohi's story who sought his lost Ady in Queen Hautia's court and thought he found her, but she turned out to be Rea. Ozonna's fate parallels that of Taji with his lost Yillah.

Paivai. *Mardi.* A Taparian on the isle of Pimminee who ignored his family tree and put faith only in his tailor.

Palaverer, Mr. *The Confidence-Man.* See the Happy Man.

Palmer. "The Encantadas." A palmer who observes the island monsters.

Palmer, The. *Clarel.* A pilgrim who in a song read by Clarel in Abdon's hotel tells of roaming over Judaea.

Pani. *Mardi.* The blind, white-bearded, materialistic guide on the island of Maramma. He publicly warns pilgrims who try to ascend the peak of Ofo without his aid, but he privately admits doubts as to his own ability.

Pansy. 'The Scout toward Aldie.' Evidently a dead Confederate soldier who wrote a song beginning "Spring is come; she shows her pass" and whose friend Archy, a soldier under Mosby, sings it when he is captured by the Colonel's men during his ill-fated pursuit of Mosby.

Paola [Paolo] of Verona. 'Marquis de Grandvin: At the Hostelry.' See [Veronese], Paola [Paolo].

Paper Jack. *Omoo*. See Guy, Captain.

Paper Jack. *White-Jacket*. A general term for an incompetent commander.

Paraita. *Omoo*. One of the four recreant chiefs whom the French governor Bruat puts in charge of the four sections into which he divides Tahiti. The others are Kitoti, Tati, and Utamai.

Parker, Captain. *Israel Potter*. The fictitious name used by the captain of the British frigate during its attack by John Paul Jones's *Ariel*.

Parki. *Mardi*. A tall, good-looking Hawaiian chief after whom the *Parki* was named.

Parkins. *Redburn*. The part-owner of Parkins & Wood warehouse in Liverpool, where Betsy Jennings and her three children starve to death.

Parsee, The. *Moby-Dick*. See Fedallah.

Parsee, The. 'The Rose Farmer.' The Persian's thin neighbor, who chops roses to make attar.

[Pasha], Ibrahim. *Clarel*. See Ibrahim, [Pasha].

Pat. *Omoo*. An Irish-born sailor, sixteen years old, aboard the *Julia*. He signs the round robin and is befriended by Irish-born Father Murphy in the Calabooza.

Pat. *Redburn*. An Irish fisherman who cleverly steals fifteen fathoms of rope from the *Highlander* when she is off the coast of Ireland.

Pat. *Redburn*. An Irish steerage passenger aboard the *Highlander*. He is punished for stealing food by being forced to wear a wooden tub.

Patella, Dr. *White-Jacket*. The *Algerine* surgeon, who with others confers with Dr. Cuticle, when that expert operates on the fatally wounded foretopman.

Patriarch, The. *Clarel*. The [Greek] patriarch who by letter authorizes the entrance of visitors into Mar Saba.

Patterson, General John. *Israel Potter*. As Colonel Patterson, the commanding officer of the Lenox regiment in which Israel Potter enrolls in 1774.

Paul. *Omoo*. The name given the narrator (also called Typee, which see) by Long Ghost, who calls himself Peter, when the two work for Zeke and Shorty, and also during their subsequent wandering toward and about Taloo.

Paul Pry. 'To Ned.' A general name for the modern maritime materialist.

Paulet, Lord George. *Typee*. A responsible British authority in Hawaii in 1843.

Pazzi, Madame. "The Apple-Tree Table." A celebrated conjuress whom Julia and Anna wish to consult for an explanation of the emergence of bugs from the table.

Pearson, Captain [Richard]. *Israel Potter*. The commander of the British *Serapis* whose surrender to Captain John Paul Jones's *Bon Homme Richard* is honorable under all the circumstances.

Pedro II, Don. *White-Jacket*. The young Brazilian emperor, who condescends to visit the *Neversink* when she is anchored off Rio de Janeiro. He is the grandson of King John I of Portugal and the brother of Maria, now queen of Portugal.

Pedro, Don. *Moby-Dick*. A Spanish friend of Ishmael's who with Don Sebastian heard Ishmael tell at the Golden Inn, Lima, Peru, the story of Steelkilt and Radney of the *Town-Ho*.

Peenee. *Mardi*. One of the twelve aristocratic Taparian families on the isle of Pimminee, entertained by Nimni.

Peepi, King. *Mardi*. The ten-year-old king of Valapee, who has inherited the diverse spiritual qualities of sundry intestate dead.

Peggy. *Redburn*. One of the waitresses at the Baltimore Clipper, managed by Handsome Mary Danby in Liverpool.

Peleg, Captain. *Moby-Dick*. Formerly the chief mate (under Captain Ahab) of the *Pequod* and now one of her principal owners. Like Captain Bildad, another part-owner, he is a Quaker. After interviewing Ishmael blusteringly, Peleg signs him aboard and then argues with stingy Bildad as to Ishmael's pay.

Pelican, The. *White-Jacket*. The thin, knock-kneed, sour-looking assistant surgeon, who once examines White Jacket and oddly asks him if he is pious. His nickname is owing to his chop-fallen expression.

[Pellico?] , Silvio. 'Pausilippo.' See Silvio.

Pence, Peter. *Pierre.* A book designer who obsequiously offers his services to Pierre, for cash.

Pendiddi. *Mardi.* A neighbor of Bardianna, mentioned in the philosopher's will.

Pennie, Miss. *Pierre.* A deaf, pious, benevolent, gossipy spinster friend of Mrs. Mary Glendinning.

Pennie, Miss. *Pierre.* Another deaf, pious, beneficent, gossipy spinster friend of Mrs. Mary Glendinning.

Peri, A. 'Marquis de Grandvin: Naples in the Time of Bomba.' A girl in Naples who lightly pins a red rose to the poet's lapel, receives a tip, dances off, and is gone.

Pericles. 'The Parthenon.' The Athenian statesman, whose mistress was Aspasia.

Pericles. 'Syra.' A Syra innkeeper who sells wine.

Perkins, Peter. *Israel Potter.* The pseudonym which Israel Potter (which see) uses to avoid detection aboard the British frigate which he rashly boards during an abortive attack on her by Captain John Paul Jones of the *Ariel.*

Perry, [Captain Matthew C. or Captain Oliver H.]. 'Bridegroom Dick.' A famous naval officer with whom Ap Catesby served.

Persian, The. 'The Rose Farmer.' A prosperous rose farmer who advises the poet to treasure his sequence of evanescent roses rather than distill them into attar.

Pert, "Milk-and-Water." *White-Jacket.* A midshipman who runs errands aboard the *Neversink.* He is disliked by the sailors, and his cockiness earns him a rebuke from the Professor in class.

Perth. *Moby-Dick.* The limping, bearded blacksmith of the *Pequod,* who was driven when about sixty years of age to sea by liquor and the wretched deaths of his long-suffering wife and three children. He forges a special harpoon with which Ahab hopes to kill Moby Dick.

Perth, Mrs. *Moby-Dick*. The blacksmith's long-suffering wife, who died before old Perth went to sea.

Perth. *Moby-Dick*. One of the blacksmith's children, who died.

Perth. *Moby-Dick*. One of the blacksmith's children, who died.

Perth. *Moby-Dick*. One of the blacksmith's children, who died.

Pesti. *Mardi*. A woman whose love for Bardianna was unrequited. The philosopher mentions her unflatteringly in his will.

Peter. *Omoo*. The name adopted by Long Ghost (which see), who calls the narrator Paul, when the two work for Zeke and Shorty, and also during their wandering toward and about Taloo.

Peter. *White-Jacket*. A handsome mizzen-top lad about nineteen years of age who is involved with Mark and Antone in a fight started by John. When flogged by order of Claret, Peter cries and loses all spirit.

Peter Paul, Sir. 'Marquis de Grandvin: At the Hostelry.' See [Rubens], Sir Peter Paul.

Peter the Wild Boy. *White-Jacket*. A young Down Easter with thick, inflexible yellow hair.

Phil. *Israel Potter*. One of Israel Potter's drunken guards during his first unsuccessful escape attempt between Spithead and London.

Phil. 'Bridegroom Dick.' A flaxen-haired sailor remembered by Bridegroom Dick.

Philanthropos. *The Confidence-Man*. A nickname which Francis Goodman (which see) gives himself when he is talking with William Cream.

Phillis. 'Marquis de Grandvin: At the Hostelry.' A kitchen maid described by Douw as picturesquely plucking a pheasant.

Philo. *Mardi*. A philanthropist in a manuscript memoir in Oh Oh's museum.

Philosophical Intelligence Office man, The; "Praise-God-Barebones." *The Confidence-Man*. The stooped little man in a cheap suit and with a brass plate saying P.I.O. suspended from his neck. He reasons Pitch out of his misanthropy against boy workers and for three dollars agrees to send him a splendidly industrious boy in two weeks.

Phipora. *Mardi*. An ancestor of King Abrazza, according to Mohi.

Phocian. 'Timoleon.' An Athenian general mentioned.

Pierre. *White-Jacket*. The "chummy" of mortally sick Shenly. He affectionately adjusted the corpse's clothing before the burial at sea.

Pierre. *Pierre*. See Glendinning, Pierre.

Piko, King. *Mardi*. The convivial ruler with King Hello of the island of Diranda. The two reduce their exploding population by holding war games on the Field of Glory.

Pillgarlic. *Redburn*. See Redburn, Wellingborough.

Pills. *White-Jacket*. Dr. Cuticle's pale, hollow-eyed, cadaverous young steward, who assists at the amputation operation performed on the fatally wounded topman and who later occasionally dispenses some vile-tasting medicines to White Jacket.

Pip (also Pippin). *Moby-Dick*. A little Alabama Negro boy who is a castaway during a chase for a whale and goes insane, after which Ahab befriends him touchingly.

Pipes. *White-Jacket*. Another name for Old Yarn (which see), the whistling boatswain.

Pippin. *Moby-Dick*. See Pip.

Pitch, "Coonskins." *The Confidence-Man*. The bear's-skin-jacketed Missouri backwoodsman bachelor who has no confidence in nature and therefore none in the herb doctor's nostrums. Pitch succumbs, however, to the analogical reasoning of the Philosophical Intelligence Office man and instead of wanting any longer to invest in machines to replace boy workers pays him three dollars to have an industrious boy—his thirtieth—sent him.

[Pius IX], Pope. 'Marquis de Grandvin: At the Hostelry.' See Pope [Pius IX].

Placido, Brother. *Clarel*. A funeral friar from Mexico with whom Don Hannibal Rohon Del Aquaviva stays while he is in Bethlehem.

Plato. 'Timoleon.' Mentioned as influencing the times while Timoleon is still in Corinth.

Platoff the Hetman. "Poor Man's Pudding and Rich Man's

Crumbs." A Cossack guest at the Guildhall Banquet in London following the Battle of Waterloo.

Palaverer, Mr. *The Confidence-Man*. The sacrcastic name by which Pitch addresses the herb doctor, who calls himself "The Happy Man" (which see).

Plinlimmon, Plotinus. *Pierre*. The mystical author of the pamphlet "Chronometricals and Horologicals," which Pierre finds and reads in the coach taking him forever away from Saddle Meadows. Charlie Millthorpe points out Plotinus Plinlimmon to Pierre in the city as the Grand Master of the Apostles. He is a combination of Apollo and Saturn, and is cheerful yet non-benevolent and inscrutable.

Poky. *Omoo*. A Tahitian native man who adopts the narrator as his friend, finds shells for him, introduces him about, and is more loyal to him than his other native friend, Kooloo.

Pollo. *Mardi*. A supercilious prosodist reader of Lombardo's *Koztanza* who suggest improvements in it, according to Babbalanja.

Pomare, Queen. *Typee*. The queen of Tahiti who is forced to flee from Papeetee to Emio by canoe to escape Admiral Du Petit Thouars's attack.

Pomaree [I], "Otoo." *Omoo*. Mentioned as the ruler of Tahiti during the time of Captain Cook. Pomaree changed his name from Otoo, after which the royal patronymic has been Pomaree.

Pomaree II. *Omoo*. Pomaree I's famous but debauched son and king of Tahiti. He died in 1821.

Pomaree III. *Omoo*. Pomaree II's son who became king of Tahiti, died in 1827, and passed the crown to his oldest sister, Aimata, the present queen, who is called Pomaree Vahinee I (which see).

Pomaree Vahinee I, Queen; "Aimata." *Omoo*. The present queen of Tahiti and ruler of the Society Islands as well. She is over thirty years of age, looks forty, and has been married twice, first to Pot Belly, a son of the King of Tahar, and then to henpecked but occasionally rebellious Tanee of Imeeo. The narrator and Long Ghost try without success to obtain an audience with her in order to be appointed officers in her navy.

Pomaree. *Omoo*. The child of Queen Pomaree Vahinee I. It is carried about by Marbonna.

Pomaree. *Omoo*. The child of Queen Pomaree Vahinee I. It is carried about by Marbonna.

Pomaree-Tanee. *Omoo*. See Tanee.

Ponce. "Benito Cereno." The Spanish servant of Don Joaquin, Marques de Aramboalaza.

Pondo. *Mardi*. A materialistic friend of Bardianna. The philosopher leaves Pondo nothing in his will.

Poofai. *Omoo*. A descendant of the kings of Taiarboo who is bold and able, and who hates the missionaries and opposes Queen Pomaree Vahinee I.

Pope, [General John]. 'The Victor of Antietam.' The Union general whose failures McClellan must rectify. 'Lee in the Capitol.' A Union general remembered by Lee as once retreating from the Capitol. Lee is now going after the Civil War to the Senate to testify.

Pope [Pius IX]. 'Marquis de Grandvin: At the Hostelry.' Mentioned as nominally supported by Garibaldi.

Pope, The. 'The New Ancient of Days: The Man of the Cave of Engihoul.' The Pontiff, urged to beat down the new ancient.

Popinjay-of-the-world. *The Confidence-Man*. The name by which Pitch first addresses Frank Goodman (which see).

Po-Po, Deacon Ereemear; "Narmo-Nana Po-Po" ("The Darer-of-Devils-in-the-Dark"), "Jeremiah," "Jeremiah-in-the-Dark." *Omoo*. The Partoowye host of the narrator and Long Ghost. Po-Po is a kind, Christianized native, the husband of Arfretee, the father of Loo and a dandified son and also twins, and the employer of Monee.

Porter, [Commander David D.]. 'Running the Batteries.' The Union commander of a fleet of gunboats and supply barges which run past the Confederate batteries at Vicksburg.

Porter, Captain David [T.]. "The Encantadas." The commander of the *Essex*, which during the War of 1812 touched at the

Enchanted Isles and unsuccessfully pursued an elusive enemy "flyaway" ship in their waters in 1813. His *Voyages into the Pacific* is one of Melville's authorities for some of these sketches. 'Running the Batteries.' Alluded to as the [Admiral] father of [Commander David T.] Porter, the Union commander of a fleet which runs the Vicksburg batteries. 'Bridegroom Dick.' A famous naval officer with whom Ap Catesby [Jones] served.

Portuguese Sailor. *Moby-Dick.* A *Pequod* sailor who interrupts his mates' dancing during the midnight festivities in the forecastle by reporting the advent of a storm.

Pot Belly. *Omoo.* The native nickname of the first husband of Queen Pomaree Vahinee I, who divorced him in spite of his being a son of the King of Tahar.

Potter, Israel; "Yellow-hair," "Yellow-mane," "Peter Perkins," "Rowser," "Snowser," "Towser." *Israel Potter.* A Berkshire farm boy who runs away from home at the age of eighteen when his love for Jenny is unrequited, goes to sea, is wounded and captured at Bunker Hill, escapes in London, becomes a courier for Dr. Franklin in Paris, joins Captain John Paul Jones on the *Ranger* and the *Bon Homme Richard* and the *Ariel*, boards a British frigate at sea during an abortive naval engagement, endures a forty-five-year exile in and near London, and finally returns to the Berkshires to die.

Potter, Mrs. Israel. *Israel Potter.* A bakery-shop girl who befriends Israel Potter when he is run over and whom he marries. They have eleven children, only one of whom lives to maturity. Mrs. Potter dies in England before Israel Potter's return to America.

Potter. *Israel Potter.* Israel Potter's farmer father, who successfully but tragically opposes his son's love affair with Jenny.

Potter, Mrs. *Israel Potter.* Israel Potter's farm-wife mother.

Potter. *Israel Potter.* The one surviving child of Israel Potter and his wife. The boy repeatedly reports his father's sad story and ultimately accompanies the old man to America.

Pounce. *White-Jacket.* With Leggs, one of the two ship's corporals under Bland. Pounce, formerly a Liverpool policeman, ferrets out illicit gamblers aboard the *Neversink*.

Poussin, [Nicolas]. 'Marquis de Grandvin: At the Hostelry.' A painter described as having an antique air about him.

Praise-God-Barebones. *The Confidence-Man*. The nickname assigned by Pitch to the Philosophical Intelligence Office man (which see).

Priming. *White-Jacket*. A nasal-voiced, hare-lipped gunner's mate, who belongs to Jack Chase's mess but does not share its tolerant philosophy. Because of his bile and superstition, he calls White Jacket a Jonah—the thirteenth in their mess— and blames him for Baldy's accident, the amputated foretopman's death, and Shenly's mortal sickness.

Primo, Lord. *Mardi*. A typical feudal lord in Dominora for whom hungry farmers toil.

Prince—. 'Rammon.' Mentioned as having wonderful philosophical conceptions.

Prince of Golconda, The. "The Marquis de Grandvin." An extravagant pseudonym for the Marquis de Grandvin (which see).

Pritchard. *Typee*. The famous British missionary consul at Papeete, Tahiti. His wife refuses to be intimidated by the French under Admiral Du Petit Thouars. *Omoo*. While absent in England, he leaves Wilson in his place.

Pritchard, Mrs. *Typee*. The brave wife of the British missionary consul at Papeete, Tahiti. She defends her flag when the French under Admiral Du Petit Thouars want to take it down.

Prodigal, The. *Clarel*. See the Lyonese.

Professor, The. *White-Jacket*. An erudite, gentlemanly, forty-year-old non-combatant aboard the *Neversink* who instructs the midshipman every other afternoon in mathematics, navigation, ballistics, and naval tactics. He rebukes Pert, Dash, Slim, and Boat Plug. This tall, thin pedant was once a West Point cadet but became disqualified because of weak eyes.

Punchinello. 'Marquis de Grandvin: Naples in the Time of Bomba.' A member of the gay Neapolitan crowd.

Purser, Mr. "Billy Budd." Captain Vere's purser, who tells the ship's surgeon that he was surprised to note no death spasm when Billy was hanged.

Putnam, [General Israel]. *Israel Potter.* The commanding officer of the rebellious American soldiers at Bunker Hill.

Queequeg. *Moby-Dick.* Ishmael's bosom friend, a tatooed Polynesian prince whose father was king of the island of Kokovoko. Queequeg becomes Starbuck's harpooneer, rescues Tashtego from a sinking whale head, becomes sick after working for a long while in the damp hold, orders the carpenter to build him a coffin, recovers, and uses the coffin for a sea chest. After the *Pequod* sinks, the coffin saves Ishmael's life. Peleg calls Queequeg Quohog.

Queen of Sheba, The. 'Rammon.' See Sheba, the Princess of.

Quiddi. *Mardi.* An improvisator, cited by Babbalanja.

[Quixote, Don]. 'The Rusty Man.' Sardonically praised for his outmoded chivalry.

Quohog. *Moby-Dick.* Peleg's mispronunciation of the name Queequeg (which see).

Quoin. *White-Jacket.* A bitter, whimsical old quarter-gunner whom Lemsford erroneously suspects of destroying his poems.

Rabbi, The; "Rabboni." *Clarel.* A Rabbi who visits Nathan, Agar, and Ruth, and gazes coldly on Clarel, brought by Nememiah.

Rabboni. *Clarel.* Agar's nickname for the Rabbi (which see).

Rabeelee. *Mardi.* A laughing philosopher cited by Babbalanja in a rare mood of humor.

Radney, "Rad." *Moby-Dick.* The ugly Vineyarder mate of the *Town-Ho*, who offended Steelkilt, one of his men, threatened him with a hammer, and had his jaw crushed for his pains by Steelkilt, whom he then tied and flogged. Steelkilt would have murdered him but for the appearance of Moby Dick, which both men chased and which savagely killed Radney.

Radney, Mrs. *Moby-Dick*. The wife of the *Town-Ho* mate. She dreams in Nantucket of the white whale which killed her husband.

Rammon, Prince. 'Rammon.' Identified as an unrobust, precocious, isolated son of Solomon's old age. Rammon is concerned with the doctrine of immortality, does not want eternal life, and is rendered uneasy when he studies Buddha.

Raneds. "Benito Cereno." Cereno's *San Dominick* mate, a good navigator, who was senselessly killed by the rebellious slaves for making a suspicious gesture with his quadrant.

Rani, Prince. *Mardi*. A Juam prince who refused to become king because he would also have had to give up roving.

Raphael [Sanzio]. 'Marquis de Grandvin: At the Hostelry.' Mentioned in a headnote as concerned because of Durer's melancholy.

Rartoo. *Omoo*. An old chief in whose house the narrator and Long Ghost stay overnight while passing through Tamai.

Rash, Captain. *White-Jacket*. An imaginary captain, typical of those who rashly try to round treacherous Cape Horn under too much sail.

Ratcliffe, Lieutenant. "Billy Budd." The *Bellipotent* officer who boards the *Rights-of-Man* and chooses Billy to impress.

Raveling. *White-Jacket*. Any stingy sailor who refuses to give a mate even a needleful of thread.

Ravoo. *Mardi*. Hivohitee's fleet-footed messenger on the isle of Maramma.

Raymonda. *Mardi*. A dead subject whose simplicity King Peepi has inherited.

Rea. *Mardi*. A maiden in Queen Hautia's court on the isle of Flozella a Nina who, according to Mohi's story, resembles the lost Ady, whom Ady's lover Ozonna vainly seeks. Mohi tells the story to dissuade Taji from continuing his search for his lost Yillah.

Reb. 'The Scout toward Aldie.' A Confederate prisoner of the Colonel's men, who offer him a drink.

Redburn, Jane. *Redburn.* One of Wellingborough Redburn's three sisters.

Redburn, Martha. *Redburn.* One of Wellingborough Redburns's three sisters.

Redburn, Mary. *Redburn.* One of Wellingborough Redburn's three sisters.

Redburn, Walter. *Redburn.* Wellingborough Redburn's father, now a deceased bankrupt. Before his financial reverses, he was an importer on Broad Street, in New York, and used to cross the Atlantic Ocean frequently. Redburn finds that his father's guidebook to Liverpool, purchased during the man's 1808 business and pleasure trip to that city, does not help the son.

Redburn, Mrs. Walter. *Redburn.* Wellingborough Redburn's affectionate mother.

Redburn, Wellingborough; "Pillgarlic," "Buttons," "Jimmy Dux," "Boots," "Jack." *Redburn.* The young man who leaves his home near the Hudson River, 180 miles north of New York, to ship aboard the *Highlander,* commanded by Captain Riga and bound for Liverpool, where he sees slum misery, meets Harry Bolton, and after a brief nocturnal visit with that friend to London sails home again, much matured by his first voyage.

Redburn. *Redburn.* Wellingborough Redburn's brother, eight years older than the sailor. He gives his younger brother a letter to a friend named Jones which aids in his finding a berth on Captain Riga's *Highlander.*

Redburn. *Redburn.* Wellingborough Redburn's infant brother.

Red Hot Coal. *White-Jacket.* Mentioned in an anecdote as a murderous Indian on the Mississippi River who collected scalps. His killing of Yellow Torch is compared to the naval habit of collecting enemy ships. Ben Browns painted hands on Red Hot Coal's blanket as symbols of victories.

Red Pepper. "Billy Budd." A red-haired forecastle mate of Billy's to whom Billy reports that the suspicious-acting after-guardsman was skulking about their area.

Red Shirt, The. 'Marquis de Grandvin: Naples in the Time of Bomba.' See Garibaldi.

Red Whiskers. "Billy Budd." A *Bellipotent* sailor whose insulting horseplay with Billy results in Billy's thoroughly beating him up. He and Billy later become good friends.

Rehoboam, King. 'Rammon.' Solomon's arrogant, disdainful, ignorant son and successor, depicted as Rammon's half-brother during whose reign troubles and disruption occur.

Reine. *Omoo.* A French assistant with Carpegna to Bruat, the governor of Tahiti.

Rembrandt (also Rembrant) [Harmens Van Rijn]. 'Marquis de Grandvin: At the Hostelry.' A painter of sooty canvases mentioned by Dolci.

Reyter, [Admiral] De. 'Marquis do Grandvin: At the Hostelry.' A sea captain under whom Van der Velde once sailed.

R. F. C. "The Paradise of Bachelors and the Tartarus of Maids." See C., R. F.

Rhyming Ned. 'Bridegroom Dick.' A sailor remembered by Bridegroom Dick.

Ribera, Giuseppe [Lo Spagnoletto]. 'Marquis de Grandvin: At the Hostelry.' See Spagnoletto.

Ridendiabola. *Mardi.* A fabulist, cited by Babbalanja.

Riga, Captain. *Redburn.* The vicious, hypocritical, Russian-born *Highlander* captain. He is a bachelor and treats Redburn abusively during and at the end of the boy's first voyage.

Rigadoon Joe. 'Bridegroom Dick.' A sailor remembered by Bridegroom Dick.

Rigs. *Redburn.* The second mate aboard the *Highlander.*

Ringbolt. *White-Jacket.* A sailor who urges Jonathan to stop shouting insults at Don Pedro II, King of Brazil, because of fear that all the main-royal-yard men will be punished.

Ringman, Goneril. *The Confidence-Man.* See Goneril.

Ringman, John. *The Confidence-Man.* The man with the weed, said by Black Guinea to be one of his character references. Ringman reminds Henry Roberts that they once met, blandly begs a bank note from him, and momentarily tempts him to buy some Black Rapids Coal Company stock. Later Ringman startles a young scholar by lecturing against Tacitus for his cynicism and destruction of one's confidence in others. Roberts tells John Truman the story of Ringman's wife Goneril.

Ringrope. *White-Jacket.* An old sailor who as sailmaker helps Thrummings encase Shenly's body in canvas for burial at sea. Ringrope argues unsuccessfully in favor of taking the last stitch through the corpse's nose.

Rob. 'Stockings in the Farm-House Chimney.' Depicted as waiting for Santa Claus.

Roberts, Henry. *The Confidence-Man.* A forwarding merchant from Wheeling, Pennsylvania, whose lack of memory of him John Ringman gently attributes to brain fever. Ringman begs a bank note from Roberts and momentarily tempts him to buy some Black Rapids Coal Company stock.

Robins. *Omoo* Apparently a London auctioneer, mentioned by the narrator when he discusses Stubbs, a Sydney real-estate auctioneer.

Robles, Juan. "Benito Cereno." Cereno's *San Dominick* boatswain, who after being severely wounded is thrown overboard with others by the rebelling slaves. He swims longest, makes the act of contrition in the water, and then drowns.

Roddi. *Mardi.* A reader of Lombardo's *Koztanza* who suggested that the work be burned, according to Babbalanja.

Rodney, [George Brydges Rodney, Baron, Admiral]. "Billy Budd." The British naval officer under whom Vere gallantly served in the West Indies as flag lieutenant, during which cruise Rodney defeated De Grasse. Vere was then promoted to post captain.

Roe. *Mardi.* One of the twelve aristocratic Taparian families on the isle of Pimminee, entertained by Nimni.

Rohon, Don Hannibal, De Aquaviva. *Clarel.* See Hannibal, Rohon Del Aquaviva, Don.

Roi Mori. *Mardi.* Dead Karhownoo's deaf, bereaved father.

Rolfe. *Clarel.* A well-traveled American sailor and brilliant humanist. He mediates between the extremes of the other pilgrims, is gracious, kind, slightly skeptical, and honest. At one point, he refers to himself as "the Dead Man" (which see).

Rondo the Round, King. *Mardi.* An ancient monarch who, according to Mohi, wanted his coffin lid to be of amber but had to settle for crystal.

Roo. *Mardi.* A rich old Taparian widow who attends Nimni's party on the isle of Pimminee.

Roonoonoo. *Mardi.* A rebel on the island of Juam whom King Marjora defeated and executed at Willamilla.

Ropey. *Omoo.* See Rope Yarn.

Rope Yarn, "Ropey." *Omoo.* A landlubber, anywhere between twenty-five and forty years of age, aboard the *Julia.* He is a former London apprentice baker who has left a selfish wife in Australia. He dies at Papeetee and is buried on the beach.

Rosa, Salvator. 'Marquis de Grandvin: At the Hostelry.' A painter described as proud and satirical. 'Marquis de Grandvin: Naples in the Time of Bomba.' Mentioned as linked with patriotic Neapolitan brigands.

Rosamond, "Rose," "Moss-Rose." 'Amoroso.' The poet's blooming love.

Roscoe, [William]. *Redburn.* The eminent historian, poet, and banker, with whom Redburn's father dined in Liverpool back in 1808.

Rose, 'Amoroso.' See Rosamond.

Rose, James; "Jimmy." "Jimmy Rose." A gracious merchant of New York who after sudden financial ruin disappears for twenty-five years, then reappears at the age of sixty-five to take tea and toast at the opulent homes of former friends. He retains the roses in his cheeks and his fine aristocratic manners.

Rosecrans, [General William S.]. 'Battle of Stone River,

Tennessee.' The Union officer whose men defeated the Confederate forces at Stone River, Tennessee.

Rose-Water. *White-Jacket.* A Negro assistant of Old Coffee, the ship's cook. Rose-Water has elegant reading tastes, once butts heads with May-Day, and is flogged for it by Captain Claret.

Rotato. *Mardi.* A sagacious, fat Mardian philosopher, mentioned by Mohi.

Rovenna, Don. *Clarel.* A friend from Seville, mentioned with a sigh by the Lyonese.

Rowland. *Pierre.* A manufacturer, with his son, of a beard-growing product, which fails to produce results for young Pierre.

Rowser. *Israel Potter.* A sailor's name invented by Israel Potter (which see) for himself when he alone boards the British frigate from the *Ariel.*

Roy, Jack. 'Jack Roy.' Praised as the captain of the maintop of the *Splendid.* He is gentlemanly, gallant, heroic, and fun-loving.

Rozas, Doctor Juan Martinez de. "Benito Cereno." The royal councilor of Lima who orders Captain Benito Cereno to testify concerning the slave revolt aboard his ship the *San Dominick.*

Ruaruga. *Typee.* Marheyo's next-door neighbor.

[Rubens], Sir Peter Paul. 'Marquis de Grandvin: At the Hostelry.' A painter who prefers to paint Venus and swans rather than kitchen maids.

Russ, The. *Clarel.* See the Russian.

Russian, The. *Clarel.* A Russian pilgrim who temporarily leaves his Greek party to chat with Clarel at David's Well outside Bethlehem.

Ruth. *Clarel.* The innocent, beautiful, considerate daughter of Nathan and Agar. Ruth falls in love with Clarel, but after her father's murder by hostile Arabs she and her mother die of grief while Clarel is on his pilgrimage.

St. Jago's Sailor. *Moby-Dick*. A *Pequod* sailor who opines that the Spanish sailor is insane to pick a fight with Daggoo during the midnight festivities in the forecastle.

Salem. *Omoo*. A knife-wielding beachcomber sailor aboard the *Julia*. He fights Bembo and signs the round robin.

Sally. *Redburn*. The Liverpool wife of Max the Dutchman, who has a wife named Meg in New York.

Salvaterra, "the Tuscan." *Clarel*. A Franciscan from Tuscany who acts as a guide at the Latin Church of the Star of Bethlehem. He is fervid and ascetic.

Sambo. "Authentic Anecdotes of 'Old Zack.'" General Taylor's confidential Negro servant, who, when an enemy shot bounces a hot pie on the General's head, says that his boss is now armed "cap a pie." Rumor has it that Sambo is selling personal items of the General's to Peter Tamerlane B—m [that is, P. T. Barnum (which see)].

Samoa. *Mardi*. The one-armed Upoluan native whom the narrator finds aboard the *Parki*. Samoa is Annatoo's husband and accompanies Taji on his voyages through the island of Mardi as far as King Borabolla's island of Mondoldo. Later Taji learns that Samoa has been killed by arrows, probably shot by Aleema's sons.

Sampson. *Redburn*. A partner in Sampson & Wilt, Liverpool, on whom Redburn's father called back in 1808.

Santa Anna, General Antonio Lopez de. "Authentic Anecdotes of 'Old Zack.'" The recipient of a sarcastic letter from General Zachary Taylor telling him to eat cannon balls like a man or cry "Enough" now. P. T. Barnum writes that he is trying to buy Santa Anna for his Museum. 'Bridegroom Dick.' The Mexican general remembered by Bridegroom Dick from old Vera Cruz days. "To Major John Gentian, Dean of the Burgundy Club." Mentioned as opposed by General Will Worth.

Sarpedon. 'A Dirge for McPherson.' See McPherson, [General James B.].

Saturnina. *Mardi*. A tall chief in the Temple of Freedom of

Vivenza, notable for his grand forehead, calm brow, and deep eyes.

Saveda, Miguel. *Redburn.* The new crew member who is brought aboard the *Highlander* drunk, dies shortly thereafter, and begins to exude flames.

Sawyer, Dr. *White-Jacket.* The *Buccaneer* surgeon, who with others confers with Dr. Cuticle when that expert operates on the fatally wounded foretopman.

Scott, [General Winfield]. 'Bridegroom Dick.' An American general remembered by Bridegroom Dick from old Vera Cruz days.

Scribe, Hiram. "I and My Chimney." A surveyor-architect hired by the narrator's wife to try to persuade the narrator to let him tear down the chimney. The narrator sends him away with a bribe.

Scriggs. *White-Jacket.* A gallows-gaited, squint-eyed old marine who cooks for the mess of the sergeant-at-arms Bland and who sells liquor smuggled aboard by Bland until their scheme is revealed by a customer when he is caught and flogged for drunkenness.

Scrimmage. *White-Jacket.* A sheet-anchor man who argues with Bungs about buoys.

Seafull. *White-Jacket.* The forecastleman who plays the part of the Mayor in the Fourth of July theatrical.

Sebastian, Don. *Moby-Dick.* A Spanish friend of Ishmael's who with Don Pedro heard Ishmael tell at the Golden Inn, Lima, Peru, the story of Steelkilt and Radney of the *Town-Ho.*

Second Nantucket Sailor. *Moby-Dick.* A *Pequod* sailor who participates in the midnight festivities in the forecastle.

Seignioroni, Seignior. *White-Jacket.* Mentioned by Dr. Cuticle as a surgeon of Seville who has recently invented a caliper-like substitute for the tourniquet.

Selkirk, The Countess of. *Israel Potter.* The lovely wife of the Earl of Selkirk, whose seat at St. Mary's Isle John Paul Jones raids in the hope of taking Selkirk hostage.

Selkirk, The Earl of. *Israel Potter.* A privy counsellor and friend of King George III. John Paul Jones wants to take Selkirk as a hostage, but he is in Edinburgh when Jones raids his seat at St. Mary's Isle.

Selvagee, Lieutenant. *White-Jacket.* A dainty, languid quarter-deck officer who never should have gone to sea. He is contrasted with Lieutenant Mad Jack.

Senior, The. 'The Scout toward Aldie.' See the Major.

Sereno, Don. *White-Jacket.* The captain of the Peruvian sloop of war aboard which Jack Chase bravely serves until he is arrested by Lieutenant Blink and returned to the *Neversink*, on orders from Captain Claret.

Sergeant. *Pierre.* See Dates.

Sergeant. 'The Scout toward Aldie.' A soldier under the Colonel, who vainly commands a group of men in pursuit of Mosby.

Shakings. *White-Jacket.* A former convict at Sing-Sing and now a forehold sailor who calls the *Neversink* a state prison afloat.

Shanks. *White-Jacket.* A long, thin, pale sailor assigned as permanent cook of Mess No. 1, presided over by Jack Chase.

Sharp-Eyes. 'A Dutch Christmas . . .' A child who looks for Santa Claus.

Shaz Gold-beak. "Under the Rose." See Gold-beak.

Sheba, The Princess of. 'Rammon.' A learned and well-traveled Indian dame, who, it is said, brings Buddhistic beliefs to Solomon's Palestine.

Shelley, [Percy Bysshe]. 'Shelley's Vision.' One who learns self-reverence.

Shenly. *White-Jacket.* White Jacket's sick messmate, a topman from Portsmouth, New Hampshire, who lamentably dies of a pulmonary complaint and general prostration aboard the *Neversink* and is buried at sea.

Shenly, Mrs. *White-Jacket.* The wife, in Portsmouth, New Hampshire, of White Jacket's messmate Shenly, who lamentably dies aboard the *Neversink* and is buried at sea.

Shenly. *White-Jacket.* One of Shenly's two children.

Shenly. *White-Jacket.* One of Shenly's two children.

Shepherd, Daniel. 'Epistle to Daniel Shepherd.' A Wall Street friend whom the poet invites to his country home for an Arcadian holiday.

Sheridan, [General] Philip [H.]. 'Sheridan at Cedar Creek.' The Union general whose timely arrival at Cedar Creek forces the belated retreat of Confederate [General Jubal A.] Early.

Sherman, [General William T.]. 'The March to the Sea.' The Union general who leads the glorious, glad, havoc-wreaking march to the sea. 'On Sherman's Men.' The Union general whose men fell attacking Kenesaw Mountain. 'Lee in the Capitol.' The Union general remembered by Lee as victorious in Washington at the close of the Civil War. Lee is now going to the Senate to testify. 'Iris (1865).' Mentioned along with his march.

Shippy. *White-Jacket.* A pale lad whom Happy-Jack Landless advises to salute officers, endure floggings silently, and drink grog.

Shirrer, Rev. Mr. *Israel Potter.* The Scottish minister of Kirkaldy who, according to popular belief, interceded to evoke a squall which prevented John Paul Jones from attacking the city.

Shorty, "The Cockney." *Omoo.* The short Cockney partner of Zeke the Yankee in a farming venture at Martair. They employ Peter and Paul—that is, Long Ghost and the narrator.

Sicilian Sailor. *Moby-Dick.* A *Pequod* sailor who dances during the midnight festivities in the forecastle and then lies down. He tries to warn Ahab when the sea hawk is about to snatch off his hat.

Sid. 'Bridegroom Dick.' A frank cadet remembered by Bridegroom Dick.

Siddons, [Mrs. Sarah]. "The Fiddler." The famous Drury Lane actress reputedly ousted from the public eye by Master Betty.

Sidonia, Alonzo. "Benito Cereno." An old Valparaiso resident who took passage aboard the *San Dominick* when he was appointed to a civil office in Lima. When he saw the mutilating of Aranda, he jumped overboard and was drowned.

Silva, The Marquis of. *White-Jacket*. A Brazilian nobleman who while attending Don Pedro II, king of Brazil, falls into the forepassage of the *Neversink*.

Silvio. 'Pausilippo.' A bent old harp player, once a political prisoner. [He may be Silvio Pellico, the dramatist.]

Singles, Jenny. *Israel Potter*. The Berkshire girl whom Israel Potter loved but lost to Singles, later a sergeant in the American army.

Singles, Sergeant. *Israel Potter*. The man who wins and marries Jenny, Israel Potter's boyhood sweetheart. When Potter later is in Falmouth, England, he sees his former rival again.

Sister Mary. *Pierre*. See Mrs. Glendinning, Mary.

Skrimshander. *Moby-Dick*. Peter Coffin's nickname for Ishmael (which see).

Skyeman, The. *Mardi*. See Jarl.

Slim. *White-Jacket*. A diffident midshipman rebuked by the Professor in class.

Slyboots, Sir. 'The Scout toward Aldie.' A Confederate prisoner of the Colonel who leads a raid to capture Mosby. Slyboots may be Mosby himself (which see).

Smart, Purser. 'Bridegroom Dick.' The fat purser aboard the ship commanded by Captain Turret.

Smith, Joe. 'The New Ancient of Days: The Man of the Cave of Engihoul.' A common man, dethroned by the new ancient.

Smyrniote, The. *Clarel*. See Glaucon.

Snarles. *Moby-Dick*. A sign painter on the island of Nantucket. Mrs. Hussey wants him to paint a sign forbidding suicides in her Try Pots Inn.

Sneak. *White-Jacket*. A hang-dog informer who replaces Bland when he is temporarily suspended from his office as master-at-arms.

Snodhead, Dr. *Moby-Dick*. A supposed authority (from the

college of Santa Claus and St. Pott's) of Low Dutch and High German who translates passages for the narrator from an ancient Dutch volume on whaling.

Snowser. *Israel Potter*. A sailor's name invented by Israel Potter (which see) for himself when he alone boards the British frigate from the *Ariel*.

Sober Sides. *Mardi*. An uninspired spectator of the war games held by Kings Hello and Piko on the island of Diranda.

Socrates. "The Paradise of Bachelors and the Tartarus of Maids." The head waiter at the sumptuous dinner of the latter-day Templars in London, attended by the narrator.

Soldier, The. 'An Epitaph.' A dead soldier whose widow keeps the faith.

Soldier, The. 'The Scout toward Aldie.' See the Colonel.

Solo. *Mardi*. A bachelor legatee mentioned in Bardianna's will.

Solomon. 'Magian Wine.' Mentioned in connection with certain Syrian charms. 'Rammon.' Mentioned [erroneously] as the son of Jethro and the aging father of unrobust Rammon. In Solomon's time, it is said, Buddhistic beliefs come to Palestine through the Princess of Sheba.

Spagnoletto, "The Don." 'Marquis de Grandvin: At the Hostelry.' A short, brawny Spanish artist who discusses the picturesque and argues splenetically with Veronese. [He is probably Giuseppe Ribera, Lo Spagnoletto.]

Spahi, The. *Clarel*. See Belex.

Spanish Sailor. *Moby-Dick*. A *Pequod* sailor who during the midnight festivities in the forecastle picks a fight with Daggoo by insulting him for being black. The storm interrupts them.

Spinoza, [Baruch or Benedict]. 'The Parthenon.' The Dutch philosopher imagined as contemplating the unity of human and architectural beauty.

Squaretoes, Squire. "Cock-a-Doodle-Doo!" One of the narrator's rural neighbors. He does not own the lusty rooster.

Squeak. "Billy Budd." One of Claggart's cunning corporals, an informer who lies about Billy.

Standard. "The Fiddler." The narrator Helmstone's friend who explains that Hautboy is a former child prodigy now happier in his anonymity.

Stanly, Glendinning; "Glen," "Cousin Glen." *Pierre*. Pierre's once-cherished city cousin, a rich youth twenty-one years old recently returned from Europe. When Pierre needs housing in the city, Glen ignores him. Mrs. Glendinning likes him and after Pierre's departure from Saddle Meadows leaves him all her property there. Stanly presses his suit for Lucy Tartan and is so enraged when she moves in with Pierre and Isabel Banford that he whips Pierre with his cowhide and is shot to death for his rashness.

Starbuck. *Moby-Dick*. The *Pequod's* chief mate's father, killed by a whale.

Starbuck, *Moby-Dick*. The *Pequod's* chief mate's brother, killed by a whale.

Starbuck. *Moby-Dick*. The chief mate of the *Pequod*. He is thirty years old and is a native of Nantucket, a Quaker by descent, and a tall, thin realist. He sees the Trinity in the doubloon nailed to the mainmast. He tries unsuccessfully to dissuade Ahab from pursuing Moby Dick, once is momentarily tempted to shoot his captain but does not, and is lost in the wreck of the *Pequod*.

Starbuck, Mrs. Mary. *Moby-Dick*. The young Cape Cod wife of Starbuck, the chief mate of the *Pequod*. They have one small son.

Starbuck. *Moby-Dick*. The small son of Starbuck, the chief mate of the *Pequod*, and his young Cape Cod wife Mary.

Starr. 'Bridegroom Dick.' An officer chided because of his affection for the donnas.

Starry Banner. 'Bridegroom Dick.' Evidently an officer remembered by Bridegroom Dick from old Vera Cruz days.

Starry. "Billy Budd." One of the nicknames of Captain Edward Fairfax Vere (which see).

Steel. *Pierre*. The publisher who, with partners Flint and Asbestos, rejects Pierre's book. They intend to sue Pierre for costs and advances.

Steelkilt. *Moby-Dick*. The proud Lakeman from Buffalo who is a

sailor aboard the *Town-Ho*. The mate Radney threatens
Steelkilt, who breaks his jaw and is flogged for the act.
Steelkilt would then have murdered Radney but for the
appearance of Moby Dick, which both men chase and
which savagely kills Radney. Steelkilt then deserts.

Steen, Jan [Havicksz]; "Jan o' the Inn." 'Marquis de Grandvin:
At the Hostelry.' A realistic painter and a shabbily dressed
spendthrift who discusses the picturesque, especially with
Veronese.

Stetson. *White-Jacket*. Evidently an official at the New York
Astor House, where Old Coffee once worked.

Steward. 'The Scout toward Aldie.' The hospital assistant who
cares for the wounded after Mosby ambushes his Union
pursuers under the Colonel.

Stiggs. *Moby-Dick*. A young sailor found harpooned to death in a
back room of Hosea Hussey's Try Pots Inn on Nantucket.
Stiggs had stopped there after a whaling voyage of more
than four years.

Still, Bob. *Redburn*. A portly drinking friend of Danby in
Liverpool.

Stribbles. *White-Jacket*. A namby-pamby midshipman who lords
it over Frank.

Stuart, [General James E. B. "Jeb"]. 'The Released Rebel
Prisoner.' A dead Confederate general thought of by the
released Rebel prisoner. 'Lee in the Capitol.' A dead
Confederate general remembered by Lee as he approaches
the Capitol.

Stubb. *Moby-Dick*. The happy-go-lucky second mate of the
Pequod. He is a steady Cape-Codman and loves to smoke
little black pipes. Tashtego is Stubb's harpooneer. Stubb
tricks the mate of the *Bouton de Rose*, a Guernseyman, out
of an unsuspected treasure of ambergris. Stubb interprets
the zodiacal arch on the doubloon nailed to the mainmast.

Stubbs. *Omoo*. A Sydney auctioneer whose rhetorical flourishes
the narrator reads about in an Australian newspaper loaned
to him by Long Ghost when both are aboard the *Julia*.

Sub-Sub. *Moby-Dick*. The grubbing sub-sub-librarian who supplies
the prefatory extracts concerning whales.

Suffrien [Suffren Saint-Tropaz], Admiral [Pierre André de].
    Israel Potter. Mentioned as the commander of a fleet
    engaging an English squadron off Coromandel. Israel Potter
    might have been involved in the engagement but for leaving
    the *Unprincipled* to join the depleted crew of a revenue
    cutter.

[S]ugar-Lips. "Under the Rose." The great Persian poet who was
    inspired while at a bridal festival at the palace of the Shaz
    Gold-beak at Shiraz to write a poem about the rose-filled
    amber vase, now owned by the Azem. A Greek renegade
    translates the poem for the Ambassador from England.

Sumner, Charles. "To Major John Gentian, Dean of the Burgundy
    Club." Mentioned as Gentian's New England friend.

Sunshine. *White-Jacket.* The hard-working, singing Negro assistant
    of Old Coffee, the cook of the *Neversink.*

Surgeon, The; "Doc." 'The Scout toward Aldie.' A bluff,
    red-faced doctor with the Colonel's men during their
    ill-fated pursuit of Mosby. The Surgeon attends a Confed-
    erate prisoner, evidently Mosby himself, who feigns injury
    following a fall.

Surgeon, The. 'Bridegroom Dick.' The grave physician who stands
    by before the ordered flogging of the Finn, according to
    Bridegroom Dick's reminiscence.

Surgeon of the Army in Mexico, A. "Authentic Anecdotes of
    'Old Zack.'" A physician who elaborately describes
    General Taylor's face, figure, and uniform.

Susan. *Pierre.* A pretty girl in the Miss Pennies' sewing circle.

Swain(e), Nathan; "Nat." *Moby-Dick.* A whaler from Nantucket
    and Martha's Vineyard who fifty years earlier killed fifteen
    whales in one day and whose lance is now on a wall in Peter
    Coffin's Spouter-Inn. Peleg says that Nat lost his daring
    after he joined the church and became pious.

Swanevelt. 'Marquis de Grandvin: At the Hostelry." A good
    Dutchman who discusses the picturesque.

Swede, The. *Clarel.* See Mortmain.

Sweeny. *Redburn.* The proprietor of the Turkey Cock, a
    restaurant on Fulton Street, in New York, where Redburn
    takes Harry Bolton for breakfast.

Sweet Wrinkles. 'Bridegroom Dick.' See Bonny Blue.

Sydney Ben, the Ticket-of-Leave-Man. *Omoo.* A convict from New South Wales who is a sailor aboard the *Julia.* He does not sign the round robin.

Syrian, Monk, The. *Clarel.* A thin, ascetic Dominican monk whom the pilgrims encounter at Quarantania while he is enduring a forty-day temptation in imitation of Christ's.

Taff the Welshman. "Billy Budd." A former shipmate whose burial at sea Billy remembers, according to the poem "Billy in the Darbies," written by Billy's friend.

Tahar, The King of. *Omoo.* The father of Pot Belly, Queen Pomaree's first husband, whom she divorced.

Tahitan Sailor. *Moby-Dick.* A golden-hued sailor who is reminded of his native island when he watches his mates dancing during the midnight festivities in the forecastle. Later he and the grizzled Manxman heave the log, which breaks its rotten line.

Taji. *Mardi.* The sailor who deserts the *Arcturion,* boards the *Parki,* kills Aleema and rescues Yillah, and fruitlessly pursues her after she disappears from the isle of Odo. On his quest he visits King Peepi of Valapee, King Donjalolo of Juam, the island of Nora Bamma, King Uhia of Ohonoo, King Borabolla of Mondoldo, the pontiff Hevohitee of Maramma, Nimni of Pimminee, Kings Hello and Piko of Diranda, King Bello of Dominora, the country of Vivenza, the philosopher Doxodox of Hamora, King Yoky of Hooloomooloo, King Abrazza of Bonovona, the land of Serenia, and Queen Hautia of Flozella a Nina. His companions include Jarl, Samoa, King Media of Odo, Babbalanja, Mohi, and Yoomy. At the end, Taji is still seeking Yillah, his lost love.

Talara. *Mardi.* Donjalolo's friend, who comforts the young prince when his father commits suicide to force him to become king of Juam.

Talbot, John. *Moby-Dick.* A sailor lost at the age of eighteen off

Patagonia, in 1836. His sister erected a tablet in his memory in the Whaleman's Chapel in New Bedford.

Talbot, Miss. *Moby-Dick*. Drowned John Talbot's sister, who erected a tablet in his memory in the Whaleman's Chapel in New Bedford.

Talus. "The Bell-Tower." See Haman.

Tamatoy, King. *Omoo*. The king of Raiatair, one of the Society Islands, and the father of Tooboi.

Tammahamaha III. *Omoo*. The present king of Hawaii, who was a mere lad in 1835 but who now expansively keeps at his court a rabble of foreigners, including Billy Loon, Joe, and Mordecai.

Tammaro, King. *Mardi*. The king in Babbalanja's nursery story who rebuked the blind men for fancying that they could find a tree trunk which men with eyes could not identify.

Tanee, "Pomaree-Tanee." *Omoo*. Queen Pomaree's henpecked second husband, from Imeeo.

Taquinoo, King. *Mardi*. A fugitive king whose royalty was presaged by an eagle, according to the anonymous manuscript read in northern Vivenza.

Tartan, Frederic; "Fred." *Pierre*. Lucy Tartan's brother, three years her senior and a naval officer. He tries with Glendinning Stanly to prevent Lucy from going to live with Pierre and Isabel Banford in the city, but without success. Tartan and Stanly then challenge Pierre, who kills Stanly, after which Tartan tries to find his sister and does so, but only when she is dead in Pierre's prison cell.

Tartan, Lucy. *Pierre*. The beautiful, fair-haired, blue-eyed fiancée of Pierre Glendinning. When he abandons her to go to the city with Isabel Banford, who he pretends is his wife, Lucy follows and lives with the couple and their maid Delly Ulver. But when she learns—after Pierre has killed Glendinning Stanly (who wanted to marry her) and is in prison awaiting execution—that Isabel is Pierre's half-sister, she falls dead.

Tartan. *Pierre*. Lucy Tartan's deceased father, who was a friend of Pierre's father.

Tartan, Mrs. *Pierre*. Lucy Tartan's mother, a well-to-do, purse-proud widow who lives in a seaport city with her only daughter, is a matchmaker, and initially approves of Pierre Glendinning for Lucy. Later, after Lucy follows Pierre and Isabel Banford to the city, Mrs. Tartan visits them to urge her daughter to depart, but to no avail, upon which she curses Lucy and sees her no more.

Tartan. *Pierre*. Lucy Tartan's second brother, two years her junior and a naval officer.

Tashtego, "Tash." *Moby-Dick*. A proud, pure-blooded Indian from Gay Head, in Martha's Vineyard, and the harpooneer of Stubb aboard the *Pequod*. Tashtego sights the first sperm whale pursued. He is rescued by Queequeg when he later falls into a whale head which then drops from its hooks into the ocean. When Tashtego perishes in the wreck of the *Pequod*, he carries a sky hawk with him.

Tati. *Omoo*. One of the four recreant chiefs whom the French governor Bruat puts in charge of the four sections into which he divides Tahiti. The others are Kitoti, Utamai, and Paraita.

Tawney. *White-Jacket*. An old Negro sheet-anchor man, who reminisces about being impressed off a New England merchantman during the War of 1812 aboard the British frigate the *Macedonian* and forced at gunpoint by Cardan, her captain, to toil at guns aimed at the United States man-of-war the *Neversink*, then commanded by Decatur. Tawney is now old, sober, intelligent, frank, and able.

Taylor, General Zachary; "Zack," "Old Zack," "Old Rough and Ready." "Authentic Anecdotes of 'Old Zack.'" The American Mexican War hero who defuses an enemy shell, washes and mends his own clothes, has his pants ripped by a nail put in his saddle as a joke, in a terse letter invites General Santa Anna to surrender, has a pie flung onto his head by a Mexican shot, and is the subject of various rumors.

Teamster, Squire. "Poor Man's Pudding and Rich Man's Crumbs." The rich farmer who hires William Coulter at seventy-five cents a day and times him with watch in hand.

Tedds. '[Fragment of a poem].' The cook of Billy [Budd]'s mess.

Teei, King; "The Murdered." *Mardi*. The king of the island of Juam whose brother Marjora killed him and set up his own residence at Willamilla.

Tempest, Captain Don. "To Major John Gentian, Dean of the Burgundy Club." A navy friend of the Marquis de Grandvin.

Teniers, [David the younger?]. 'Marquis de Grandvin: At the Hostelry.' A painter of inn scenes mentioned by Dolci.

Thesus. 'The Archipelago.' The Athenian hero, mentioned as once roving through the Greek isles.

Thessalonian, The. *Clarel*. The Banker (which see).

Third Nantucket Sailor. *Moby-Dick*. A *Pequod* sailor who tires of dancing during the midnight festivities in the forecastle.

Thomas, Admiral [Frederick J.]. *Typee*. The commander-in-chief of the British Pacific fleet in 1843. When he receives Captain Charlton's report, he dispatches Lord George Poulet to Hawaii.

Thompson, "The Doctor." *Redburn*. The slovenly, Bible-reading Negro cook aboard the *Highlander*. He is abstemious when he goes ashore at Liverpool and therefore pockets seventy dollars in pay upon his return to New York.

Thouars, Admiral Du Petit. *Typee*. The commander of the French naval forces ordered to subjugate the Marquesas Islands and Queen Pomaree's Tahiti. His ship is the *Reine Blanche*. *Omoo*. The admiral of the *Reine Blanche* in the harbor of Papeetee. He leaves hated Bruat as the governor of Tahiti behind him.

Thrummings. *White-Jacket*. An old sailor who as sailmaker helps Ringrope encase Shenly's body in canvas for burial at sea. White Jacket persuades Thrummings not to take the last stitch through the corpse's nose.

Thule, The King of. 'The New Ancient of Days: The Man of the Cave of Engihoul.' Mentioned as riding a sleigh drawn by reindeer from Pole to Wetterhorn in May.

Thumb, General Tom. "Authentic Anecdotes of 'Old Zack.'" P. T. Barnum's main feature, who is floored when General Taylor's tack-torn pants are put on exhibition.

Ticket-of-Leave-Man, The. *Omoo*. See Sydney Ben.

Tidds. *Israel Potter*. A midshipman aboard the British frigate which Israel Potter boards alone off the *Ariel*.

Tight, Lieutenant Tom. 'Bridegroom Dick.' A fine brig-o'-war officer, remembered by Bridegroom Dick as involved in trying and hanging a mutineer.

Tilly, [Count Johann von]. *Clarel*. Mentioned as the commanding officer of one of Ungar's ancestors. The ancestor helped settle Maryland and later married an Indian.

Timoneer, The. *Clarel*. See Agath.

Timoleon. 'Timoleon.' Timophanes's younger brother, who is not favored by their mother. To preserve right in their native city of Corinth, Timoleon permits his tyrannical brother's assassination and is exiled for it. When appealed to by Corinth, he fights successfully in Sicily but then remains there in exile.

Timophanes, "Wrong." 'Timoleon.' Timoleon's older, tyrannical brother. Timoleon permits his assassination for the good of their native city of Corinth.

Tinor. *Typee*. Marheyo's wife and Kory-Kory's mother. She is a typical home-loving, bustling housewife.

Tintoretto, [Jacopo Robusti]. 'Marquis de Grandvin: At the Hostelry.' A lolling and leonine painter who discusses the picturesque with Franz Hals and Van Dyke.

Tior, The King of. *Typee*. The ruler of the valley of Tior, near Nukuheva, of the Typees, and of the Happars. Admiral Thouars confers with this imposing monarch.

Tistig. *Moby-Dick*. A Gay-Head squaw who said that the name Ahab, which the future captain's widowed and crazed mother gave him, would prove prophetic.

Titonti. *Mardi*. A dead subject whose thrift King Peepi has inherited.

Tobias. "To Major John Gentian, Dean of the Burgundy Club." A rosy-cheeked Burgundy Club waiter.

Toby. *Typee*. An athletic, quick-tempered young sailor who deserts the *Dolly* with the narrator, shares some of his experiences with the Typees, goes to the beach for help, and then disappears. In a sequel, the narrator explains that

Toby went into debt to a native named Jimmy, was unable to obtain help, and had to ship as a sailor to New Zealand. Toby and the narrator met again, in 1846.

Tom. *White-Jacket.* A sailor killed aboard the British frigate the *Macedonian* in an engagement with the United States man-of-war the *Neversink* during the War of 1812, according to the reminiscences of Tawney.

Tomasita. *White-Jacket.* A lovely Castillian belle of Tombez, Peru, who, says Jack Chase, used to caress his fine beard.

Tom, Happy. *The Confidence-Man.* See Thomas Fry.

Tom [Melville]. 'To Tom.' The poet's brother, aboard his ship the *Meteor* and therefore missed at home this Christmas.

Tommo. *Typee.* The narrator who with Toby deserts the *Dolly* when she is in the bay of Nukuheva in the Marquesas Islands, makes his way to the valley of the Typees, suffers a mysteriously infected leg, resides with Marheyo and Tinor for about four months, evidently consorts with Fayaway, is served by Kory-Kory, and finally escapes with the aid of Marnoo and Karakoee.

Tompkins. "Hawthorne and His Mosses." Evidently an imagined British author, to whom American authors should not be unflatteringly compared, as, for example, in saying that someone is an American Tompkins.

Tom Tight, Lieutenant. 'Bridegroom Dick.' See Tight, Lieutenant Tom.

Tom Thumb. "Authentic Anecdotes of 'Old Zack.' " See Thumb, General Tom.

Tonans, Jupiter. "The Lightning-Rod Man." The lightning-rod man whom the narrator tosses out of his house at the end of a wild thunder storm.

Tongatona. *Mardi.* A dead subject whose pusillanimity King Peepi has inherited.

Tonoi. *Omoo.* The chief of the fishermen who works sleepily for Shorty and Zeke at Martair.

Tooboi. *Omoo.* The heir of Tamatoy, the King of Raiatair. Poky introduces the narrator to a charming girl in Papeetee whom Tooboi is courting.

Tooboi. *Mardi.* A *Parki* sailor from Lahina, at Mowee, Hawaii, who is lost to sharks while he is bathing.

Tooke, Rev. Mr. Horne. *Israel Potter.* The pro-American British clergyman who plots with Squire John Woodcock and James Bridges to use Israel Potter as a courier to Dr. Franklin in Paris.

Tooroorooloo. *Mardi.* An orator whose jawbones are in Oh Oh's museum.

Too-Too. *Typee.* A very young Typee native who has built a baby house in the branches of a coconut tree and who sings when aloft.

Top-Gallant Harry. 'Bridegroom Dick.' A sailor remembered by Bridegroom Dick.

Topo. *Mardi.* A legatee mentioned in Bardianna's will.

Tot. *Omoo.* See Old Mother Tot.

Toulib, "A Horror." *Clarel.* A crippled beggar whom Nehemiah befriends near the Gate of Zion in Jerusalem.

Towser. *Israel Potter.* A sailor's name invented by Israel Potter (which see) for himself when aboard the British frigate which he boards alone from the *Ariel.*

Tranquo. *Moby-Dick.* The King of Tranque, one of the Arsacides islands. Ishmael visited him once and saw there a glen decorated with carved whale bones.

Tribonnora, Prince. *Mardi.* A mad prince of three islands near Mondoldo who enjoys submerging small canoes by dashing over them with his large canoe.

Triton, A. 'Marquis de Grandvin: Naples in the Time of Bomba.' See Carlo.

Truman, John. *The Confidence-Man.* The Black Rapids Coal Company president and transfer agent, who sells stock to the college man, to the merchant Henry Roberts, and to the coughing miser. The herb doctor identifies Truman to the miser as coming from Jones Street, in St. Louis.

Truxill. "The Encantadas." The brother of Hunilla, who when he and his brother-in-law Felipe drowned while fishing became the wretched Chola widow of Norfolk Isle.

Tryon, Corporal. 'Lyon.' A brave soldier from Iowa led with his men by Lyon.

Tubbs. *White-Jacket.* A sailor who was once a whaler, for which reason Jack Chase abominates him and drives him from his chatty maintop.

Turbans. *Clarel.* The general name for Turks, among whom the saintly Nehemiah, called the Hat, wanders safely.

Turkey. "Bartleby." The Wall Street lawyer's short, British-born scrivener. He is almost sixty years old and—unlike his fellow-worker Nippers—is irritable only after the noon hour.

Turret, Captain; "Old Hemlock." 'Bridegroom Dick.' The Kentucky captain remembered by Bridegroom Dick as colossal, fond of drink, and obliged once to come close to flogging the Finn.

Tuscan, The. *Clarel.* See Salvaterra.

Typee. *Omoo.* The narrator, who rebels against Captain Guy of the *Julia,* instigates and signs the round robin, goes to the Calabooza Beretanee, then wanders with Long Ghost to Martair, Tamai, Imeeo, Loohooloo, Partoowye, and Taloo, and finally ships aboard the *Leviathan.* At one point he is called Paul (which see).

Uhia, King. *Mardi.* The unnaturally ambitious monarch of Ohonoo, who worships the god Keevi in the valley of Monlova. On a rock over the valley Uhia once stood to prove his right to the throne. He envies bedridden Manta.

Ulver, Delly. *Pierre.* One of Mrs. Mary Glendinning's servants, who has evidently been seduced by Ned, another of Mrs. Glendinning's servants, and must therefore be dismissed. She passively accompanies Pierre Glendinning and Isabel Banford to the city and serves them as a maid in their cramped quarters among the Apostles.

Ulver, Walter. *Pierre.* Delly Ulver's old father, who rents the red farmhouse by the lake where Isabel Banford lives for a short while.

Ulver, Mrs. Walter. *Pierre.* Delly Ulver's aged mother, who is grief-stricken when her daughter is seduced by Ned.

Una. "The Bell-Tower." The garlanded hour of one on the clock bell, beneath which Bannadonna dies.

Ungar. *Clarel.* A scarred former Confederate officer descended from Maryland Catholics. He is also part Indian. He now irregularly serves in the armies of Egypt and Turkey. He joins the pilgrims at Mar Saba and leaves them at Bethlehem. He is bitterly anti-democratic, admirably stoical, pessimistic, but also deeply Christian.

Unknown, The. *Clarel.* The first name by which Celio (which see) is referred to, at lower Gihon.

Urania. 'After the Pleasure Party.' A Mediterranean girl who devotes much of her life to intellectual pursuits and is then annoyed when a man, whom she suddenly wants sexually, prefers a simple peasant girl. Urania is tempted to join a nunnery but instead prays, probably without effect, to the armed Virgin, which represents cold knowledge and art.

Ushant, John. *White-Jacket.* The brave, philosophical, well-traveled, sixty-year-old captain of the forecastle, who refuses to trim his magnificent, Neptune-like beard, is put in the brig, and undergoes a flogging by order of Captain Claret. Ushant retains his beard.

Usher, The. *Moby-Dick.* The fictitious grammar-school grammarian who supplies the prefatory etymology concerning whales.

Utamai. *Omoo.* One of the four recreant chiefs whom the French governor Bruat puts in charges of the four sections into which he divides Tahiti. The others are Kitoti, Tati, and Paraita.

Van. *Omoo.* A quiet old Finnish sailor who at one point truthfully predicts that within three weeks few of his mates will remain aboard the *Julia.* He signs the round robin.

Van der [de] Velde, [probably Willem I]. 'Marquis de Grandvin: At the Hostelry.' A dreamy painter, formerly a sailor, who reminisces on dead Van Tromp and De Reyter. Van der Velde is then joshed by Douw.

Vandyke [Van Dyke, Sir Anthony]. 'Marquis de Grandvin: At

the Hostelry.' A painter who urges Franz Hals to come to England and paint, and who also discusses the picturesque with him.

Vangi. *Mardi.* A promising young legatee mentioned in Bardianna's will.

Vangs, Captain. *Typee.* The tyrannical, neglectful captain of the *Dolly*, from which the narrator escapes while she is in the harbor of Nukuheva in the Marquesas Islands.

Van Lord, Mrs. *Pierre.* A fictitious dead widow's name in a German prince's proclamation imagined by Pierre.

Van Tromp (also Trump), [Admiral Cornelius Van]. 'Marquis de Grandvin: At the Hostelry.' The captain of the *Dunderberg*, remembered by Van der Velde.

Van Winkle, Rip. 'Rip Van Winkle's Lilac.' The Kaatskill loafer who returns to his rickety house and confusingly finds a big lilac in front of the door where a willow used to be. The lovely lilac immortalizes him.

Van Winkle, Mrs. Rip. 'Rip Van Winkle's Lilac.' Rip Van Winkle's shrewish wife, now deceased.

Varnopi. *Mardi.* An agent sent with Zuma to the Mardian island of Rafona by Donjalolo for information.

Varvy. *Omoo.* An old native hermit who pretends he is deaf and dumb, and who keeps contraband liquor in old sheds near Taloo.

Vavona. *Mardi.* A blind, mystical Mardian poet, much celebrated but thought by some to be obscure. He is described as sublime by Babbalanja in his conversation with Abrazza.

Vedder, E[lihu]. ' "Formerly a Slave." ' The painter of the idealized picture of Jane Jackson, the former slave.

Vee Vee. *Mardi.* King Media's boy dwarf.

Velasques [Velasquez, Diego Rodrigues de Silva y]. 'Marquis de Grandvin: At the Hostelry.' A painter described as quiet and sedate.

Velluvi, Queen. *Mardi.* Donjalolo's third-night queen.

Verbi. *Mardi.* A critic who, according to Babbalanja, denounced Lombardo's *Koztanza* for slightly inaccurate punctuation. Lombardo ignored him.

Vere, The Honorable Edward Fairfax, Captain; "Ed," "Starry."

"Billy Budd." The short, bookish, stern, courageous forty-year-old captain of the *Bellipotent*, aboard which Billy Budd kills John Claggart. Captain Vere advises the drumhead court to find Billy guilty and then hangs him.

Vere, Captain. "Billy Budd." Captain Edward Fairfax Vere's distant senior relative, also a naval captain.

[Veronese], Paola [Paolo] of Verona. 'Marquis de Grandvin: At the Hostelry.' A genial, richly arrayed painter who urges Douw to visit Venice.

Vestris, Madame. *Redburn*. Presumably a high-society acquaintance of Harry Bolton in London.

Victor. *Omoo*. A knavish adventurer from Marseilles on whose premises the outraged Tahitians find some liquor and confiscate it, thus precipitating an incident which Admiral Thouars uses to his political advantage.

Victor, The. 'Magnanimity Baffled.' A soldier who magnanimously tries to shake the hand of his defeated enemy but finds him dead.

Viking, The. *Mardi*. See Jarl.

Vine. *Clarel*. A curious, ambiguous, withdrawn pilgrim who makes the acquaintance of Clarel and Nehemiah at the Sepulcher of Kings in Jerusalem. He is both aesthetically sensitive and highly if quietly moral.

Viner. *Omoo*. A former shipmate of John Jermin's. When the two after fifteen years meet again in the harbor of Papeetee, they become convivial, and ultimately Viner signs as third mate aboard the *Julia*, of which Jermin is the first officer.

Vineyarder, The. *Omoo*. The tall, robust captain of the *Leviathan* who signs the narrator aboard at Taloo but who refuses to take on Long Ghost.

Virginian, A. "Hawthorne and His Mosses." The mask which Melville—saying that he is spending July in Vermont—assumes when he praises Nathaniel Hawthorne as a superb American author.

Viscaya, Manuel. "Benito Cereno." A boatswain's mate thrown alive overboard with Roderigo Hurta from the *San Dominick* during the slave revolt.

Vivia. *Pierre*. The name of the author-hero about whom Pierre writes when he is at the Apostles'.

Vivo. *Mardi*. A sophist paraphrased by Babbalanja.

V., L. A. "Fragments from a Writing Desk. No. 1." The author of a letter from the village of Lansingburgh [in New York] to his friend M— describing three lovely girls. "Fragments from a Writing Desk. No. 2." The man who follows the bearer of a letter signed Inamorata, only to discover in a villa in the woods that the peerlessly beautiful woman is deaf and dumb.

Voluto. *Mardi*. An authority on ambergris cited by Mohi.

Volvoon, Professor Monsieur. *Pierre*. A philosophical lecturer whom Charlie Millthorpe accompanies.

Vondendo. *Mardi*. An authority on amber cited by Mohi.

Voyo. *Mardi*. A dead subject whose cunning King Peepi has inherited.

W—. "Fragments from a Writing Desk. No. 1." A mutual friend of L. A. V. and M—.

Wahabee, A. *Clarel*. An evil Mohammedan whom Agath the Timoneer smuggled aboard *The Peace of God* to enable him to avoid the plague. But the Wahabee accidentally wrecked the ship because in his sea chest were blades which turned the compass.

Wallace, [General] Lew. 'Donelson.' A Union officer who participated in the siege of Donelson.

Warbler, The. *Mardi*. See Yoomy.

Washington, General [George]. *Israel Potter*. The leader of the American Revolutionary forces whose taking of command in July, 1775, after Bunker Hill, Israel Potter witnesses. "The Cincinnati." Mentioned as the General-President of the Society of the Cincinnati.

Waterford, The Marquis of. *Redburn*. Presumably a madcap acquaintance of Harry Bolton in London.

Watteau, [Antoine]. 'Marquis de Grandvin: At the Hostelry.' A French painter courteously addressed by Veronese.

Weaver. *The Confidence-Man.* A Virginia family which migrated with their cousins the Wrights to Kentucky but were treacherously killed with them by the perfidious Indian Mocmohoc.

Wedge, Dr. *White-Jacket.* The *Malay* surgeon, who with others confers with Dr. Cuticle when that expert operates on the fatally wounded foretopman.

Wellingborough, Senator. *Redburn.* Wellingborough Redburn's great-uncle, who died a member of Congress in the days of the old Constitution.

Wellington, The Duke of. *Redburn.* The heroic Duke whom Redburn thinks Harry Bolton may take him to peep at in Apsley House, in Hyde Park, London. "Poor Man's Pudding and Rich Man's Crumbs." One of the aristocratic guests at the Guildhall Banquet in London following the Battle of Waterloo.

Wen. *Pierre.* An affected tailor turned publisher, who with his partner Wonder offers to publish Pierre's writings at Pierre's expense.

White, Deacon. "I and My Chimney." One of the neighbors of the narrator, who likes the fellow because he is old.

White Jacket. *White-Jacket.* The narrator, a common seaman aboard the *Neversink*, commanded by Captain Claret. White Jacket joins Jack Chase's maintop crew and his mess, admires Mad Jack and Lemsford and Tawney and Ushant, goes ashore on liberty at Rio de Janeiro, despises Bland, fears and loathes the Articles of War, keeps watch over the dying Shenly, falls from the weather topgallant yardarm and nearly drowns, and disembarks at Norfolk, Virginia.

Wilkes. "Billy Budd." One of Captain Vere's midshipmen.

Will. 'Bridegroom Dick.' A sailor of the ward-room mess recalled by Bridegroom Dick. The *Cumberland*, which Will was aboard, was later sunk by the *Merrimac*, which his former shipmate Hal was aboard.

Willi. *Mardi.* King Normo's fool in a story by Babbalanja. Willi was ordered to go to a tree but was free to walk there on

his feet or on his hands. He chose his hands because he
practically had to do so.

William. *Omoo.* A sick sailor in the Calabooza to whom Dr.
Johnson sends some liniment, which William promptly
drinks. (William may be Bill "Liverpool" Blunt [which
see], who signs the round robin.)

William, "Bill." *Omoo.* A runaway ship's carpenter who has much
work at Taloo and whose love for Lullee is unrequited.

William. "To Major John Gentian, Dean of the Burgundy Club."
A Burgundy Club waiter.

Williams. *White-Jacket.* A former Yankee peddler and pedagogue,
whose wit and gay philosophy White Jacket values. Williams
later unsuccessfully tries to stimulate the bidding at auction
on White Jacket's jacket.

Williamson, Lieutenant. *Israel Potter.* An officer suspicious of
Israel Potter when he boards the British frigate alone off
the *Ariel.*

Willie. 'Stockings in the Farm-House Chimney.' Depicted as
waiting for Santa Claus.

Wilson. *Omoo.* Consul Wilson's old, white-haired, saintly father,
who lives at Point Venus in Papeetee.

Wilson. *Omoo.* The small, contemptible, pug-nosed acting British
consul at Papeetee. He is a friend of despicable Captain Guy
of the *Julia.*

Wilt. *Redburn.* A partner in Sampson & Wilt, Liverpool, on whom
Redburn's father called back in 1808.

Winsome, Mark. *The Confidence-Man.* A blue-eyed, red-cheeked,
mystical-looking transcendentalist about forty-five years
old. To Goodman he describes Noble as a Mississippi
operator.

Winwood, Ralph. *Pierre.* A cousin of Pierre's father, whose
portrait—the one showing the subject as young and rakish—
Winwood secretly painted and then gave to Miss Dorothea
Glendinning.

Womoonoo. *Typee.* See Wormoonoo.

Wonder. *Pierre.* An affected tailor turned publisher, who, with his partner Wen, offers to publish Pierre's writings at Pierre's expense.

Wood. *Redburn.* The part-owner of Parkins & Wood warehouse in Liverpool, where Betsy Jennings and her three children starve to death.

Woodcock, Squire John. *Israel Potter.* The elderly, pro-American British squire who with Rev. Mr. Horne Tooke and James Bridges plots to use Israel Potter as a courier to Dr. Franklin in Paris. Squire Woodcock conceals Potter in a secret room behind his heavy stone chimney and then dies of apoplexy.

Woodcock, Mrs. *Israel Potter.* Squire Woodcock's widow, whom Israel Potter terrifies when he marches past her dressed in her late husband's finest clothing.

Wooloo. *White-Jacket.* The Commodore's sedate and earnest Polynesian servant who thinks that snow is flour, hailstones are glass beads, and raisins are bugs.

Worden, [Lieutenant John L.]. 'In the Turret.' The commander of the iron-clad *Monitor,* which engaged the iron-clad *Merrimac.*

Wormoonoo (also Womonoo). *Typee.* Mentioned as a native whose property, like that of all other Typees, is respected by all.

Worth, General Will[iam J.]. "To Major John Gentian, Dean of the Burgundy Club." An American Mexican War general whom Gentian knew personally.

Wright. *The Confidence-Man.* A Virginia family which migrated with their cousins the Weavers to Kentucky but were treacherously killed with them by the perfidious Indian Mocmohoc.

Wrong. 'Timoleon.' The name which Timophanes (which see) calls himself.

Wymontoo-Hee, "Luff." *Omoo.* A stalwart native of the island of Hannamanoo who ships aboard the *Julia,* soon becomes seasick, and is christened Luff by the crew. He signs the round robin but ultimately remains aboard ship.

Wynodo. *Mardi.* A neighbor of Bardianna, mentioned in the philosopher's will.

X—. "Billy Budd." A probably fictitious friend of the author. The personality and intellectual make-up of X— were baffling.

Xiki. *Mardi*. The god Doleema's butler, in a story by Mohi which concerns the isle of Maramma. Xiki javelined to death a reluctant sacrifice to the god.

Yambaio. "Benito Cereno." An Ashantee slave who polishes hatchets during Delano's visit aboard the *San Dominick* and is killed during the attack led by Delano's chief mate.

Yamjamma. *Mardi*. Quoted by Babbalanja as a sage but ambiguous-talking lawgiver.

Yamoyamee. *Mardi*. One of the twelve aristocratic Taparian families on the isle of Pimminee, entertained by Nimni.

Yankee, The. *Omoo*. See Zeke.

Yankee Doodle. "Authentic Anecdotes of 'Old Zack.'" The boss of the newspaper *Yankee Doodle*, for whom the correspondent goes to General Zachary Taylor to report authentic anecdotes.

Yarn. *White-Jacket*. See Old Yarn.

Yau. "Benito Cereno." A vicious Ashantee slave who polishes hatchets during Delano's visit aboard the *San Dominick*. He prepared Aranda's skeleton for use as a warning figurehead.

Yellow-hair. *Israel Potter*. See Potter, Israel.

Yellow-mane. *Israel Potter*. See Potter, Israel.

Yellow Torch. *White-Jacket*. Mentioned in an anecdote as the victim of Red Hot Coal, a murderous Indian on the Mississippi River who collected scalps.

Yillah. *Mardi*. A beautiful, white-skinned, golden-haired, blue-eyed girl who was born at Amma, was taken at an early age to Oroolia (where legend says that she became a flower), and was enshrined as a goddess in the temple at Apo in the glen of Ardair. Her guardian, the priest Aleema, is taking her by ship toward Tedaidee when Taji encounters them, kills Aleema, and rescues her. She and Taji go to the isle of Odo and make love. But she disappears, and he fruitlessly pursues her. She may be drowned or may be disguised as a maiden in Queen Hautia's court at Flozella a Nina.

Yoky, King. *Mardi*. The misshapen monarch of Hooloomooloo, the isle of Cripples. He gives Taji and his party a feast.

Yola. "Benito Cereno." An African-born slave, a calker by trade, between sixty and seventy years old, killed during the attack on the *San Dominick* led by Delano's chief mate.

Yoomy, "the Warbler." *Mardi*. The minstrel from the isle of Odo who accompanies Taji, along with King Media of Odo, Babbalanja, and Mohi, on his long and fruitless search for Yillah. Yoomy and Mohi leave Taji on the isle of Flozella a Nina but return from Odo to try to rescue him from Queen Hautia of Flozella.

Yorpy. "The Happy Failure." The faithful old Dutch-African Negro servant of the unsuccessful inventor-uncle of the young narrator.

Young Man, The. 'The Scout toward Aldie.' See the Colonel.

Youth, The. 'The Scout toward Aldie.' See the Colonel.

Zack. "Authentic Anecdotes of 'Old Zack.' " See Taylor, General Zachary.

Zardi. 'Rammon.' An urbane, well-traveled, shallow, unthinking Tyrian improvisator who visits philosophically inquisitive Rammon in Jerusalem.

Zeke, "Keekee." *Omoo*. The tall Yankee partner of Shorty in a farming venture at Martair. They employ Peter and Paul—that is, Long Ghost and the narrator.

Zenzi. *Mardi*. A mercenary Mardian poet mentioned by Yoomy.

Zenzori. *Mardi*. A reader who told Lombardo that his *Koztanza* was trash. Lombardo ignored him, according to Babbalanja.

Zmiglandi, Queen. *Mardi*. A collateral ancestor of King Abrazza, according to Mohi.

Znobbi. *Mardi*. A runaway from Dominora who is now an enthusiastic inhabitant of Vivenza.

Zonoree. *Mardi*. A dead subject whose prodigality King Peepi has inherited.

Zooperbi. *Mardi*. The fallen son of Tarquinoo, according to the anonymous manuscript read in northern Vivenza.

Zozo. *Mardi.* An enthusiast whose back tooth, which he knocked
  out in grief, is now in Oh Oh's museum.
Zuma. *Mardi.* An agent sent with Varnopi to the Mardian island
  of Rafona by Donjalolo for information.

APPENDICES

APPENDIX A

Poems Considered in This Volume

From *Battle-Pieces and Aspects of the War*, 1866

The Portent (1859)

Lyon, Battle of Springfield, Missouri (August, 1861)

Dupont's Round Fight (November, 1861)

Donelson (February, 1862)

The Temeraire

The Battle for the Mississippi (April, 1862)

Malvern Hill (July, 1862)

The Victor of Antietam (1862)

Battle of Stone River, Tennessee, A View from Oxford Cloisters (January, 1863)

Running the Batteries, as Observed from the Anchorage above Vicksburgh (April, 1863)

Stonewall Jackson, Mortally Wounded at Chancellorsville (May, 1863)

Stonewall Jackson (Ascribed to a Virginian)

Chattanooga (November, 1863)

The Armies of the Wilderness (1863-4)

On the Photograph of a Corps Commander

The Battle for the Bay (August, 1864)

Sheridan at Cedar Creek (October, 1864)

The College Colonel

A Dirge for McPherson, Killed in Front of Atlanta (July, 1864)

At the Cannon's Mouth, Destruction of the Ram Albermarle by the Torpedo-Launch (October, 1864)

The March to the Sea (December, 1864)

The Fall of Richmond, The Tidings Received in the Northern Metropolis (April, 1865)

The Surrender at Appomattox (April, 1865)

The Martyr, Indicative of the Passion of the People on the 15th Day of April, 1865

"The Coming Storm": A Picture by S. R. Gifford, and Owned by E.B.: Included in the N.A. Exhibition, April, 1865

Rebel Color-Bearers at Shiloh: A Plea against the Vindictive Cry Raised by Civilians Shortly after the Surrender at Appomattox

The Released Rebel Prisoner (June, 1865)

A Grave near Petersburg, Virginia

"Formerly a Slave": An Idealized Portrait, by E. Vedder, in the Spring Exhibition of the National Academy, 1865

Magnanimity Baffled

On the Slain Collegians

An Epitaph

On Sherman's Men Who Fell in the Assault of Kenesaw Mountain, Georgia

Presentation to the Authorities by Privates, of Colors Captured in Battles Ending in the Surrender of Lee

The Scout toward Aldie

Lee in the Capitol (April, 1866)

Clarel, 1876.

From *John Marr and Other Sailors*, 1888

John Marr

Bridegroom Dick (1876)

Tom Deadlight

Jack Roy

The Haglets

To the Master of the "Meteor"

Old Counsel of the Young Master of a Wrecked California Clipper

To Ned

The Berg (A Dream)

From *Timoleon*, 1891

Timoleon (394 B.C.)
After the Pleasure Party: Lines Traced under an Image of
    Amor Threatening
The Margrave's Birthnight
Magian Wine
The Garden of Metrodorus
Lamia's Song
Monody
Buddha . . .
C—'s Lament
Shelley's Vision
The Marchioness of Brinvilliers
The Age of the Antonines
Pausilippo (in the Time of Bomba)
The Parthenon
Off Cape Colonna
The Archipelago
Syra (A Transmitted Reminiscence)
The Apparition (The Parthenon Uplifted . . .)
In the Desert
L'Envoi: The Return of the Sire de Nesle. A.D. 16—

From *The Works of Herman Melville* (1924, XVI, *Poems* . . .)

The Loiterer
The Lover and the Syringa Bush
The Chipmunk
Stockings in the Farm-House Chimney
A Dutch Christmas up the Hudson in the Time of Patroons
Time's Betrayal
Iris (1865)
Rip Van Winkle's Lilac
Amoroso
Hearth-Roses
Under the Ground
The Vial of Attar
The Devotion of the Flowers to Their Lady

The Rose Farmer
L'Envoi
Marquis de Grandvin: At the Hostelry
Marquis de Grandvin: Naples in the Time of Bomba as Told by
    Major Jack Gentian
The New Ancient of Days: The Man of the Cave of Engihoul
The Rusty Man (by a Soured One)
Camoens
Montaigne and His Kitten
Falstaff's Lament over Prince Hal Become Henry V
Shadow at the Feast: Mrs. B—
Honor
Pontoosuce

From *Collected Poems of Herman Melville*, 1947

Epistle to Daniel Shepherd
The Admiral of the White
To Tom
Suggested by the Ruins of a Mountain-Temple in Arcadia, One
    Built by the Architect of the Parthenon
Rammon
Ditty of Aristippus

From *Melville's Billy Budd*, 1948

[Fragment of poem]

APPENDIX B

Characters, Probably Historical, Incompletely Identified in This Volume

Carpegna
Charlton, Captain
Fergus, Major
Lefevre
McCloud, Colonel
Reine